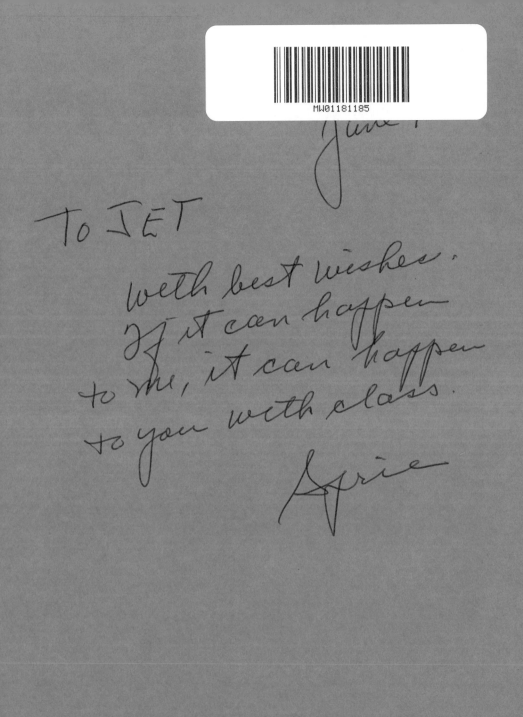

TO JET

with best wishes.
If it can happen
to me, it can happen
to you with class.

April

The Way It Was

D. C. SPRIESTERSBACH

The Way It Was

The University of Iowa,

1964–1989

UNIVERSITY OF IOWA PRESS Ψ Iowa City

University of Iowa Press, Iowa City 52242

Publication of this book was made possible in part
by a grant from the Office of the Vice President for
Research, the University of Iowa.

Library of Congress
Cataloging in Publication Data
Spriestersbach, D. C.
    The way it was: the University of Iowa, 1964–1989 /
by D. C. Spriestersbach.
        p.   cm.
    Includes index.
    ISBN 0-87745-666-6
    1. University of Iowa—History—20th century.
2. Spriestersbach, D. C.   3. College
administrators—Iowa—Iowa City—Biography.
I. Title.
    LD2568.8.s77   1999
    378.777′655—dc21   98-32003

99   00   01   02   03   C   5   4   3   2   1

*This book is dedicated
to the memory of*
HOWARD BOWEN,
*whose confidence in me
made this account possible.*

CONTENTS

ACKNOWLEDGMENTS

To the students, faculty, and staff during the years 1965–1989 who gave the substance and context to the period; to Jerry Loewenberg, whose gentle urging convinced me that I should make the effort; to Les Sims and David Skorton for the generous assistance from their offices; to the faculty and staff who took the time for the interviews; to the dedicated professional staff of the University Libraries archives: Earl Rogers and Fran Murphy; to my colleagues who read drafts for completeness and fact: Tom Bauer, Marge Hoppin, and Charlie Mason; to my longtime colleague and friend, Hugh Morris, who used his editor's pen generously; and to Joan Taylor and Barbara Olson — two talented and dedicated colleagues without whose help, encouragement, and critical comments this book would never have been started, much less finished.

This book is both an institutional and a personal history involving the University of Iowa during the period 1964–1989. It is an institutional history to the extent that the events described here reflect the status of the university as it responded to internal and external forces that caused it both to reaffirm and modify its priorities and modes of management. In addition to my perspective, it is told from those of a number of key players at the time.

The book is necessarily a personal account to the extent that my various administrative duties frequently placed me at the center, or near it, of those institutional events. To acknowledge that this is a personal account, I have frequently used the first-person singular in describing them.

Because this is a personal account, developments related to the Offices of the Dean of the Graduate College and the Vice President for Educational Development and Research are typically highlighted. However, the evolution of those offices clearly occurred in a temporal context, and so the discussion extends to other aspects of the university as well as to state and federal developments that shaped them.

The book is intended to illustrate the means by which a research university of moderate size is led to recognize state and federal goals, priorities, and opportunities, and to take advantage of them when possible. As indicated later, this obviously was, and is, the case for such federal programs as those of the National Institutes of Health and the National Science Foundation.

My personal account begins on a sunny Thursday afternoon on October 29, 1964. The place was Macbride Auditorium. The occasion was President Howard Bowen's first "fall speech" to the faculty. He had just come to the university from the presidency of Grinnell College on July 1, 1964, to be the university's fourteenth president after Virgil Hancher's twenty-four-year tenure. He said that he intended, through fall appearances before the faculty, to give them an opportunity to learn about his hopes and plans for the University of Iowa.

I was a professor of speech pathology and principal investigator of a multidisciplinary "program project" investigating the social, psychological, and physical consequences of cleft lip and palate, having successfully competed for several grants from the National Institutes of Health to support the research.

I had been happily engrossed in my professorial duties since 1948 and only dimly aware of committees and ad hoc groups of faculty that kept tabs on the inner workings of the university. But President Bowen's appearance was enough of a unique event that I decided to attend the convocation. In fact, it was the first time that I had attended this sort of university-wide function.

In his talk, "A Report to the Faculty," Bowen laid out to us some of his plans for the university in the months and years ahead. His presentation was without rhetorical flair. Rather it was given somewhat flatly, almost as though he was giving a report to a committee. Yet the points he made were thought-provoking, exciting:

> I came to my new job on the assumption that the University of Iowa has before it a period of potentially great advancement.
>
> I would not be surprised if, in the next few years, we would need to employ as many as 150 new full-time faculty members each year. . . . At this rate of employment fully half the entire faculty of 1970 will have been employed in the next five years. . . . Everyone must help convey to prospective new people the idea that Iowa is the kind of place which is congenial to capable people, where they are appreciated, and where they can do their best work.
>
> The obvious need we have in the months ahead to chart the long-range course of this institution provides an excellent opportunity for us to begin working together on problems of great importance that will require of all of us the best ideas, the clearest vision, and the greatest wisdom we can muster.

Bowen's vision of what the university could become, and the quiet dignity and conviction with which he presented it, captured my attention and intrigued me so much that I wrote a note to him, the president of the university! — something I had never done in the sixteen years I had been on the Iowa faculty — expressing my appreciation for the ideas in his speech. Maybe I was ready and waiting for a new challenge. In any event I told him that I wrote to him with feelings of great humility, given courage to do so because of the invitation extended in his talk. I offered to help him achieve his objectives in any way that I could. I closed the note by asserting that "I think I am an idealist, a person with imagination, and a guy in a hurry. I believe investigation will show that I am a person with competitive administrative and executive abilities." How brash can a young professor be!

Little did I know when I wrote the note that it would kick off a series of events that would change my life and that I would soon join the central administration of the university to live through and adapt to unprecedented times for higher education in the United States. This book is about those times.

The materials that have been drawn upon for this book come from three sources: my personal files, the university archives, and my interviews with fifty-six faculty and administrators who were involved, one way or the other, in university affairs during the 1965 to 1989 years. Of these three, the archives proved to be the primary source. I found the *Daily Iowan* archives to be especially helpful because they not only described university events but enough of national/international events to provide the necessary global orientation for local happenings.

The interviews typically took an hour and a half, using a common format: the nature of the interviewees' association with the university during the period under review, their relationships with the Offices of the Vice President for Educational Development and Research and Dean of the Graduate College, other university relationships during the period, national/international developments that impinged on the interviewees' university responsibilities during those years, university highs and lows during the period, and any additional remarks that the interviewees wished to include.

The persons interviewed between September 1995 and July 1997 were: Stephen Arum, assistant dean, International Programs; Thomas Bauer, associate director of the Technology Innovation Center, formerly associate director of the Office of Public Information; Samuel Becker, professor emeritus, communication studies, formerly acting vice president for academic affairs; Randall Bezanson, professor of law, formerly vice president for finance and university services; Arthur Bonfield, professor of law; Willard Boyd, professor of law and president emeritus of the University of Iowa; George Chambers, professor of education, formerly executive vice president; John Colloton, vice president for statewide health services; Paul Cooper, university veterinarian; William Decker, associate vice president of research, director of information technology services; Lyle Dickinson, captain and area commander retired, Iowa State Patrol; John Eckstein, professor emeritus, internal medicine, formerly dean of the College of Medicine; Dorsey Ellis, dean of the College of Law, Washington University, St. Louis, formerly vice president for finance and university services; Robert Engel, professor emeritus, education, formerly special assistant to the president; Geraldine Felton, professor of nursing, formerly dean of the College of Nursing; James Freedman, president of Dartmouth College, formerly president of the University of Iowa; Richard Gibson, associate vice president for finance and university services, director of facilities services group; Brian Harvey, director of sponsored programs; Ray Heffner, professor emeritus, English, formerly vice president for academic affairs; Lyell Henry, formerly assistant to the vice president of educational development and research; Robert Hering, professor emeritus of engineering, formerly dean of the College of Engineering; Margery Hoppin, formerly director of sponsored programs; Frank Horton, president of the University of Toledo, formerly dean for advanced studies; Philip Hubbard, vice president and professor of mechanical engineering emeritus; James Jakobsen, associate dean of the Graduate College; Phillip Jones, vice president for student services and dean of students; Gerhard Loewenberg, professor of political science, formerly dean of the College of Liberal Arts; Casey Mahon, formerly associate vice president for finance and university services; Charles Mason, professor emeritus, education, formerly associate dean of the Graduate College; Deirdre McCloskey, professor of economics and history; James McLeran, formerly dean of the College of Dentistry; Michael McNulty, associate provost for international affairs; Julia Mears, formerly legal assistant to the president; Kim Merker, professor of English and director of the Center for the Book emeritus; Kenneth Moll, professor emeritus, speech pathology and audiology, formerly associate and acting vice president for academic affairs; Rex Montgomery, professor emeritus, biochemistry, formerly associate dean of the College of Medicine, and acting vice president for research; Hughlett Morris, professor emeritus, speech pathology and audiology; Ray Muston, professor emeritus, education, formerly president of ICAD (Iowa City Area Development Group); Mary Parden, formerly administrative assistant to presidents; Hunter Rawlings III, president, Cornell University, formerly president of the University of Iowa; Lawrence Rettig, assistant to the vice president for research; Ann Rhodes, vice president for university relations; Rudolph Schulz, professor emeritus, psychology, formerly dean for advanced studies; Jay Semel, director of Obermann Center for Advanced Studies; Lee Shope, director of Information Technical Services Financial Planning emeritus, formerly acting director of Weeg Computing Center; David Skorton, vice president for research; Mary Jo Small, associate vice president emeritus for finance and university services; Howard Sokol, formerly special assistant to the vice president for academic affairs; Gordon Strayer, formerly director of the Office of Public Information; William Stwalley, head of the Department of Physics, University of Connecticut, formerly professor of chemistry and physics; William Trease, formerly legal advisor to the vice president for educational development and research; James Van Allen, professor emeritus, physics and astronomy; David Vernon, professor of law, formerly acting vice president for academic affairs; Bruce Wheaton, director of the University Research Park; Derek Willard, associate vice president for research; and Paul Zimmer, formerly director of the University of Iowa Press.

The assembled materials from which this book has been drawn have been deposited in their entirety, along with the 687-page original draft of the book, in the university archives.

The Way It Was

1. THE BOWEN YEARS

1964−1969

1964−1966: THE NEW DEAN'S INITIATION

Defining the Graduate College and Recruiting the Dean

When President Howard R. Bowen arrived on the Iowa campus in the summer of 1964, John Weaver, the incumbent vice president for research and graduate dean, had recently resigned after serving three short years, to accept the position as vice president for academic affairs and dean of faculties at Ohio State University. Orville Hitchcock, professor of speech and dramatic art, who had been serving as the assistant dean, was appointed acting dean of the graduate college by the acting dean of faculties, Willard Boyd, until a replacement for Weaver could be chosen. A committee of deans and other university leaders had been appointed by President Bowen to recommend Weaver's replacement.

President Bowen moved quickly to fill the vacancy. After meeting with the search committee, he outlined his views of the position of graduate dean on December 28, 1964, in a three-page memo. (It's not clear with whom he shared the memo, if anyone.) Its contents reveal that he had thought at length about the position of graduate dean, apparently because he foresaw the need for strong leadership in the light of the anticipated growth in both the number of graduate students and the importance of graduate education and research on the national front, a growth already begun. Nevertheless, it seems remarkable to me that a university president would take the time to articulate the job description of the graduate dean with such completeness. Perhaps he felt that some of his university colleagues needed such a statement to grasp fully the scope and responsibilities of the position. In the memo he emphasized the traditional influential position of the dean under Dean Carl Seashore's dominant and imaginative leadership (1908−1936, 1942−1946), his hope to restore the deanship to one similar to that of Seashore's legacy, and the inclusion of research policy as part of the dean's responsibilities. He went on to comment on the special tact and diplomacy required by the dean when working with the other colleges, emphasizing the relationship with the College of Liberal

Arts in particular. He closed by saying: "I want to make clear that the graduate dean is subordinate to no other academic officer. Moreover, the graduate dean is a member of the central administrative staff and a close advisor of the academic vice president and president."

But not everyone agreed on the importance of the graduate dean's role. Dewey B. Stuit, dean of the College of Liberal Arts, apparently had some question about the future of the Graduate College and the graduate dean. In a letter to President Bowen on December 18, 1964, he advocated asking the Graduate Council to study the future role of the Graduate College, continuing with Acting Dean Orville Hitchcock in the interim. He also recommended that, if Mr. Bowen decided to retain the Graduate College with a role similar to that of the past, a local faculty member should be appointed. President Bowen, however, ignored Dean Stuit's counsel, which seemed to suggest the appointment of a weak person, if indeed anyone at all. Bowen clearly was committed to the appointment of someone with strong leadership credentials and wanted to aim higher.

The committee conducted its search during the fall of 1964 with apparently no clear results, and, in the end, President Bowen took over the search himself, interviewing several people from off and on the campus. In fact, he made an offer to someone from off campus but nothing came of it. And it was toward the end of this process, following his fall speech, that he received my October letter out of the blue. Apparently it piqued his interest.

One day I got a surprise phone call — maybe it was late November or early December in 1964 — in which President Bowen asked me to come over and talk to him. I thought, Oh, my God, what have I done? During the meeting he broached the subject of my possible interest in the graduate deanship. I was shocked; I had been brought up by my mentor, Wendell Johnson, in the shadow of Carl Seashore. It had never occurred to me to aspire to Seashore's former job. But I was brash enough to say that I'd be interested in thinking about it.

He didn't offer me a job at the time, and a number of weeks went by during which I didn't hear anything. I really didn't expect anything to come from the conversation. I don't recall that I felt sad about it, but I was curious to know what was going on. Then I got another call from President Bowen to come see him. This time he was very serious about proposing my name as graduate dean. I am sure that many said, "Spriestersbach? Who's he?" Up to that time I'd been very insular in my activities at the university.

At some point in late January, President Bowen called me to arrange a third meeting. It turned out that we would both be in Washington at the same time the last of January. We agreed to an early morning meeting before our separate meetings of the day. Over breakfast (I had one egg up and bacon) he offered me the job as dean, which I accepted. Part of my reasoning for doing so was that I was already so consumed in the administration of my grants that I had effectively ceased being a bench researcher. I felt that I might as well expand my administrative responsibilities beyond that of my research group.

A handwritten note for his files, dated February 3, 1965, noted that he had met with the Graduate Council and Research Council (dates unclear), presented the recommendation that I be appointed graduate dean, and asked if they wished to consider further candidates. Apparently the overwhelming recommendation was against further consideration. The Board of Regents approved my appointment, effective February 15, 1965, during its February 10–12 meeting.

I appeared at the Graduate College offices in the basement of Old Capitol (the original seat of Iowa's state government) on the morning of February 15, 1965, and was shown to the dean's office, my new home. The secretary to the dean, Gertrude Unrath, a quiet, unassuming, and gracious lady, appeared shortly and placed all the incoming mail, including second, third, and fourth class, on my desk. I looked at the pile, nearly a half-bushel basket of documents; what the hell was I to do with it? Fortunately Orville Hitchcock, whom I had known since our times as faculty members in the Department of Speech and Dramatic Art, helped and advised me, generously giving context for the tasks at hand. Not that there was a huge operation to oversee; there were two other secretaries in addition to Gertrude and that was it.

Routines were already in place, of course — meetings of the Graduate Council, meetings of the Academic Board (the academic deans and other central administration officials), and conferences with President Bowen and Willard (Sandy) Boyd, vice president for academic affairs — which soon started to fill my schedule. Most of my attention was focused on the Graduate College, since the advent of major external funding was yet to come.

While the official title of my position was dean of the Graduate College, it was clear to me from the first that I was expected to deal with both graduate education and research, and that this larger mission was consistent with President Bowen's conception of the position. Indeed, he later recommended to the Board of Regents, and they approved, inclusion of "research" in my charge by changing my title to vice president for research and dean of the Graduate College. Here is what he said in his notes to the Board of Regents, March 7, 1966:

> When Duane Spriestersbach was appointed dean of the Graduate College, I withheld the conventional title for the position, which is vice president for research and dean of the Graduate College. I did so because I wished

to use the title "vice president" sparingly. [Or did he want to wait and see what this unknown quantity could do?] I now believe I made an error in his case. He is heavily involved on behalf of the university in activities on the national scene, especially in Washington, and in educational circles. In these activities, the lack of the title of vice president is a handicap to him. Virtually every one of his counterparts in other comparable institutions is known as vice president, as was his predecessor, Dean Weaver. Therefore, I recommend the change in title. . . . I should mention parenthetically that Dean Spriestersbach has already been responsible for raising far more money for the university than his entire lifetime salary.

Opportunities for Federal Funding: The Trend Begins

President Bowen had pointed the way to this expanded charge in earlier remarks. For example, even at a meeting of the Research Council on April 16, 1964, before my tenure as dean, during a campus visit when he was president-designate, he had expressed keen interest in the newly announced National Science Foundation (NSF) program to support the establishment of "Centers of Excellence" in selected universities. The purpose of these centers was to move programs from good to excellent with major NSF grants. He suggested that an ad hoc committee be formed to map out the application contents and strategy. Subsequently, a number of faculty groups met, but a specific plan did not emerge. Hence, one of the very first directives that he gave me when I came on board was to review what had been done to date in getting an application developed and to move it forward. More will be said about this later, but it was clear at the outset that my experience in successfully competing for external funding for my own research was expected to carry over to the entire university.

Until World War II ended, the University of Iowa, like most state-supported universities, depended on state appropriations, tuition, and some very modest private gifts for its operating support. Following the war, it became federal policy to provide funds to universities for support of research, students, and demonstration programs, mostly in the view that it was in the national interest to insure the continuation of the intellectual activity that had begun during the national buildup of World War II. Thus, external funding, especially from federal agencies, became increasingly available, albeit on a competitive basis. During his tenure as president (1940–1964), Virgil Hancher and his colleagues had been relatively cautious at best about actively seeking such funds, apparently wary of the obligations that might be attached to them. But by the time President Bowen came on the scene, the growing availability of federal funds could no longer be ignored.

Bowen had only been in office two and a half months when Phil Connell, assistant to the president, wrote to Dean Zenor, director of the Institute for Public Affairs, indicating that, while President Bowen knew of the efforts of the institute to keep various departments and divisions informed of federal legislation, he wanted occasionally to write to the deans, directors, or department heads, asking them to consider actions that might eventually bring outside support to existing programs or funds for new programs. Connell went on to say that eventually President Bowen planned to center the responsibility for local action in the hands of an associate dean for research in the Graduate College, but that, in the interim, Bowen intended to take the initiative. Clearly, it was his intention to provide focus and responsibility for increasing the amount of external funds coming to the university.

Indeed, as early as the meeting of the Academic Board on February 17, 1965, just two days after I had begun my new appointment, Professor Lewis Wagner, director of the Bureau of Business and Economic Research, mentioned the existence of the governor's Scientific Advisory Committee, which was affiliated with the Iowa Development Commission. He reported that he understood that these groups appeared to want to be the "focal point for all federal research and development support but that . . . we ought to tread lightly in endorsing this position because the university's interest and the interest of Iowa industry may not always be identical." Further discussion revealed a high degree of agreement that it was important to give some indication to both groups that there should be an official point of contact between such agencies and the university.

Apart from President Bowen's initial charge to me to explore external funding opportunities, this was my first introduction to the existing university structure that might be relevant to my duties. There was clearly much for someone to do, and I assumed that I was the person to do it. We would need to develop a single university unit with the capacity for the aggressive pursuit and dissemination of external funding opportunities for the faculty and staff; we would be facing calls from a variety of sources to play a role in fostering support for business and industry; and we would need to be vigilant in our review of possible competing interests of the groups. Each of these issues became central to planning and decision making in the years ahead.

Soon after that meeting President Bowen led a related discussion of the Academic Board.

The university has moved cautiously in the direction of using federal grants for salary purposes because . . . it is not always easy to ascertain the extent upon which federal money can be depended for continuing support; and it is difficult in budget-making to have to pick up positions in the regular budget which have been initiated and then dropped because of lack of continued support. However, the changing pattern very definitely indicates that federal support is a part of the scene in American higher education and our experience indicates that we need to be less cautious than perhaps we have been in the past.

He proposed that the funds released through the use of federal funds should be placed in a contingency account to be used to reinstate the portions of salaries covered from federal sources when they were no longer available and for use for additional salaries, equipment, and general expenses if balances from this source accrued.

Some departments reacted negatively to the proposed policy. James Van Allen, then professor and chair of the Department of Physics and Astronomy, wrote to Dean Stuit:

> The announced policy is doubtless a reasonable and proper one for deal-ing with institutional grants which are made, in effect, to the board of re-gents for use at its discretion, or for grants or contracts which are for specific activities of a non-academic character. But I submit that it is an unreasonable and improper one for dealing with grants and research con-tracts which are obtained by individual investigators or alliances of inves-tigators for academic work in specific areas. The purpose of such grants and research contracts is to increase the resources of personnel, equip-ment, supplies, etc., in a specific area, and especially to make possible significant graduate research programs for which, as is almost always the case, state appropriations are inadequate. Almost all such grants and con-tracts are obtained by the efforts of individual faculty members . . . to a very large extent as entrepreneurs. The announced policy subverts the purpose of such grants by diverting a portion of the support to purposes for which it is not intended. It does so, moreover, in the most destructive possible way — that is, by making it impossible to increase the faculty in the very areas which the support is designed to strengthen.

I had yet to develop an "institutional" position, but at this point I reacted sympathetically to Van Allen's position.

A number of other departmental executive officers (DEOs) seconded Pro-fessor Van Allen's protest. While the proposed policy was not implemented as such, resource allocations at collegiate and university levels were dealt with on a case-by-case basis. Typically, the DEOs and faculties of departments that are successful in generating external funds have not been bashful in parlaying the information to their advantage in the allocation of resources. The issue of indirect cost lay buried in these exchanges, as I would later discover.

This was, of course, not the first time that the central administration acknowledged the growing level of external funding by announcing university-wide policies for managing the seeking and spending of such funds. In fact, back in November 1961, John Weaver issued a memo to DEOs and faculty that outlined the procedures to be followed in making applications for external funds. He explained its rationale in part as follows:

> It does cost money to accept money through grants and contracts, and if the institution's always limited resources of funds, space and personnel are to be used equitably and effectively, some all-university picture of need and opportunity must be assembled and given regular review. . . . The functions of the vice president's offices in regard to application approval are those of assuring an ever current inventory of commitments being made, of assuring that proper and consistent forms and procedures are being observed, and that the all-university concerns for distribution of financial, space and personnel resources are being given adequate review.

This policy was a harbinger of what was to follow as the policies of funding agencies grew more complex — in part because of their requirements for cost sharing, mandated university programs for the use of human and animal subjects, control of toxic materials in research, and the provision of safe environments for the researchers and student and faculty colleagues.

At a meeting of the Research Council on March 18, 1965, discussions that would ultimately shape the outreach functions and the enlargement of the administrative umbrella of the Graduate College continued. To quote from the minutes: "It was agreed . . . that the Graduate College office could render a real service to the university by continuing and extending its function as a central source for information about research programs sponsored by governmental agencies and private foundations." The council concluded that there was no need for the university to have a permanent representative stationed in Washington, D.C. There was general support for "the suggestions that the Graduate College be given further funds for use in helping beginning researchers try out new ideas."

The Need for Additional Personnel
At the time we were faced with the development of applications for construction funds. (There truly were some in those days!) But the backup files were bare. There was no material on the University of Iowa — mission, size, budget, accomplishments, etc. — the inevitable material that is included in

the background pages of external fund applications, the "boilerplate" as it's called in the trade. After only two months in the office, it was clear to me that the responsibilities of the office were going to grow and that I would need help beyond that of an assistant dean and three secretaries.

The gods were with me the day that Margery Hoppin walked into my office, inquiring about a possible staff opening for her. I may have made a couple of calls to references that she gave, but it took me only a day or two to decide to hire her. I liked her quiet but self-confident manner. She seemed to be a person who would follow through with a minimum of prompting. It was one of the most fortuitous employment decisions that I made during my entire twenty-five years in central administration, since Marge was destined to become "sponsored programs" at the University of Iowa during my tenure. Of course, we had little basis for understanding the potential magnitude of the new university posture that called for the aggressive pursuit of external funds and the follow-through management that would grow out of funds we received.

The number of graduate students grew and the responsibilities for research and development funds were increasingly vested in my office. I recommended (and subsequently received approval for) the addition of an assistant dean for administration, an associate dean for special projects (ultimately named the dean for advanced studies), a funds research specialist (ultimately to become the director of sponsored programs), and a graduate examiner. Hard on the heels of this announcement, Charles Mason, then the director of student aid, was approved by the regents at their May meeting as the assistant dean for administration. While all these positions and more continue in some form today, supporting the validity of my need assessment then, I am taken aback at my audacity in moving so far so fast in augmenting the staff. However, I felt a sense of urgency to keep ahead of the incoming tide, and President Bowen and Vice President Boyd obviously agreed with me.

President Bowen buttressed his view that Iowa faced an unusual period of growth with data contained in the September 1965 *President's Report*. (These annual reports came to be known as the "green books" because of the color of their covers.) In it he projected that total student enrollment would grow from 15,850 in 1965 to 28,865 in 1990 (a remarkably astute projection: the actual 1990 figure turned out to be 28,045), requiring an additional increase in faculty from 1,314 in 1965 to an estimated 2,405 in 1990. When he took account of vacancies created by retirements and resignations, he estimated that the university would need to recruit approximately 125 new faculty members per year. These projections were then used widely in planning for the future, which seemed hard upon us.

When the 1965–1966 budget year began, the Graduate College staff had been increased over the previous year by three additional professional positions. In addition, the office had funds for fifteen research professors and stipends for graduate student fellowships, research assistantships, and scholarships. While I was pleased with the increases, I didn't think very much about them in view of what I felt I had been charged to accomplish: anticipate growth and exploit all supporting opportunities without sacrificing quality.

The Graduate College: A University-Wide Unit

Defining new policies for the Graduate College evolved almost daily. It's helpful to remember that when Seashore became dean in 1904, graduate education was in its infancy in this country. At Iowa many departments were unsure what master's and doctoral degrees entailed and what their obligations were in mounting graduate programs. Since Seashore had very definite ideas about these matters, coupled with a very strong personality, he told departments what to do and expected them to conform. If I had used some of the Seashore practices during my tenure, I would have been sacked.

During the years that followed Seashore's tenure, there hadn't been any major changes proposed or made in the policies or procedures of the Graduate College until I became dean. It had been a given for the faculty that the college was there. Most of the faculty, however, didn't quite know what it was about; it was just there. The consensus was that the college wouldn't bother you so long as you followed its picky rules and regulations.

I was aware that the Graduate College had been viewed by many primarily as a kind of arm of the College of Liberal Arts. After all, that is where the traditional graduate programs were. Most administrative traffic involved those departments and still does. I was also aware that some of my predecessors had assiduously attended the meetings of the departmental executives of the College of Liberal Arts. I chose not to follow that custom, quickly sensing that, as the graduate dean, I was obligated to relate equally to the departments of all our colleges.

Of course, the faculty directly involved determine how to package knowledge into which kinds of academic units. In dealing with them, we set a posture of excellence — of being concerned, providing gentle assistance when it was needed (maybe not always enough), readily recognizing good things, expressing unhappiness with the failures, and scrutinizing the inadequacies. We developed comparative data that we publicized. Unit X could see that it was at the bottom and that Y was at the top. We would say to unit X, "Is that where you want to be?" Additionally, we sought to influence decisions in other ways:

the notes we wrote to faculty; the notes we didn't write to faculty; the ones we chose to congratulate, etc. All of this had a cumulative effect.

Revision of the *Graduate College* Manual

Urgency was in the air. In my first appearance before the graduate faculty on May 26, 1965, I reviewed projections that the graduate student body would grow from 3,332 (23 percent of the total university enrollment) in 1965 to 13,500 (46 percent of an estimated enrollment of 28,865) by 1990. While the percentage of graduate students in total enrollment did not increase over time, remaining at approximately 25 percent during the entire twenty-five years of my tenure, the estimates at the time called for us to look to our enrollment and retention procedures to insure that such massive enrollment increases would not result in a watering down of the quality of the graduate student body.

The Graduate College *Manual*, the bible of rules and procedures governing the operations of the Graduate College, had last been revised in 1962. Early in the fall of 1965, a consensus grew among the members of the Graduate Council that some changes were in order. I was fortunate to have inherited a particularly dedicated and experienced group of council members. We decided to review the thirty-seven-page *Manual* line by line. Copies of similar governing documents were assembled from other universities for comparison. Our goal was to have a revised *Manual* in place at the beginning of the 1966–1967 school year.

The council worked assiduously in subcommittees and as a council through the fall semester of the 1965–1966 academic year on revising the *Manual*. Finally, the council had a draft in place to share with the faculty for comment, and a special meeting was held on April 26, 1966. Not surprisingly there were reactions, even some with passion. The two proposals that drew most fire were changes in the grading of research work and in graduate faculty membership. In addition to proposing that letter grades for research work should be changed to S and U (satisfactory and unsatisfactory), we proposed that the existing regulation specifying automatic membership in the faculty of those who were appointed and held the rank of assistant professor or above be changed to require that new members should instead be nominated by their departmental executive and approved by a college-wide committee on elections, using research and scholarship as the prime criteria for making suitability judgments. Both proposals were in line with the practices of many universities throughout the country.

At the regular meeting of the graduate faculty on May 24, 1966, the graduate faculty membership proposal was dropped. In the case of grading research work, language was inserted that permitted departments to use the S/U system if they wished, but it was not required. Other changes were made, the most contentious of which required that applicants for admission must take the Graduate Record Examination (GRE) or similar national examinations established for specific fields, such as the Admission Test for Graduate Study in Business (ATGSB). A motion to strike the requirement lost. The new regulations went into effect at the beginning of the 1966–1967 academic year, and we felt that we were better prepared administratively and academically to handle the onslaught that appeared to be around the corner.

More Adjustments to a Changing World

It had been the custom at Iowa for many years that any graduate student with a teaching or research appointment of a quarter time or more would be assessed in-state tuition; that policy continues. In addition, there had been many tuition scholarships for graduate students. In my view the keen competition for top-quality graduate students from the nationwide pool, along with the significant contributions that they made to the departments and the university, argued for only a minimal level of tuition fees. Unfortunately, in the ensuing years the relative increases in graduate tuition for nonresidents have been steadily greater than those for resident graduate students, raising questions in my mind about the level of appreciation for the need to recruit the finest young intellects without regard to geography to serve the best interests of the university.

At the January 27, 1966, regular meeting of the graduate faculty, I expressed my strong opposition to a differential in tuition between resident and nonresident graduate students, a policy that was generated by the regents. In fact, the Graduate College staff prepared an exhaustive thirty-six-page paper entitled "The Case for a Single Tuition Rate for All Graduate Students." I felt that an important policy issue was at stake. However, I was unable to generate support for my position at any level.

Other changes were under way. One, only in its beginnings, had to do with the admission of women to graduate school. In 1965 an attitude existed among some of the professoriate that university resources should not be "wasted" on women unless it was clear that they were committed to a full-time profession rather than to becoming a housewife and mother. Although spurred on by World War II, the two-income family had not yet become the norm. And for those of either sex who intended to work as professionals, they found that, increasingly, advanced degrees were required for professional advancement and sometimes for entry into the professions as well. In 1931, 15 percent of

Iowa's graduate students were women. That percentage had grown to 24 percent in 1965. (The percentage in 1997 was 52 percent.) Consideration of gender, at least as a shadow criterion for admission to graduate work, has officially disappeared from the admission processes today. But it was not that way even thirty years ago.

Tooling Up for Federal Funding

During my first year as dean, opportunities for applying for external funds, primarily from federal government sources, were announced almost daily, so much so that Marge Hoppin, our funds resource specialist, and I had difficulty cataloging them, much less recruiting, advising, and helping faculty and staff with the necessary follow-through applications. But we had some early hits that tended to solidify the validity and necessity of a "research" office at the central administrative level of the university.

In 1963 the Higher Education Facilities Act became law. Its provisions included funds for the building and renovation of academic buildings that would advance the undergraduate programs, under Title I, and the graduate programs, under Title II. In addition to boilerplate about the university, applications for the funds needed to provide convincing demonstrations that the academic programs had established merit, that the need for additional or improved space was necessary if the programs were to thrive and improve, and that university funds were available to pay some portion of the building costs. For example, in 1963 the state legislature had appropriated $2 million for the construction of the English-Philosophy Building. We requested $366,514 from the Office of Education to cover part of the "graduate project development" costs. In due course we had a site visit composed of persons from the English departments of other universities and representatives from the Office of Education. Subsequently, we received the full amount requested in the application. In his December 1965 letter to the Board of Regents President Bowen called it a windfall.

We then applied for funds to cover both undergraduate and graduate construction costs for portions of the Art and Music buildings. In addition, NASA, NSF, and HEW provided funds separately or in combination for portions of the construction costs of the Bowen Science Building, a Chemistry Building addition, the Biology Building, the Hardin Library of Health Sciences, and Van Allen Hall. Earlier similar awards had been received for partial support of the construction costs of the Spence Laboratories and the Wendell Johnson Speech and Hearing Center. The availability of these funds provided powerful arguments for the university administration as it sought the vital matching funds from the state for construction of the buildings. All too soon these federal programs were abandoned, and the unmet needs for adequate university building programs have grown steadily.

In his December letter to the regents, President Bowen reported that we had received eighty-five new National Defense Education Fellowships for the 1966–1967 academic year, in contrast to twenty in the current year. Not only did these awards involve multiple-year stipend support for the fellows, but they also provided "cost of education" allowances to the university that could be used to support departmental and university needs for program enhancements. During the four years from 1965 to 1969, Bowen estimated that the total for the cost of education allowances for the NDEA awards then approved or scheduled to be approved would be over $1.3 million. All other fellowship programs from NSF, NASA, NIH, etc., carried similar allowances. In the years that followed, these funds became the source of early support from our office for "development."

We weren't always successful, of course, in our efforts to get external funding for university and related programs. One of our failures had to do with the proposed multimillion-dollar "Atom Smasher" that the Atomic Energy Commission had proposed to build. The AEC sought a 3,000-acre site on flat land with the availability of large quantities of electricity and water. There was also the unspoken acknowledgment that the facility would attract a supporting community built by private investors that would add millions of dollars to the local economy. Sites in Iowa were identified in the vicinity of North Liberty and between Iowa City and Davenport. Planning meetings were held involving area business, state, congressional, and education leaders, and an application was made under great time constraints. Site visits were duly held, which included presentations and luncheons with Professor James Van Allen as our spokesperson. We were competing with applicants from forty-three other states offering 110 sites. While we didn't make the cut (Batavia, Illinois, was ultimately chosen), we were in good company, and we had our first taste of the kind of concerted community planning that would be required in the years ahead.

Cost sharing was one of the requirements of applications for federal funds. Sometimes these could be "in kind" contributions — portions of time, principally. However, sometimes the university had to be willing to contribute funds earmarked to support the needs cited in the applications. In February 1966 I wrote a memo to Vice President Boyd consolidating for him the matching commitments ($75,000) that we had made in our applications for undergraduate and research equipment funds during the year so that he could use the information in his budget planning for the coming year.

Such matching funds were a constant source of modest tension between the funding agencies and the universities and their faculties and staffs. All tried to get favorable numbers, with the faculty frequently feeling strongly that the greater the university match, the better their chances for getting an award. The funding agencies frequently implied agreement with the faculty and sometimes joined forces with them against the universities. In any event, at Iowa we gradually developed review processes that attempted to ask the hard "what if" questions during the time applications were being written to insure that all concerned understood the commitments that were being made when applications left the university. To be sure, we weren't always successful in getting the applicants to reveal the potential hidden obligations!

Given the growing number of programs announced and funded by federal agencies, insuring that we were in position to strike at funding opportunities in Washington ahead of the pack was an early and recurring issue. Although many sister universities did establish offices in Washington, we were steadfast in the belief that we could do a more effective job of "selling" the university directly from campus. Subsequently, however, we did assign leadership duties associated with that mission to a director of agency liaison, later to be renamed associate vice president, in our research office.

The End of Year One

Toward the end of the 1965–1966 fiscal year, I wrote a memo to President Bowen and Vice President Boyd in which I shared what I had written at the end of a Teachers Insurance and Annuity Association (TIAA) survey of university administrator benefits in response to an opened-ended invitation to comment about my job. I noted that there had been a major increase in the complexities of administering an office such as mine, particularly resulting from federally supported programs. I indicated that departments resented this intrusion on their autonomy and the mounting reporting requirements. I closed by saying: "I think most people involved in administration get some personal rewards by doing a job well and being able to complete it in a reasonable length of time. Too often, however, there is too much to do — too many demands, too many meetings — that few tasks are really completed well. As a consequence, frustration, depression, and demoralization develop. These feelings are intensified by the fact that few people in academia have any great attraction for 'The Administration.'" President Bowen replied with a sympathetic note, saying in effect that "some days are like that." It was, of course, the proper response. He endured me while, at the same time, providing me with perspectives that I needed as I worked into my administrative harness.

1966–1967: CONSOLIDATIONS, IMPLEMENTATIONS, AND MORE PLANNING

The new future seemed to be bearing down on us. We all — students, staff, and faculty alike — were more than usually aware of our ourselves and our educational and social structures. We would see manifestations of that awareness in the months ahead.

Still More Dealing with the Feds

The tempo of activity surrounding the seeking of external funds for all purposes had started to accelerate at the university, and across the country, and ultimately would require a major portion of the time and resources of our office. We were able to report to Bowen on August 10, 1966, that the dollar amounts for applications forwarded during 1965–1966 ($44.7 million) had increased 45 percent (from $24.6 million for 1964–1965). Since the number of applications approved for funding relates to the number of applications forwarded, it was reasonable to assume that the amount of funds ultimately accepted would jump the ensuing year, which it did (28 percent). That pattern of increases would continue throughout the next twenty-five years and beyond, and governed the messages that I transmitted to the faculty and central administration throughout the period, colored by my constant reminders that we must anticipate and prepare for handling these sources of university revenue without missing any beats and without causing the university to veer from its central purposes of teaching, research, and service.

This activity was not without its consequences, of course. There were restrictions of varying degrees on expenditures from the awards made, governed by the applicants' statements of purpose and proposed budgets. Furthermore, all expenditures were subject to audit by the federal agency in charge of auditing these awards. (At the time the navy had that responsibility for the University of Iowa.)

One of our problems related to levels of cost sharing. On April 25, 1967, a memo went to the faculty from Vice President Boyd, Vice President Elwin Jolliffe, and me, reminding the faculty that current federal regulations prohibited agencies from covering the entire costs of supported research grants. In essence the memo prohibited cost sharing from indirect costs but allowed it through salaries or equipment in a form that must be part of the audited record. In the main we had few problems in identifying appropriate university cost sharing. Many times our problems were in the other direction, too much sharing, since sometimes faculty perceived that their chances of having their applications approved would be enhanced by higher levels of institutional cost sharing. Most agencies were aware of this possibility and established policies that divorced cost sharing from the consideration of the merits of proposals. Once a proposal was approved for funding, the agency staff would then negotiate the level of cost sharing with the recipient institution.

On July 1, 1966, the Public Health Service ordered that certain policies and procedures must be implemented by institutions applying for funds for research with human subjects as safeguards for the subjects' rights and welfare. Consequently, in September 1966 we announced the establishment of three committees: one with jurisdiction primarily over the health colleges other than dentistry, one for dentistry, and one for the balance of the departments, mainly those in the social sciences. Subsequently, a fourth committee was added to cover research involving human subjects that was done without external funding, because of the consensus that it was a proper safeguard to take when doing any type of research involving humans. Some adjustments in the jurisdictions of the committees have been made over the years, but they all continue to function today. Their original, and continuing, charge is to insure "an independent determination (1) of the rights and welfare of the individual or individuals involved, (2) of the appropriateness of the methods used to secure informed consent, and (3) of the risks, and potential medical benefits of the investigation."

Over the years the review process has become more bureaucratized and complex. Review committees have spent major amounts of their time in the reviews. Still, the consensus continues to be that it was and is a justified and necessary function.

My Concerns

At the first meeting of the Research Council of the new academic year on September 28, 1966, I alerted the council to some of the pending agenda items. They included the balance between teaching and research in programs with large research grants, priority issues for the use of flexible funds in support of research and creative work, classified research and restrictions on publication stemming from federally sponsored research, conflict of interest regulations, regulations concerning research involving human subjects, cost sharing on research grants, patents, and copyrights, and the allocation of funds recovered from indirect cost charges. Perhaps it should not come as a surprise that almost all these topics are still under review and evolution.

With the unprecedented expansion of graduate programs across the country in response to the country's optimism over the "new world order," competition was keen for bright graduate students. Stipends were raised along with other support programs. We knew that if we raised our academic standards, which we did, in the face of this competition, we would end up with a diminished supply of good applicants for our graduate programs. At the time slightly less than a third of the students we were admitting actually enrolled. Consequently, we felt compelled to devise better support programs to entice our very best applicants to follow through.

Some New Programs and Some Old Ones Revised

One of the programs that we devised and ultimately got a budget allocation for was the Teaching-Research Fellowship Program. It was based on the following premises:

1. Teaching and research are synergistic in their effect.

2. The whole structure of the graduate programs at the University of Iowa depends upon attracting scholastically superior students.

3. Since teaching and research stimulate each other, the graduate student would benefit from continuous exposure to both.

We took the position that there were important educational values in teaching for all persons seeking the Ph.D. degree regardless of their career objectives. Many of us felt that teaching something to someone else inevitably improved one's understanding of the subject. In addition we were mindful of the clamor at the time for teachers for junior colleges, community colleges, and liberal arts colleges. We were being pressured to develop new programs and intermediate degrees, yet we remained convinced that our departments were capable of preparing persons for these positions without new courses, new requirements, and new degree procedures. We managed to maintain this position in spite of the adoption by some of our sister institutions of related new programs and new degrees specifically designed for these positions. In most instances the degrees that were established elsewhere during this period have gradually disappeared.

The spring of 1967 brought harbingers of disquiet that would explode several years hence into major disruptions at many universities across the land, including the University of Iowa. On April 13, 1967, the Student Senate voted to hold a special university-wide meeting to support the National Mobilization to End the War in Vietnam. A peace march, announced for the following day — to coincide with marches to be held in New York and San Francisco — would end with a public rally in front of Old Capitol. Campus and city police took cognizance of the plans and announced that they would be present to "assure peace and order." Several weeks later the Student Senate passed a resolution calling for President Bowen to suspend classes at 2:30 one afternoon for a "campus-wide teach-in on the east steps of Old Capitol." President

Bowen denied the request. The contentions over the Vietnam War were to escalate to major proportions in the springs of 1969, 1970, 1971, and 1972. By each spring, studying, for many, had become a drag; the warming weather enticed outdoor activities, and built-up frustrations gave birth to what would become contentious expression.

1967–1968: THE PLOT THICKENS

Strengthening the Graduate College

In addition to continuing to organize our offices for expected growth in student enrollments and competition for external funds, I attempted to get my arms and head around the "Graduate College." The college consisted of eighty departments offering ninety-eight degrees at the master's level and fifty-three degrees at the doctoral level. It had 998 faculty members (only six of whom were paid from the college budget) and 4,770 graduate students. Its programs ranged from the traditional fields of scholarship to those with a strong professional orientation. Even so, were there areas of common interest and mutual concern among these fields and orientations? What was the proper balance between collegewide and departmental regulation? During graduate faculty meetings I tried to frame questions that would pinpoint our common agenda.

I had, after all, earned my professorial spurs in the Department of Speech Pathology and Audiology, which felt strongly, as did the majority of other university departments, that it was, and should be, the principal architect of its own graduate programs. It took a dim view of outside interference in them. I had already learned that some departments were more assiduous in the development and monitoring of their graduate programs than others. Thus, I tried to lead rather than direct, inform where possible, and even inspire a few.

The Selective Service Draft and Campus Unease

The scope of the war in Vietnam escalated, swallowing increasing numbers of young men, including college students, into the draft. By and large, college students in 1967 were exempt as long as they were enrolled in college and making satisfactory progress in completing requirements for a degree. On November 2, 1967, a group of demonstrators gathered at the student union to protest and prevent, if possible, Marine recruiters from interviewing potential applicants for Marine officer candidate school. A melee ensued in which 108 demonstrators, including a faculty member and a state senator, were arrested and taken to the Iowa City police department for arraignment. President Bowen issued a statement that was to guide university policies in the months ahead:

> As it has sought to make abundantly clear, the university must continue to fulfill its clear responsibility to protect the rights of individual students in seeking access to placement facilities. In relation to the current situation, this means that the university will continue to assist students who wish to interview recruiters, including officers of the U.S. Marine Corps. If their help is not sufficient to assure access to all who wish it, assistance will again be sought from peace officers of the city, the county and the state of Iowa.
>
> Students involved in violations of university regulations concerning these rights of fellow students will be subject to disciplinary action through regular university procedures.

Later, on January 15, 1968, he wrote in a piece entitled "University Students and the Advancement of American Society":

> The chief weakness of American society, as I see it, is a malaise, or sickness, of the individual human spirit rather than a breakdown of social machinery. That is why I think the under-thirty generation may be right in concentrating on ethical and humanistic considerations. . . . The one place where I disagree profoundly with some members of the under-thirty group is on the value of orderly democratic procedures, and especially on the value of the basic principles of university life which include thoughtful search for truth, free expression for all, tolerance toward differing opinions, and rational discourse. . . . There is no place for [direct action] at the University of Iowa.

On December 6, when recruiters from the Dow Chemical Company, manufacturer of napalm, were on campus, another demonstration took place in which eighteen persons were arrested following several disturbances. On December 15, 1967, the Board of Regents embraced Bowen's statement and made it applicable to ISU and UNI as well.

The selective service draft continued to be an unsettling force throughout the year as federal draft policies were revised several times. Newly enrolled male undergraduate and graduate students, except those in medical, dental, and veterinary fields and the ministry, were no longer to be deferred. Students who graduated at either level became subject to the draft; those in the oldest bracket (twenty-six years) were to be drafted first. There were, of course, blocks of men, for example, veterans and those not passing the physical standards, who were not subject to the draft. The position of the Graduate College was that it could not defend the need to defer individual half-time teaching assistants as critical to the operation of the undergraduate programs of the university. Further, we urged all to keep calm and counseled departments to appoint draft-eligible, competitive applicants to assistantships, traineeships, and fellowships. The consequence of the draft on university enrollments both at the undergraduate and graduate levels was minimal, but its existence was a very personal reminder to many students that an unpopular war was going on, which they felt required changes in national policies.

In addition to laws and presidential directives relating to the draft, general campus unrest was undoubtedly the basis for "flags" in new federal laws. An example is the antiriot clause that appeared in the 1967 appropriation for the Department of Labor and HEW. It prohibited the use of funds appropriated under the act from being used "to provide payments, assistance, or services, in any form, with respect to any individual convicted in any federal, state, or local court of competent jurisdiction, of inciting, promoting, or carrying on a riot or any group activity resulting in material damage to property or injury to persons found to be in violation of federal, state, or local laws designed to protect persons or property in the community concerned." Despite the many protest activities that were to follow on campus, no federal funds received during the period were ever challenged as a result of this clause, but again it reveals the state of mind of the majority of legislators at the time.

Working with the Iowa Congressional Delegation

In the light of our increasing involvement with federal agencies and federal funding, I proposed to President Bowen, and he agreed, that some members of the university administration should visit the Iowa congressional delegation in Washington, D.C., on an annual basis for give-and-take discussions of the state of the university. As part of that strategy, we arranged a luncheon meeting in Washington for the congressional delegation in December 1967. President Bowen carried the brunt of the discussion, some of which was anything but friendly since several of the members of the delegation felt that the university, and President Bowen in particular, was not "controlling" the war-dissenting students adequately. During similar luncheons in succeeding years during the Vietnam War era, the level of criticism in that vein would increase in intensity. But we lived through them, and arranging congressional luncheons continues in the belief that the exchanges of views and information between the members of Congress and university representatives is worthwhile. The practice is testimony to how far we have come from being "only" a state university.

Nationally, there was a growing articulation of the issues surrounding the university/federal partnership. The following is excerpted from "Life with

Uncle," which appeared in the February 5, 1968, issue of the *Chronicle of Higher Education*:

> To that end [the enlargement of the partnership between], colleges and universities may have to become more deeply involved in politics. They will have to determine, more clearly than ever before, just what their objectives are — and what their values are. And they will have to communicate these most effectively to their alumni, their political representatives, the corporate community, the foundations, and the public at large.
>
> If the partnership is to succeed, the federal government will have to do more than provide funds. Elected officials and administrators face the awesome task of formulating overall educational and research goals, to give direction to the programs of federal support. They must make more of an effort to understand what makes colleges and universities tick, and to accommodate individual institutional differences.

This dialogue continues in one form or another. Most of the time the issues are not clearly presented on either side. The universities are expected to be dependable anchors for advanced learning and creativeness. Yet they are expected, unreasonably in my opinion, to withstand abrupt funding changes brought about by changing federal programs, policies, and priorities.

New Program Initiatives

In large part as the result of cost-of-education allowances stemming from fellowships from federal programs, we were able to respond to a number of initiatives generated by faculty and staff. They were varied in purpose and came from persons throughout the university. In the end I made the final funding decisions, usually after consultations but without systematic review by a committee of faculty or staff peers. While there were no formally stated criteria, I was usually influenced by the thoroughness of the proposal, the track record of the proposer, and my judgment of the potential impact on the university. I needed to be persuaded that there would be follow through to an established activity within the university that would contribute a benchmark to the aspirations of the university as a whole. Karl (Kim) Merker, director of the Windhover Press, recalls:

> I did not know D. C. Spriestersbach that well at the time, so with fear and trembling I made an appointment and went to his office to see if I could get some money. The budget I had set up was not any great amount of money. I remember very well what he told me. He said, "It's yours." And then he said, since he had no idea what I was about any more than I had

an idea of what he was about, "You might think of this as a big piece of string. You can either weave it into a beautiful tapestry or you can turn it into a rope with which you can hang yourself."

A number of new programs were brought into being by drawing on such allowances. They have now been imbedded into the university's structure. A sample of them are: the Windhover Press (part of the Center for the Book), the Social Science Data Archive (part of the Political Research Laboratory), the Center for Biocatalysis and Bioprocessing, and the University Press.

In addition, one-time funds were given to numerous faculty members to support specific activities or to purchase specific items of equipment that would provide a special boost for their research efforts. For a promoter of development, it was a heady time!

Patents

In 1968 Congress began to discuss the rights of the federal government to patents stemming from university research that had been supported by federal funds. Some advocated that the existing policy granting federal agencies the primary responsibility for determining rights and options for pursuing patents supported by federal funds should be maintained. At the same time there was a growing awareness that moving such intellectual property to the marketplace could have a positive impact on the national economy that would be in the national interest. Each agency had its own rules; there was no standard policy. It wouldn't be until 1980 that patent law was modified to give patent rights to the universities for those inventions made as the result of federal funding of the research at the universities. The federal government has retained the right to a paid-up, royalty-free nonexclusive license to such patents. However, this does not prohibit universities from giving exclusive licenses to industry. The government has rarely, if ever, exercised its licensing option. The economic-good-in-the-national-interest argument has prevailed.

Classified Research

One of the consequences of the growing opposition by university students and faculties to the Vietnam War was a review of university practices for accepting federal funds to conduct either "secret" research (the existence of which cannot be revealed) or "classified" research (the existence of which is made public including the source and amount of funds and a general description of its purpose but with restrictions on the disclosure of its design and results). Debates on the matter raged in universities across the country. Many university policies were modified. In some cases federal contracts were canceled. In March 1968 the University Research Council accepted the distinction between secret and classified research and concluded that secret research had no place on the campus but that classified research should be left to the judgment of the investigator. The council went on to endorse the prohibition of theses and dissertations based on classified research.

Center of Excellence Award

As I mentioned earlier, one of President Bowen's first actions when he came to the campus in 1964 was to call a representative group of the science faculty to a meeting to discuss making an application to the National Science Foundation for a Center of Excellence award. Later the group held a number of meetings but arrived at no consensus concerning the focus and contents of such an application. President Bowen grew impatient. Then I arrived on the scene with the charge to get the process moving promptly.

In a 1996 interview, I queried Sandy Boyd about that time (when he had been the vice president for academic affairs and dean of faculties). Here is his recollection of it:

> I was concerned about the match [the NSF requirement that the university pick up the funding of all programs initiated as the result of the award] that was going to have to come ultimately. Howard used to say, "Don't worry about the match. It will all come. This is deterring to think how you are going to match these things up." Well, this possibly could be a big grant and so we figured out how we were going to do it. When it came due, even though we were in a tight budgetary situation, we were able to do the match.

The NSF statement of the purpose of the Center of Excellence awards was that they were a "major effort to increase the number of first-rate science institutions in the United States by helping a limited number of already good institutions advance rapidly to a higher level of quality." The awards could be used for faculty and staff salaries, graduate stipends, equipment, construction or renovation of facilities, and supplies. Ultimately, we sought funds for all of the above.

One of the early decisions had to do with the focus of the application and which science programs should be included. We were sophisticated enough to know that, while the Center of Excellence grant program was designed to move good academic programs to excellent ones, we needed some programs with established track records; others could be less than stellar. Eligible departments in the natural and biological sciences all wanted to be included and were in on the early discussions of application strategy. But a focus was missing, and hard choices limiting participation had to be made, taking into account the established departmental track records and their potential for major improvements. After consultation we recommended that the focus be limited to the biological sciences. It was, of course, a disappointment for the natural science departments.

Once we had decided who the players were, we had to come up with an intellectual focus for lashing the programs together. Three interdisciplinary programs emerged: endocrinology, genetics, and neurobiology. We then proceeded to plan for the organization of those programs and their support, and for the resources necessary for the eight supporting departments. There followed a lot of dreaming, then paring that led to budgets and programmatic statements. Surprisingly, the process went along with dispatch and civility. In sum, we sought funds for forty new faculty members and supporting staff, stipends for thirty graduate students, specialized equipment (some of it very expensive), and construction funds to help in building the new basic science building (now the Bowen Science Building) and an addition to the then zoology building. It totaled $7.952 million for the five years of the program, with a request for an initial award of $5.1 million. It also required a pledge from the university that it would pick up and sustain the programs at the end of the NSF award. At the time of the impending site visit Boyd had to be prepared to convince the visitors that solid plans were in place for the pick-up by the university at the end of the grant period.

The application went forward. It was the culmination of my first major task as a university administrator, and the president was watching closely. I don't think I appreciated at the time what a large personal stake was riding on the outcome. The site team came to the campus on October 17 and 18, 1966. They talked to the DEOs of the eight departments, the leaders of the three interdisciplinary programs, the deans and central administrators. Recalled for a final session by myself, I was asked to explain the process by which we had developed the application and to express my opinion on the viability of the proposal. It was a subdued, almost somber meeting. Several of us were later called to the NSF headquarters in Washington, D.C., to go over portions of the application in greater detail. Then we waited months to learn the outcome. How well did we, and most particularly I, do?

August 1967 was a banner month for the fledgling research office. Word came that our application for a Center of Excellence award in the biological sciences had been approved by NSF in the time and amounts requested. We were the first and only university, as subsequent events were to show, to receive such a grant in the biological sciences. All of us stood a little taller that day. And President Bowen's charge had been fulfilled!

Not surprisingly, the program moved ahead with fits and starts, but it did move ahead. Today, the biological sciences are one of Iowa's recognized strengths. They continue to expand, and we continue to build more space for them. The doctoral programs in genetics, neuroscience, molecular biology, and immunology — direct or indirect outgrowths of the award — are well established, producing outstanding doctoral graduates and outstanding science.

The initiatives of the faculty and staff in seeking external funding grew. During this year there was a 23 percent increase in the number of applications forwarded ($62,519,905) and a 78 percent increase ($35,404,346) in funds accepted. Not only were there funds for the support of research but also for traineeships, fellowships, and scholarships as well as for capital improvements.

While the research office had never been given a specific charge, its role and purviews were being redefined almost daily as a result of additional assignments of responsibility. I asserted repeatedly to Messieurs Bowen and Boyd that I and my staff were running as fast as we possibly could and that expansions to the staff were imperative. In spite of the relative inflexibility of university budgets, my requests were largely implemented, sooner or later.

Animals in Research

The use of animals in research grew as our funds for research grew. The management of animals in a humane and cost-effective way appeared on the agendas of several university groups. The College of Medicine already had an animal facility that it had built largely out of practice-fund earnings, and it had been generous in sharing the facilities with other members of the university community. Dean Donald Galagan of the College of Dentistry predicted that the use of research animals by his faculty would shortly overwhelm the facilities of the college and recommended that a central university facility be established. The health deans resolved that a committee of users from throughout the university should be established. That initiative would start a tortuous journey that would result in the appointment of a university veterinarian and the establishment of a university-wide animal care facility, ultimately located in the Medical Laboratories and on the Oakdale campus.

1968–1969: CONSOLIDATIONS

*Continuing Efforts to Strengthen the Graduate College
and the Graduate Student Senate*

The new Graduate College regulations were now in full effect and were in the process of being implemented: tools of research, higher grade points for admission, and moving away from the "unclassified student" category by limiting the students' option of acquiring significant hours of completed graduate work without being identified with a particular field of study. In the past, students had petitioned to become degree candidates primarily because of the graduate hours of work that they had been allowed to complete.

The Teaching-Research Fellowship Program began with thirty-four of the fifty-two departments that offered the doctorate participating. We began an outreach program designed to recruit students with potential for doing graduate work who came from educational backgrounds that might have deterred them from admission to the Graduate College otherwise. The interdisciplinary programs in endocrinology, genetics, and neurobiology now supported by the Center of Excellence award were being organized, a new doctoral program in cultural anthropology and linguistics, and research programs in transportation safety and urban and regional planning had begun.

An article in the *Daily Iowan* on September 18, 1968, characterized the Graduate College as "the fastest growing academic unit." In the article I reported that the enrollments in the college had increased from 10 to 20 percent each year since 1964, reaching 4,889 in 1968, composed of 3,492 (71.4 percent) male students and 1,397 (28.6 percent) female students, with male enrollment dropping slightly from the previous year. However, future enrollments were uncertain in view of the announcement in June 1968 that male graduate students with few exceptions would be subject to the draft. I predicted that approximately 10 percent of the male graduate student body could be lost as the result. Iowa State University predicted that its graduate enrollments would decrease by 60 percent. As I indicated earlier, none of these dire projections proved to be correct. Nevertheless, they added to the unease of our current male graduate students.

The graduate students joined the chorus of students across the country in petitioning to have a voice in programming their course of study. They came to see me several times to talk about establishing a recognized student organization that could represent graduate student issues to the Graduate College administration. I responded by insisting that I would support the establishment of such an organization only if it was representative of the university-wide graduate student body and not limited by default to a few departments of the College of Liberal Arts on the east side of the Iowa River. I made clear to the students that our recognition of the student group would apply only to matters of interest and concern to the college and that, if they wished recognition as a university-wide organization, they would have to follow university procedures for gaining it.

The Graduate Student Senate was ultimately organized and provided a channel for easy communication between the students and the college administration. The net effect was that we understood each other better and were prepared to respond in constructive rather than knee-jerk reactive ways to changes proposed by both sides. Over the years the relationship has proved to be a very positive one.

On November 14, 1969, I wrote a note to Dean for Advanced Studies Alvin Scaff indicating that President Bowen harbored the feeling that, despite our tightening of admission and retention standards and instituting the requirement of the GRE as part of the application documentation, the quality of our graduate students was not what it might be. The president was particularly interested in information on the admissions standards of the various departments — which were the highest and the lowest. In time we generated such data and found, hardly to anyone's surprise, that the standards varied greatly by programs. Some of our programs clearly enjoyed national reputations, receiving large numbers of applications for admission from throughout the country, from which only a select few were chosen. Other programs were quite the contrary, usually drawing from a limited local geographical area and some even admitting every minimally qualified applicant that applied. Later, as we developed increasingly sophisticated data to be used in allocating funds to departments for graduate student support, we used these data as one of several indices in making allocation decisions. We were trying to send a message that the quality of our graduate students mattered.

Vice President Boyd wrote to us on a theme that he would later articulate during his presidency, his support for "a single graduate college and faculty at the University of Iowa." In a letter to us on January 8, 1969, he said:

> I favor the single graduate college . . . and believe that it would be a mistake if the various colleges were to award their own professional degrees. Sufficient flexibility can be provided for in a single graduate college so that it is not necessary to have separate graduate colleges of education, law, business, engineering and so forth. I urge you to continue your consideration of techniques for accommodating the disparate needs of many disciplines within the graduate college and at the same time maintain a university-wide standard of quality and sound educational practice for advanced degrees.

Boyd coupled this view with his belief that the University of Iowa was a single university that derived a considerable amount of its special character from being one academy in one physical space (in contrast, for example, to the

Universities of Illinois and Indiana, whose health colleges are on campuses geographically separated from their main campuses). I wholeheartedly supported Boyd's view and sought to insure that the Graduate College was appropriately flexible, for example, substituting the ATGSB for the GRE in the case of students applying for admission to some of the advanced programs in the College of Business Administration, modifying criteria for evaluating programs in which special educational objectives existed, and providing funds in support of advanced students with atypical degree objectives.

Interdisciplinary graduate work had been a hallmark of our graduate policies for many years, one of Dean Seashore's legacies. As early as 1908, during his tenure as dean of the Graduate College, Seashore saw the university as one academy, one unified body of scholars. He encouraged advanced graduate students to seek out those faculty members whose interests and expertise were especially relevant to the students' study plans. In that context Seashore had little time for departmental boundaries, which he saw as borders to be ignored. (In fact, my own field of speech pathology and audiology grew out of that environment with strong encouragement from Seashore.) On March 7, 1969, the Graduate Council felt called upon to reaffirm the policy in view of the reluctance of some departments to support appropriately individual student's interests:

> We call attention to a long and distinguished tradition in the Graduate
> College established years ago by Dean Seashore of approving an individual
> plan of study where this was endorsed by the student's major department
> even if the plan was interdisciplinary in content. . . . The flexible approach
> to graduate programming, especially the doctorate, has rested on the con-
> viction that many significant research problems extend across depart-
> mental lines. . . . The council wishes to reaffirm this tradition.

The Graduate College staff sought to support this policy in every possible way. In fact, we identified a portion of our funds for allocation to departments with specific proposals for support of graduate students involved in interdisciplinary research to make sure that the students didn't fall through the cracks in the allocation of resources.

Strengthening Research and Scholarship

From its earliest days the Graduate College, again under the strong leadership of Dean Seashore, had interpreted "research" to include creative work in all its forms, from art to zoology. For example, in the mid-1920s, during Seashore's tenure as dean, the Graduate College began to accept creative works in writing, theater, and music in lieu of research projects toward the fulfillment of the requirements for master's degrees. The move created a national furor among graduate deans, but Seashore and Iowa stood fast.

Today we view that move as a benchmark in documenting Iowa's leadership in advanced teaching and research. Since I had been steeped in that philosophy by my mentors, it was very natural for me to carry it forward into my role as a university administrator. The staff of the vice president for research willingly made special efforts to find external resources to assist faculty and staff outside the sciences in their creative efforts, for example, in assembling and studying special collections in the arts, developing a new system for dance notation, and using computer technology in teaching art appreciation courses. Since the funds available from the National Endowment for the Humanities and the National Endowment for the Arts were modest, we made special efforts to find niches of support from privately supported foundations and even businesses willing to support creative work in the arts.

The issue of classified research continued to be discussed and debated; should it be allowed and, if so, under what circumstances. On February 21, 1969, President Bowen wrote to me, "I am particularly concerned about the reference to research conducted for private companies [referring to a draft policy then under review]. I do not think it is ordinarily proper for university research workers to be involved with the research programs of private companies on terms that would involve even temporary suppression of information. And I am also concerned about involvement with the federal government which leads to classification of research results."

Faculty attitudes divided over the issue, some arguing for prohibiting classified research under all circumstances and others arguing for pragmatic accommodations in specific instances. The Research Council was persuaded to the latter view, provided that information was made available to the public about the purposes of such research, the identity of the investigator(s), the amount and sources of funds expended, and the university facilities used in the research. It also confirmed that graduate student theses and dissertations should not incorporate research that could not be made public at the time of the final examination.

The policy of resisting efforts to suppress information about ongoing university research continues today, stemming from the conviction that a distinctive characteristic of a university is that it is a place that allows and encourages the free exchange of information within the academic community. Any activity that abridges that exchange diminishes the unique and distinctive character of the academy of scholars.

Early in the fall, we tried to cope with an NSF policy that required it to keep its fiscal 1969 expenditures for sponsored programs below a designated ceiling that it had set. All recipients of NSF funds were in turn given ceilings. We chose to adjust spending levels on a project-by-project basis in an attempt to extend the time of completion of the projects. By November 1 we had negotiated revised spending plans for all of our NSF-supported investigators.

NIH took a different tack, negotiating reductions directly with principal investigators. Understandably, most investigators did their best to accommodate the requests of the NIH negotiators in the belief that it was necessary for them to do so in order to hold the remaining portion of their awards and to assure the chairs of the various study sections that they (the investigators) were reasonable people. The consequence was that the investigators pressed the university to pick up the funds they had negotiated away. In response, President Bowen wrote a letter to the deans, departmental executive officers, and principal investigators, directing that all revised budgets should be reviewed and approved through regular application channels. The cause of these many readjustments was a mandate from Congress that the federal expenditures for fiscal 1969 must be reduced by $6 billion.

The exchange of information between similar institutions, largely through national meetings, convinced us that we were effectively keeping in touch with developments in Washington. We had quickly come to the view that we must do that if we wished to play in the big leagues. For example, congressional proposals were continually being developed that could affect student aid, institution of new programs of funding for research and demonstration projects, and establishment of new controls over funds for which universities competed. We needed to get our views heard at the right times and to alert the university community about new funding opportunities that were coming in a very competitive world. Consequently, we developed the staff capability to provide our faculty and staff with in-depth reviews of all available sources of support in specific areas. In some cases we scheduled training seminars to assist faculty in developing proposals appropriate to the interests of individual agencies. We were alerted even then to the probability that the agencies were looking to computer technology for disseminating information about funding opportunities and updates in rules and regulations; over time we took actions to prepare our staff and then the faculty for these opportunities.

Through it all we continued to hold steadfast to the view that we should not establish a resident representative in Washington. Rather, we believed that it was more effective in the long run for our office to provide the most complete possible information about funding opportunities, rules, and regulations to our faculty, who would then represent their own causes directly, rather than having our staff mediate between the agencies and our faculty. A few universities did establish resident offices in Washington; most did not.

This atmosphere of change was far reaching. Given the increased levels of funding for sponsored research, expectations heightened that scientific discoveries needing patent protection would follow. After two years of studying patent policies of similar universities and many hours of discussion within the Patent Committee and with the faculty, a new patent policy was developed and recommended by the university to the Board of Regents, which adopted it at its February 1969 meeting. The policy, while making explicit the rights and privileges of the faculty and the university, was designed to encourage faculty to come forward with ideas, inventions, and discoveries that might be patentable. The new policy mandated disclosure of "all ideas, inventions, or discoveries" made by the faculty using university time, materials, or facilities. Earnings were first to be used for covering the cost of investigating, evaluating, and protecting the discovery. After that the earnings were to be distributed equally among a fund in the vice president's office to cover other patent development expenses, the department from which the discovery originated, the person or persons making the discovery, and the vice president for research for furthering research and creative work at the university. That policy continues essentially unchanged.

Another program receiving our support during this period was the University of Iowa Press. In 1938 the Board of Education approved "The University of Iowa Press" imprint, but the paper shortage during World War II and later a lack of funds delayed a regular publishing program. In 1963 the press embarked on a modest program of monograph publications. In the spring of 1969 we restarted the University Press to "enhance the scholarly activities of the university." This followed representations from a number of faculty that it was a proper thing for a university of stature to do. The Faculty Senate concurred. The first book of the press, *The Myxomycetes*, was a classic work on slime molds, illustrated with forty-one color plates, and written by Professor Emeritus W. W. Martin of our Botany Department and Professor S. J. Alexopoulos of the Zoology Department of the University of Texas. Since then, the press has earned a highly respected place among university presses.

Early in the year I began to press for yet another expansion of the staff of the Office of the Vice President for Research. We needed to fund two new positions, one for university-federal projects (later absorbed into sponsored programs) and one for agency liaison (later to become the associate vice president for research). These were in addition to the director of the Office of Research Services and Administration (later to become the Division of Sponsored Programs) with Hoppin already in place. I reminded President Bowen of his statement that he hoped we would get $10 for every $1 invested in the office. We had exceeded that expectation manyfold. Ultimately, funds for the positions were provided since, if we did not receive them, the specter of lost funding opportunities seemed undeniable.

Increased Student Unrest

Throughout the year student protests over the Vietnam War increased, resulting in sit-ins, demonstrations, the use of tear gas, and arrests by the police. During it all the university community carried on its work almost on a business-as-usual basis.

President Bowen, always mindful of the nature of universities and the University of Iowa in particular, presented some thoughtful remarks in his address to the faculty on October 8, 1968. Given against a background of the issues raised directly and indirectly as a result of student protests, his remarks highlighted fundamental questions about the ultimate essence of a university. In leading up to his discussion of the Code of Student Life, which had been rewritten, not without some controversy, especially from the students, he said:

> The autonomy of the university which we value highly — the academic freedom, the tenure system, the determination of our own curriculum and educational methods, the selection of our own research subjects, the privilege of making our own internal allocation of funds — all of these things we enjoy only because we are a community that is capable of responsible self-government. . . . If those of us in the universities are to defend academic freedom, if we are rightfully to expect to be exempt from outside interference and direction, it behooves us to make sure that we are living by our principles.

A Sudden Resignation

On January 22, 1969, President Bowen unexpectedly wrote to President Redeker of the Board of Regents, resigning as president of the university effective September 1. He made clear that he had done so voluntarily and for personal reasons. "When 'personal reasons' are given as the cause for a university president's resignation it is often assumed that there are undisclosed issues or problems in the background. I should like to allay such speculation by assuring you there were no untoward circumstances leading to my decision. I have simply made a choice about how I wish to extend my professional activity and career in higher education at a time which seemed to me to be opportune. . . . Specifically, I expect to become chairman of the faculty in economics at the Claremont Graduate School in California."

I felt then and continue to believe that student unrest was a factor in pushing President Bowen to his decision. An incident took place outside the president's home involving two students, one of whom had laid on the hood of his car, blocking him from leaving for a Board of Regents meeting. The students required removal by the police. It's probable that the incident was the precipitating event for President Bowen's resignation. This supposition was confirmed during my 1995 interview with George Chambers, then assistant dean for academic affairs, who reported hearing it from President Bowen while talking to him months later. Apparently, the times were simply not Bowen's cup of tea.

His decision surprised the university community. If I had any prior knowledge of his decision, it was only a day or so before it became public. In my view his unease in informal communication situations, such as one-on-ones with students, and several "dirty word" confrontations by students in public meetings, which some persons in the legislature and others held him accountable for, clouded the significant impact he had made in arousing the university family from the inertia of earlier years and turning it squarely toward the future. As a consequence, his successor could take over and keep on the course Bowen had already charted.

A Successor Is Appointed

The Board of Regents wasted little time in identifying President Bowen's successor. Hoping to have his replacement named by July 1, the board asked the university faculty, students, administrative council, and alumni to consult with them on February 15, 1969, in Iowa City. But extended consultations were not to be. On March 20, 1969, the board announced its unanimous decision to appoint Willard Boyd as president, because, I assume, they felt that he was the right person to lead the university in those turbulent times.

Not everyone agreed. Six state representatives and two senators indicated that they were disturbed by the appointment in the light of Boyd's failure to take any action several weeks earlier, when some students had used four-letter words during a symposium on student power, of which he was a member. On the whole, however, his appointment was greeted with great enthusiasm. It provided me with an occasion for taking stock of my role as a university administrator.

I had now been in office about four years, time enough for my administrative style to begin to take shape. It was not determined as a result of a predetermined plan but mostly by "feel." I was taking from my years as a college leader (appearing before groups with prepared agenda), my military training (the elements of effective staff work and span of control), my experience working in industrial relations (listening to and melding different points of view), and my experience as a professor (careful assessment and presentation of data). When occasions presented themselves, I enunciated these principles to the staff:

> This office has been charged by the president to protect the name of the university. . . . We can all stand to be run out of town because we stand for excellence but we can't stand to be run out because we stand for mediocrity. So we must constantly be involved in making evaluations and when we do that we are treading in sensitive areas.

> We are primarily a service organization. . . . We relieve the faculty of nonproductive responsibilities. We help them organize and systematize those administrative responsibilities which they have so they require as little of the faculty's time as possible.

> Good staff work . . . involves research on an issue and proposed solutions or options for solutions. It's not enough to delineate the problem and stop there. You need to propose solutions.

> If this office has been successful, it has been in part because we have done our homework and done it better than anyone else. We must continue to function in this way.

> Universities are complex structures because of the wide diversity of activities of their components and because of the need for a delicate balance between them. We must be extremely careful that we evaluate the judgments of all components of the institution, not just the aggressively vocal ones. This means that . . . expressions of some will have to be solicited while others will have to be discounted.

The responsibilities of the Offices of the Graduate College and of the Vice President for Research were defined gradually, not by formal charges, which I requested but never received — probably, in retrospect, for good reasons. The ambiguity allowed me to receive assignments without regard to the particular segment of the university that might be affected. This practice was to become the basis for adding "educational development" officially to my title down the road.

2. THE BOYD YEARS
1969–1981

1969–1970: THE NEW LEADER AND CHANGING TIMES

On September 1, 1969, and with essentially no fanfare, Willard L. Boyd was promoted from vice president for academic affairs and dean of faculties to president of the university. The *Daily Iowan* of August 26, 1969, noted: "He explained his interest in the challenging post in terms of the question of whether it is more desirable to be a member of the 'silent majority' . . . or whether to become subject to criticism. Saying that he did not seek a snug harbor, Boyd added, 'I shall try to do my best.'" The events that were ahead would find that his "best" was indeed equal to the challenges.

Sandy brought with him a change in style from his more reserved, somewhat formal predecessor. Accessible and easy to approach, Sandy related comfortably to groups as well as individuals, usually smiling as he did so. He rarely raised his voice and rarely chewed someone out. He didn't need to; his facial expressions could tell it all. One of his dirty looks could send you to the dungeons. We learned that he always knew what he wanted to accomplish in any setting. However, he could be the master of circumlocution when he wasn't ready to reveal a strategy, frequently leaving us wondering after such meetings what he had really said. In a very short time he had molded those of us on his central staff into a dedicated and loyal group of advisors who were expected to engage in friendly but candid exchanges during the weekly meetings of what he called the "docket" group, typically starting at eight-thirty on Monday mornings.

Sandy did not move his family into the president's home, 102 Church Street. He had three school-age children, and he and his wife, Susan, wanted them to grow up in a normal home environment. The Boyds reserved one room on the second floor of 102 Church Street for an office for Susan to use in taking care of the many functions expected of a university's first lady. The rest of the space on that floor was fully utilized later in the fall by the Institute for Urban and Regional Research. All the usual presidential social functions were held on the first floor, of course. In addition, Sandy not infrequently invited small groups of his staff there for noon meetings at which he himself, sometimes with the assistance of a physical plant handyman who did odd jobs at the house, typically served Campbell's split pea soup, toasted cheese sandwiches, and perhaps an orange. To him the work at hand was the important item, the lunch necessary but almost incidental, and frugality was his characteristic approach to such working sessions.

Student Unrest

Tensions among the students, stemming largely from the Vietnam War, grew to a crescendo by the end of the 1969–1970 academic year. Associated with the tensions were continuing concerns of some small groups of students and faculty over university policies that permitted faculty to accept awards from the Department of Defense to conduct alleged "war research." Again, the great majority of faculty recognized that determining a priori what was "good" research based on the source of funding was inappropriate. For example, several faculty members in the College of Medicine were supported by the Department of the Army to study the problem of schistosomiasis, a disease spread by worms that infest the waters in Asia, South America, and Africa. While the army's interest was clearly based on its concern for the health of its troops that might be stationed in those areas, the results could have enormous beneficial effects on the populations endemic to the areas. There was no majority sentiment for removing the "appropriateness" test from the individual investigator. Thus, the policies concerning secret and classified research that had been extensively reviewed and modified by the Research Council the previous year were aired again for the media and the Faculty Senate and sustained.

Then came the Kent State episode in May, and the university, in the interest of personal safety in light of sporadic destruction of property, bomb threats, and arson, gave students the option of leaving school immediately, taking grades for the work that they had completed to that point; many did. However, the university did not close and commencement was held as usual. More will be said about student unrest in chapter 8.

The Graduate College

The Graduate College enrollment for the 1969–1970 academic year reached 5,019, up from 4,889 the previous year. There were indications that many students were seeking "relevance" in their courses of study, moving away from the physical sciences toward the humanities and the social sciences. Many of them were joining the undergraduates in a search for studies that would help them deal in constructive ways with their perceptions of society's needs.

With growing enrollments in programs of higher education and growing demands for expensive equipment to support much of the research involved in advanced study, the graduate enterprise came under increased scrutiny. Newspaper articles and editorials asked if such programs were really necessary. Were we overeducating our people? Were we concentrating too many resources on the research aspects of that education? Proposals for degrees intermediate between the master's and doctorate degrees surfaced in response to such questions. All of this prompted me to write an article published in the October–November 1969 edition of the *Iowa Alumni Review* entitled "A Curse on Both Your Houses," in which I argued that the issue wasn't one of either-or. It was one of balance, and neither teaching nor research could prosper without the other.

New Initiatives

At the beginning of the year President Boyd wrote a letter to Provost Ray Heffner indicating that he had asked me for suggestions about the area of foreign study. In response to his observation that our office was getting a number of inquiries about foreign study, he was looking for suggestions for better coordination "so that we will be able to maximize the opportunities available to students and faculty overseas in a period of declining support for those activities." The assignment was the beginning of our involvement in the international arena and the soon-to-be-established Office of International Education and Services (OIES), which would be a part of our responsibilities during my tenure in the office.

The Oakdale Campus

In July 1965 the Oakdale campus, consisting of approximately 500 acres and thirty-five major buildings located six miles west of the main campus, was transferred to the University of Iowa by the Iowa General Assembly. The College of Medicine was given primary responsibility for the campus since there were still some eighty tuberculosis patients at the Oakdale Hospital. It was the long-range goal of the college to turn the campus into a medical research and training center concerned with community-oriented and chronic medical problems. Those plans were publicized in the summer of 1969. Outpatient medical and dental training programs were implemented but failed to progress. Ultimately the campus and its facilities would come to be viewed as one open to all for special programs and new initiatives.

Federal Programs

The Public Health Service (PHS), beginning in 1968 and continuing until 1992, provided funds to the university based on the amount of awards we had received the previous year from PHS. Initially, the grants were known as General Research Support Grants; later, the name was changed to Biomedical Research Support Grants (BRSGs). The Colleges of Medicine and Dentistry were the chief beneficiaries. However, the vice president for research received the funds associated with awards to faculty in the other colleges. The amount varied, reaching a peak of $100,000 per year. There were very few restrictions on their use other than the requirement that they be used to support other health-related research. We chose to limit the awards to junior faculty to assist them in preliminary research that showed promise of developing into full-scale investigations. We solicited applications annually, and the Research Council made recommendations for allocating the funds. It was another of the funding sources that made the vice president's office the place to go for funds to launch new programs.

The NSF Center of Excellence award for the biological sciences was in its third year, and the three interdisciplinary programs of endocrinology, genetics, and neurobiology had been established. Faculty were recruited, equipment purchased, and facilities were being built or renovated. We submitted a progress report and a request to NSF for supplemental funds for the fifth and sixth years of the plan. It had been understood at the time of the original award that, if we had made sufficient progress, NSF would entertain such a supplemental request. Obviously, we felt that we had made enough progress to deserve the additional funding. In the endorsements accompanying the proposal, Dean Robert Hardin of the College of Medicine spoke about academic integration: "Medical schools are often isolated even though physically present on the same campus with the rest of the 'parent university.' The present College of Medicine administration has had integration with the university as a prime goal. The Biological Science Plan has acted as a catalyst to accelerate this process."

I had come from a background of working with colleagues in the health colleges, and had served on the master's committees of graduate students in the College of Dentistry. I had worked with my colleagues in the Department of Otolaryngology and Maxillofacial Surgery on joint research projects and directed the master's theses of residents in the department, joined them in the clinical assessment of patients, and continued to interact with them until the time demands of my new job required me to withdraw from regular faculty responsibilities both in otolaryngology and speech pathology. It was only after

I'd had the opportunity to attend meetings with my counterparts from other universities that I came to appreciate the uniqueness that Iowa enjoyed by functioning so easily as a single institution.

The Council on Federal Relations

Early in the year I had been appointed by the president to serve as the university's representative on the Council on Federal Relations (CFR), a newly formed group of the American Association of Universities (AAU), an association of approximately sixty-two of the leading research universities in the country. I was chosen because our office had been delegated the responsibility for liaison with federal executive agencies and the Congress. For a number of years the AAU had held meetings twice a year, attended only by its presidents, who met to discuss common problems and issues. The need for the AAU to take a more active role in affecting public policy grew as the federal government became increasingly involved in funding the institutions and promulgating directives that affected the operations of its members. For example, some of the matters on the agenda of the council meeting of April 20, 1970, were university-DOD relations in ROTC matters and means of improving them, status and prospects for legislation and appropriations for federal support of education for the health professions, employment of members of minority groups by universities (affirmative action programs), and the establishment of a quick response network among universities.

The Research Office

The Office of the Vice President for Research had to deal with a constantly increasing universe. Opportunities for external funding of faculty and staff projects, coupled with increasing requirements for monitoring the progress and expenditures of the federal funds obtained, kept us busy. Increased competition for the available funds required increased sophistication in the quality of the proposals that went forward from the university. The small staff in sponsored programs worked long hours, even seven days a week, to keep up. Visitors from sister institutions expressed amazement that we accomplished so much with such a small staff. Needless to say, I was not silent about our needs, making representations bordering on harassment to the provost and president concerning them. It was a catch-22 situation for them. The university's budgets were always tight, yet we needed to compete successfully for external funding to augment the budget. Ultimately funds were pried loose to allow us to enlarge our operation — never, of course, approaching what we thought we needed. The enormous dedication and loyalty of the staff kept us trudging along.

This year began in the shadow of the Vietnam War, and student unrest demanded more time in our day-to-day agendas. Its end was not in sight, but we were determined to keep the university functioning despite its distractions. Recounted here are some of the events of note from the "regular" agenda of the university.

New Agendas and New Arrangements

President Boyd started the new year by announcing some assignment changes in the central administration group, and changed my title to Vice President for Educational Development and Research and Dean of the Graduate College. The addition of "educational development" to my title, as explained by the president, "reflects the responsibilities his office has for generating various proposals for federal, state and private support for research and instruction. In addition, he will now be responsible for coordinating various internal and external information activities in conjunction with the Office of Public Information and University Relations," which was to report through me to the president. In my cynical moments I characterized the "educational development" part of the title as a rationale for assigning me a variety of activities that were only tangentially, if at all, related to graduate education or research. However, I didn't object, since the additional responsibilities took me into new worlds filled with interesting challenges.

Outreach

In February 1971 President Boyd asked me to chair a new group, the Seminar on University Relations, which replaced the Seminar on External Relations and the Committee on University Relations. Its purpose was to interpret university policy to its several constituencies in and outside the university and to advance good public relations practices. It met once a month with an agenda distributed in advance of the meetings. In practice its goal was to stimulate the development of agreed-to messages and their effective dissemination.

Our growing financial needs would have been enough to cause more than usual scrutiny of the university by the public; the student unrest tended to heighten it, which prompted me to try to put the "service" part of the teaching, research, and service triad of university functions into perspective in a statement issued by the University News Service on January 15, 1971:

Teaching has public support because it is understood that the young must learn, and research survives because the public knows that knowledge is not static and must be increased if society is to progress. . . . It would be parochial and shortsighted for the academic community to assume that there are no new principles to be discovered by organizing service activities which lend themselves to critical examining and evaluation. . . . More attention to service can improve the effectiveness of both teaching and research. . . . It can prevent professors from hiding in a kind of vacuous, abstract world. . . . It is reasonable for the public which supports us to assume that sooner or later the knowledge which comes from the research laboratory will be tested and applied in the real world. . . . In many ways, the ivory tower has been too much of an academic reality.

More Concerns about State and Federal Funding

In May 1971 we received word that our application for a supplemental grant to our Center of Excellence award had been approved. We were awarded $1.6 million in addition to the $5.1 million received in the original award. It was a terrific boost to our plans to put the biological sciences at Iowa on a competitive basis with the best in the country.

Nevertheless, I worried aloud about the slowing down and, in some cases, the cutting back on federal programs in addition to those devoted to advanced graduate training. I saw inflation, cutbacks, and increasing interest of federal agencies to support applied research as producing a crisis in money, momentum, and manpower. The movement of federal agencies to contracts for prescribed studies, rather than grants, meant that we had to compete with industries to do prescribed research, some of which might not be high on the research agendas of the faculty. Basic research was especially vulnerable. I also worried about the lack of funds to support junior faculty and high-risk proposals.

Federal budgets were not the only ones that were being cut back; the state also cut back to keep its budgets balanced. University appropriations were cut by 5 percent, and each of our units was asked to submit budgets to the provost that were 95 percent of those of the present year. In the process, provisions were made for dealing with high-priority developments and opportunities. Needless to say, I made a strong case for relief in view of the increased activity in the sponsored programs office (enlargement of data-processing support, costs associated with the newly established unit in our office concerned with the acquisition of surplus property from the federal government for use in a wide variety of our research laboratories, and demands for increased services from our staff), and the needs of the emerging programs in computing, urban and regional planning, and international student services. In the main the problem was dealt with throughout the university with reasonably good grace, since we all assumed that the slowdown was temporary.

Graduate Education

Peter Drucker, a noted educator and writer, called the times the "age of discontinuity." The apparently insatiable need for persons with advanced degrees that was the basis of much academic expansion in the 1960s had been largely satisfied. At the national level there were calls for an abrupt change of educational course. There were concerns about the "overproduction" of Ph.D.'s and calls for programs of study geared to jobs outside of academe, as well as designing courses of study with greater "relevance" to the needs of society. There was talk of placing caps on the admission of graduate students. Some of these concerns were on the agenda of the graduate faculty at our end-of-semester meeting on January 14, 1971.

We discussed new tracks and options. We considered opportunities for students to demonstrate their mastery of content through examination and changes in the criteria for admission to graduate and advanced professional programs to take into account demonstrated capacity, maturity, and motivation through successful work experience; the intensification of the advising system, including the development of lifetime plans of study; the reduction in highly specialized courses and an increase in attention to basic principles that would provide for the student's capacity to adapt to change more easily; and increased attention to programs of continuing education.

In the late 1800s advanced degree programs existed in only a few U.S. universities; since then, many new, specialized degrees have been added — approximately 1,600 — largely as a consequence of professional certification requirements. By placing such a multitude of academic and professional objectives within a very limited degree superstructure, the significance of the degrees had become confused, if not meaningless. Earlier, Lyell Henry, then a staff member in our office, and I created quite a stir with a paper entitled "Servant or Master," which raised questions about the role of the dissertation in some fields of study. We did so out of our concern that the Ph.D. degree umbrella had been applied to some areas where it really didn't fit; we were concerned that, in the process, the degree was ceasing to be the highly respected research degree that we thought it should be.

Other topics on our agenda included review of our admission policies in order to improve our admission of women and minority groups, the development of new curricula to encompass new bodies of knowledge and new combinations of existing bodies of knowledge, and the rationale for graduate education to answer better the allegation that graduate education was an expensive frill.

These comments were made during times when the type and amount of federal support for graduate students had changed. Traineeships and fellowships had shifted to more loans for graduate study. We faced a 43 percent reduction in fellowship awards. In fact, based on the assumption that the goals for the programs had been reached, NASA terminated its program in August 1970, and NSF announced that its traineeship programs would be terminated by 1974. The status of NDEA fellowships was uncertain. There were cutbacks as well in state appropriations for higher education.

Our doctoral enrollments had leveled off. We predicted a continuing increase in students in the humanities and social sciences, however, with admission applications increasing along with rejections. Since Iowa had not moved into highly vocationally oriented doctoral programs, there was no local phasing out to be done. Enrollments in our master's programs continued to show modest gains. We felt that most of our graduate programs would remain in 1980 but that the content of some of them would change. We saw an increase in the number of interdisciplinary programs aimed at large basic problems such as environmental pollution and urban and regional planning. We looked forward to a more realistic understanding federally of the importance of graduate education to the nation. In the long term, we were optimistic about graduate education.

I was impressed by the resilient way in which the academy dealt with these issues. Certainly our sensitivities to the new universe were heightened. I tried to help intensify them by writing a column called "As I See It" in *Research and Graduate News*. During this year I commented about the projected oversupply of Ph.D.'s, the rationalization of the place of research training in doctoral degree programs, preparation for tomorrow, offering students more options especially designed for vocational objectives, the implications of the rating of graduate faculties and programs by the American Council on Education, the need to reduce our levels of awards of the Ph.D. degrees, and the supply-and-demand issues of graduate degrees. These topics suggest the nature of the zeitgeist of the times.

1971–1972: CHANGES OF PACE

Leave

This year was highlighted by the only leave I ever had during my entire forty-one-year university tenure, including every intervening summer session, both as a professor and administrator at the university. The leave extended from October 1, 1971, to May 31, 1972, without pay.

I had been offered a position as one of three consultants to advise a commission in Brazil during October and November 1971 on the formulation of a plan for graduate education for the country. At the time Brazil was one of the largest recipients of USAID funds and had made education one of its highest priorities in the light of a 70–80 percent illiteracy rate. That being so, it needed to establish graduate programs to instruct the thousands of teachers who would be required to teach both youngsters and adults to read; clearly it was not feasible for this education to take place outside Brazil. USAID was anticipating an application from Brazil for an additional loan to assist it in its heroic education intentions; hence, the need for consultants.

Prior to my leaving for Brazil, I had become concerned about finishing a report on the results of a major study of families with children with cleft lips and palates that had been supported by the National Institute of Dental Research (NIDR), for which I had been the principal investigator. I received a special six-month fellowship from NIDR to complete the report in the form of a small book. Following my return from Brazil, I completed the draft in good time and chose to go back to my regular job in early April, even though I was technically still on leave.

The Graduate College

The brakes continued to be applied to the exuberant expansion of graduate programs seen in the 1960s. The problem appeared to be one of overproduction. President Boyd sent down the word that we needed to give attention to defending and justifying our graduate programs. Among the suggestions of the Graduate Council in response were: conduct program reviews and make adjustments suggested by them, justify the use of teaching assistants as part of quality instruction, and defend the admission of out-of-state students as essential to the quality of the university's educational programs.

At Iowa, Ph.D. enrollment declined modestly from 1969 (2,038) to 1972 (1,862), while the rejection rate for admissions to the Graduate College increased slightly. Some departments took a second look at their graduate admission practices. In the end, however, there were no new policies emanating from the Graduate College, only the resolve to join the other colleges in more proactive program reviews.

This resolve was not universally applauded by all of the collegiate deans. Several deans were understandably sensitive to their roles in defining and supporting the graduate components of their departmental programs. Some were pleased to have the additional involvement; others were quietly resistant. ("We can manage our own affairs without outside oversight, thank you!") Clearly, it was a new era. Generating data to serve as indices of student quality and effectiveness of departmental procedures was a part of the expanded agenda of the college. Some of the data were disquieting, suggesting that standards and procedures in some departments needed improvement. It quickly became apparent to us that considerable disparities existed between our several programs and that they ranged from superior to just barely adequate, a circumstance that we did not find acceptable.

The College of Liberal Arts was home to the largest number of graduate programs. Dean Stuit saw the Graduate College in a staff relationship to the other colleges, charged with "coordinating requirements for graduate degrees and providing important assistance of various kinds, for example, research, publications, lectures, etc. . . . In the years ahead I think the master's degrees will be seen as being more and more a post-graduate (fifth undergraduate) year which can be readily administered by the individual colleges."

President Boyd had another view:

> It is my position that the Graduate College stands in a line relationship rather than a staff relationship to the central administration. . . . I feel that there are two things to be gained by having a university-wide graduate school. It is the one opportunity for the faculty of the entire university to come together and come to grips with university-wide educational programs. I think this develops a sense of university and guards against insularity within a given program. I am also convinced that . . . we should guard against excessive professionalism which I consider to be a narrowing educational process. I do not believe that graduate work should simply be another year of course content; rather, I am strongly committed to research as an instructional tool and firmly believe in the dissertation both at the master's and doctoral levels. I deeply regret that so many master's degrees are now without thesis.

Over the years procedures for the involvement of Graduate College staff in reviews have evolved to include sharing with the respective colleges the appointment of departmental review committees, evaluation of their reports, and determination of appropriate responses. In the main the process has been working well.

During the year the graduate faculty reaffirmed its commitment to interdisciplinary studies and approved a statement that encouraged the establishment of individual ad hoc interdisciplinary Ph.D. programs outside existing degree programs. While such programs are to be found in other universities, the support given to them by Iowa is unusual, clearly the result of the tradition vigorously fostered by Dean Seashore.

The number of international students at Iowa grew from 377 in 1965 to 511 in 1972. They had been and were being welcomed through the good offices of the Foreign Student Advisor. I used to remark that in earlier years we had given these students tea and sympathy. But the increased numbers required that we do more. The Graduate College was given the assignment, since back then the students were nearly all graduate students. Given the authority to hire a person to head our program, I chose Stephen Arum. One of his first tasks was to establish a philosophy for having foreign students at Iowa. He and I delivered talks on the subject, arranged meetings with deans and faculties, and gradually put in place a plan for receiving, advising, and supporting our international students — tasks which, over time, have become increasingly complex because of closer federal monitoring of students' work status and progress toward degree objectives. Although we encountered little resistance to what we were trying to do, we certainly didn't create a groundswell of eager support. Typically, the response was a kind of "what's the fuss about?"

The year was marked by the departure of Alvin Scaff, dean for advanced studies. He had come to Iowa on February 1, 1966, at a time when the college was gearing up to play a more active part in the academic life of the university. During his tenure we began gathering data about our graduate programs and negotiating with the collegiate deans about ways in which we could become involved in program reviews. The college began to receive a host of proposals for new graduate programs and for modifications of existing ones. They all had to be examined with care. Some were discouraged from further development. Many were incomplete. These evaluations had to be conveyed with frankness and with a keen sensitivity to the enthusiasm of the proposers. Alvin was a master in playing the role of diplomatic messenger.

My "As I See It" contributions to *Research and Graduate News* dealt with anticipating the graduate education realities ahead, including the need to relate to the "outside" in preparing graduates for the world of work, the value of education in a changing world, graduate students as a source of faculty renewal, and postsecondary education outside colleges and universities.

Excess/Surplus Property
Early in 1971, universities became eligible to receive excess/surplus property from the federal government for the cost of packing and shipping the items. After reviewing the inventories of available property, we concluded that

we should make a concerted effort to obtain some of it. We assigned one of our staff full time to the task. At the end of the 1971–1972 fiscal year we had placed 698 reservations for items with a total acquisition price of $5,004,388, although not all the items reserved were subsequently received. The items we did receive included such things as computers, aerial camera components, oscilloscopes, machine-shop tools, and a truck, and went to eighteen academic departments from Anatomy to Zoology, the physical plant, and Lakeside Laboratory. All the recipients seemed pleased with our efforts. Our office continued to administer the program until 1977, when it was transferred to the purchasing department; ultimately, the federal government closed the gates, presumably because the surplus yard was empty. During the height of the program, when we were providing staff support for it, we acquired equipment worth $16,709,802 (based on the original cost to the government), just by paying the shipping costs.

Keeping Up

The complexities related to seeking and managing external funds increased exponentially, so much so that we found it necessary to codify the information. The sponsored programs staff prepared a manual covering policies affecting sponsored programs, guidelines for preparing and routing proposals, and guidelines for administering awards. However, it was such a fast-moving scene that we revised and expanded the manual almost on an annual basis. In fact, the current voluminous document (more than two hundred pages in length) is no longer published on paper but is made available to university applicants on the Research and Technology Transfer home page on the university's site on the World Wide Web. As the funding agency bureaucracies have grown, so too have those of the receiving institutions, many times to the chagrin of both university faculties and administrations. The reality remains, however, that funding agencies, like universities, have to account for their decisions.

Indirect Costs

The expenditure of recovered indirect costs festered as an issue, as it did at research universities across the country. Some of our academic units that had been successful in competing for large amounts of funds, such as physics and astronomy, felt that they were not being dealt with fairly for their aggressive and successful work. It was a divisive issue that pitted faculty against administration. I was torn by the arguments. Although I felt that faculty should be rewarded for their special efforts, I also harbored the view that their efforts were a legitimate part of their commitment to advancing their research by all appropriate means and thus that they should not be given special treatment in an accounting sense.

From the first days of my time in central administration to the present, the issue of the recovery of indirect costs (overhead, now F&A — Facilities and Administrative Costs) related to external grants and contracts has been a contentious and frequently misunderstood matter in the academy countrywide. When federal agencies started making awards to support research, demonstration, and training projects, the university acknowledged that it should pay its appropriate share of *all* associated costs. Those related to payment of faculty, staff, and students, required equipment and renovation of laboratory spaces, consumable supplies and necessary travel were identified in the application and reimbursed in advance, subject, of course, to subsequent audits to insure that the funds had been spent as budgeted.

Then there are other costs related to the funded activity — heat, light, general administrative support, library resources, custodial services, etc. — to be reimbursed after the fact by the funding agencies. To reduce the amount of book work involved, the federal government developed a formula for each institution receiving funds based on documented institutional historical costs. Thus the word "recovered" indicates that these payments are made after the fact and that, until that time, the institution "advances" the resources to do the work agreed to by the university and the funding agency.

There has been confusion among investigators, members of Congress, and federal agency administrators because of variations in the indirect cost rates among institutions receiving awards. The differences are not surprising, since institutions have different accounting procedures and provide different products and services directly or indirectly.

One source of contention is the manner in which recovered funds are administered by universities. Frequently, researchers who have funded research projects believe that they should benefit directly in some way from the recovered indirect costs, which most universities place in university-wide accounts rather than dedicating them solely to the research labs being supported. In some instances the feelings of the researchers are quite bitter because, in their view, they have gone the extra mile in obtaining the awards in the first place and therefore should get the rewards for their efforts — efforts that are beyond those that would be required of them to do an "adequate" job in their teaching and research.

During my time we resisted any direct pledging of recovered indirect costs. However, we were very much aware of the faculty who were aggressively and successfully seeking external funding. Not surprisingly, we tried to be responsive when they needed additional staff support or remodeling of space or whatever. And there were those who preferred this arrangement because they knew that there might be times when they would not be successful in obtaining external funding and would need some special support to carry on their work. Formula sharing would likely result in no special institutional support in hard times; they preferred to have the university rather than themselves as their "bank."

I also knew that, in many instances, the university was contributing significant amounts of faculty time to sponsored work that was not being charged to the grants and contracts, and I knew that, even at best, the university was recovering only a portion of the indirect costs (69 percent in 1971). In addition, there were horror stories about how some universities used recovered indirect costs. To be sure, there was nothing illegal when universities chose to use these funds to build athletic facilities and presidents' homes. However, doing so placed the universities in a bad light since the recovered funds were to cover costs for heat, light, library, computer facilities, etc., that were part of the infrastructure support routinely provided, but at a cost, by the institution in support of sponsored research. Moreover, sometimes the "advances" for institutional services had to be covered by funds for which the university paid interest, a cost that could not be charged back to the grants and contracts.

Here are some 1996 recollections about the issue. James Van Allen (professor and head of the Department of Physics and Astronomy, 1951–1985; professor emeritus, 1985 to present):

> My main problem was where, as we were bringing in quite a bit of money, we had the feeling that it was being piped off into the general fund and distributed for unrelated purposes to departments and individuals who had no such enterprise and determination that we had in developing this support. They were kind of freeloaders and, furthermore, we did need a significant fraction of that indirect cost to be piped back to develop the infrastructure in our department for things like machine shops, computers, and technical help, which were not, by and large, supportable by grants or contracts. But it was necessary in order to compete successfully for proposals for certain classes of work. That great conflict persists, as you know, to the present day.

Randall Bezanson (professor in the College of Law since 1973; vice president for finance and university services, 1979–1984):

> You and I and May [Brodbeck, then vice president for academic affairs] had a kind of arrangement with people that we would occasionally waive

some of those costs if we felt it was a way of investing in these people's future scholarly and research productivity. Sometimes we had arrangements for sharing those revenues with departments that could make the case that they would like to make the decisions about how to invest in equipment and facilities and that sort of thing. We were all philosophically inclined on two points: One, not to want to treat everybody the same, just for the sake of doing that. Secondly, if somebody wanted to be able to make a decision more locally, we were all inclined to think that was a good idea. There was no formal connection between the indirect cost revenues on the one hand and the budgetary assistance that would be provided on a non-recurring basis as needed on the other hand. It was not lock-stepped.

The payment of indirect costs was also an issue with a number of the state agencies. We felt we were on tenuous grounds when we dealt with state appropriated funds in light of the argument that the state was already covering the indirect costs through its appropriations. But increasingly states received block grants from the federal government to be disbursed for designated programs. In those instances we argued that we should also receive payment for the indirect costs associated with the programs those funds supported. Ultimately, we were only partially successful. The staffs of some state departments saw the university as being greedy; some were so understaffed that they did not have time to think through the concept. In a few cases they registered their concerns with sympathetic members of the Iowa legislature. But we pressed the principle as far as it was possible to do so without causing a major upheaval in university/state relations.

Other Developments
Computer use doubled yearly. I assume that the University Computing Center had been originally assigned to the research office during John Weaver's time because computers were used primarily for research. That was a reasonable view since the supporters for its establishment had been Jim Van Allen of the Department of Physics and Astronomy, already involved in managing the reduction of very large data sets from stratospheric research, and E. F. Lindquist of the Iowa Testing Program, whose program was expanding to a national constituency requiring the management of huge arrays of test scores.

But the doubling did not come only from these sources; it also came from the faculty who were turning in increasing numbers to the center for assistance with their research data and from a small but increasing number of faculty who were finding computers to be an important resource in their teaching, so much so that we had created an additional computer committee, the Computer-Based Education Committee (CBE).

Funding, not vision, was the issue. I was a willing cheerleader for the development, not because I had the technical background to anticipate new computer developments but because I was persuaded by Gerard (Gerry) Weeg, director of the University Computing Center, and the faculty who saw how fundamental the technology could be in support of both teaching and research. More will be said about this development in chapter 7.

University Services to Nonuniversity Organizations

At its meeting on August 12–13, 1971, the Board of Regents received a communication from Representative Gluba that questioned the propriety of the University Computing Center providing computer services to the Rock Island Arsenal. It became a two-issue matter — the provision of services to nonuniversity customers and the university's involvement in Department of Defense business — that occupied time at several meetings of the board. Neither issue was a new one. In 1960 the board had established the following policy:

Establishment or conduct of any service shall be limited to services which satisfy one or more of the following conditions:

1. The service is one peculiar to the nature of the institution and is necessary to the conduct of its educational, research or services programs.

2. The inclusion of the service in the total activity of the institution will improve the efficiency and economy of the operations.

3. The provision of the service by the institution will contribute primarily to the convenience and economy of the operations.

4. The provision of the service by the institution will contribute primarily to the convenience, comfort, health, academic, social, or recreational life of its students and staff, or others who participate in educational, research or service programs on campus.

5. The service is not otherwise available in the quantity or quality required nor conveniently available geographically.

No service shall be established or conducted solely for the purpose of profiting from the public sale of services or products. In those instances in which sales or services or products are made to the general public, that service shall be secondary and incidental to the primary functions of the institutions, and the institution shall not seek to advertise or promote for the purpose of increasing the volume of general public business.

While the involvement of the United States in the war in Southeast Asia clearly precipitated this particular event, making university services available to the public had occurred years before in relation to the operation of the Iowa Memorial Union; the same issue would keep the spotlight on the computer center because it provided specialized services to public constituents as well as computer resources to its students, faculty, and staff.

On October 12, 1971, the Faculty Senate reviewed the recommendations of the Research Council concerning the suitability of research policy that the council had crafted over several months. A senate committee had proposed three amendments to the policy, calling for rejection of any projects connected with the production of a military weapon; projects "designed to enslave or otherwise decrease the freedom, health or quality of life of U.S. or foreign citizens"; and any project interfering with "the political processes of the U.S. or any other country." All amendments to the policy were rejected on a Senate vote of forty-four to nine. The Research Council recommendations stood that, in effect, left to the individual investigator the decision as to whether the research was consistent with university policies and objectives.

The action of the Board of Regents and the Faculty Senate suggested that the heat created by the war in Southeast Asia was dropping. Several large outbursts of student unrest occurred before the year ended, followed, after the May 1972 commencement, by hardly a whimper. The student unrest of those times is treated in detail in chapter 8.

1972–1973: A TIME OF REASSESSMENT

From the Top

President Boyd addressed the faculty on August 31, 1972. It was a somber speech because the outlook for higher education had turned somber. He noted that, in the light of the depressed economy of the state, the regents universities could not expect significant increases in their appropriations. In fact, to provide some development funds they were directed to prepare their budget askings for the 1973–1974 budget year with a base budget 10 percent less than that of the 1972–1973 appropriation level. Some of the savings (the difference between 90 and 100 percent of the final appropriation) would then be used for internal reallocations for urgent and high-priority programs: increased faculty and staff compensation, and increased enrollment in the health colleges. Noting that "self-study is the best vehicle for accountability," Boyd directed that five-year annual reviews be instituted for all programs and that the Graduate College staff join with the other academic units in the self-studies.

In addition, Boyd announced that "the Department of Health, Education and Welfare requires the university to establish and implement an affirmative action program . . . to establish goals for increased participation of under-represented groups. The university must make a good faith effort to achieve those goals." He then concluded, "Iowa is unique among universities. It remains a university, not a multiversity, not a campus in a system. We are unique because we are not only present physically in one place but also because we are intellectually present in one place. The core of the university is arts and sciences surrounded by well integrated professional colleges."

Graduate College

I needed to find a replacement for Alvin Scaff as dean for advanced studies. I had watched Frank Horton move up the tenure ladder in geography and confidently recruit faculty with related interests into the Institute for Urban and Regional Planning. My recommendation that he replace Scaff was approved, and he joined our staff on July 15, 1972. While he was young (thirty-three), he had demonstrated a toughness about issues of academic quality, a high energy level, extraordinary research productivity, and effective leadership. Graduate education was being called into question at both the state and national levels; internal program reviews were the order of the day. Frank seemed to me to be the right person to fill the position.

In August 1972 we began publishing in the *Daily Iowan* the names of doctoral candidates who were scheduled to defend their dissertations. The announcement included the times and locations of the meetings. We did so in the belief that this information would increase the interactions between students and faculty of the college who had overlapping interests by enticing them to attend the defenses. We also began placing additional graduate faculty members on the examining doctoral committees from time to time. We felt that openness was one way to provide quality control and keep the issue of high standards constantly before the faculty.

From the outset we had seen one of our roles to be the monitoring — and improvement, where indicated — of the quality of the students who were admitted to our graduate programs. We knew that there was information already available to us that would serve as indices of the quality of the students. We felt that, without adding further administrative burdens to our program administrators, we could exploit the data, which included the number of faculty and graduate students, number of admission applications received and percentage admitted, mean GRE scores of those admitted, resident/nonresident admissions, success ratios of applications/awards of external funds, etc. The array proved to be impressive as we sought to make judgments, advocate the establishment or change of collegewide policies, and provide feedback to our departments for developing policies and making judgments at their levels.

For example, we were interested in the data concerning the mix of resident/nonresident students within our programs. We examined the data for the 1971 fall enrollment and found that 53 percent of our 4,941 graduate students were nonresidents. But the mix varied widely by departments; those with more-established national reputations had, not surprisingly, the highest numbers of nonresidents. These data, coupled with wide variations in the numbers of admission applications received and rejected, provided us with important background for our work with the departments. None of the data would have been readily available five years earlier, before the advent of computers for data management.

Budget Retrenchment

As I noted earlier, it was a time of budget retrenchment both at the national and state levels. Consequently, appropriations for education, especially higher education, were among the many targets. Graduate education in particular came under scrutiny.

Little did we know at the time how deep some of the retrenchments would be. The worst blow came in January 1973, when President Nixon announced that funds for certain training and research grants would be impounded, effective immediately. Students currently supported from the affected programs were to be allowed to continue, but no new appointments could be made. In our case we estimated that $2.2 million from HEW alone would be lost during the fiscal year, a cut made more significant because many of the programs to be cut had been scheduled to be continued for several years. The ultimate impact of the impoundments would have been devastating to some of our training programs, particularly in the health fields. However, President Nixon and Congress had some second thoughts and decided for the coming year to fund the National Defense Student Loan Program and the Federally Insured Student Loan Programs at essentially their current levels, and extended the work-study and Supplemental Education Opportunity Grants programs at approximately half their current funding levels.

President Boyd sent a memo to deans, directors, and departmental executive officers on February 12, 1973, dealing with the impoundments and recommended reductions. He noted in the memo that our office was in the process of documenting the fiscal impact of these cuts for every university unit. He closed the memo by saying: "I assure you that we intend to take all necessary steps to convey to the federal and state executive branches, and to the Congress and the General Assembly of Iowa, the full extent of our problem when it is defined, and we shall press for all necessary help." While we ran up the distress flags, we didn't panic but set about to control the damage as best we could. In due course we produced documentation that did, indeed, show the full impact of the cuts and, as we shall see, it paid off.

Nevertheless, the graduate education community geared up for a debate on a national policy toward higher education, and graduate education in particular. Charles Kidd, then executive director of the AAU, distributed a list of topics in 1973 for that debate. They are still timely.

Can the case be made that social benefits from graduate education are so significant and broadly diffused that support of graduate education should be publicly financed?

To what extent does the desirability of equality of access to graduate study establish a case for public support of graduate education?

What philosophy of the role of government justifies provision of graduate fellowships in all fields of study?

What weight should be given to the existence of a high degree of mobility among doctorates?

To what extent and by what means (if at all) should federal support of graduate education be designed to alter the goals of graduate education?

To what extent should needs generated by federal activities themselves influence the content and volume of federal support?

What weight should be given to manpower considerations?

All these developments had heightened our awareness of the need to become more visible to our supporting publics to insure their continuing support. In October 1972 President Boyd wrote to me in response to some comments that I had made at a health deans' meeting: "I want you and Phil Hubbard to give high priority to innovative proposals for teaching and research grants. You might specifically limit funding to proposals involving off-campus instruction and model service enterprises. These would encourage faculty to broaden into new areas. . . . I do by this letter want to indicate that you have great freedom in the expenditure of the funds that have been specifically protected in times of retrenchment in order to provide for a more vital faculty." One of the very rewarding aspects for me in working for President Boyd was that, having gained his confidence, I was given great freedom to dream the dreams and hawk their merits.

In the midst of our travails President Emeritus Howard Bowen gave a speech entitled "Manpower and Higher Education" before the Association of Graduate Schools on October 19, 1972, reminding us of our common goal:

Perhaps my most far-reaching conclusion is that education is not designed to prepare people to do whatever work flows from the blind and pre-destined imperative of technology; rather it is intended to educate people of vision and sensitivity, who will have the motives to direct technology into humanly constructive channels. Our society clearly needs to conquer poverty, achieve racial justice, renew our cities, restore order, improve health and education, renew the environment, develop the arts, keep the peace, restrain world population growth, and aid developing nations. These tasks will require great cadres of dedicated and professionally competent persons. They will stretch our resources in educated, sensitive, insightful people. Education is still our main hope for coping with these problems. The limits of education have by no means been reached.

Research

As an institution we were acquiring highly sophisticated research equipment and specialized facilities. Increasingly, we were asked to certify to funding agencies that the funds requested in proposals for equipment did not duplicate resources that we already had. As a response we decided to publish a directory to encourage equipment sharing among faculty and noncampus users in those instances when the principal facility director felt that usage time could be made available for problems of mutual scientific interest. While the response was not overwhelming, there were positive anecdotes about researchers discovering each other; in our view even one such discovery was worth our efforts. But in the long run, publication of the directory did not deal effectively with the growing — embarrassingly so — duplication of expensive items of equipment when one unit would do. The publication foreshadowed our decision later to establish central research support facilities as a means of limiting the proliferation of unnecessary facility duplication.

Development

Computer technology increased by leaps and bounds, growing exponentially in capabilities and capacities. Those in the "know" in education saw the potential for computers in teaching as well as research. But it was a new toe in a budget door that opened with great resistance. By this time I was convinced that institutions such as the University of Iowa could never stand still; the only options were to move forward or backward.

Times were difficult for higher education. Yet all of us knew that we had to keep moving ahead by every available means. Reallocation, difficult as it was, was our final recourse to keep a sense of movement in the academy.

Changes at the Top

The Board of Regents, at its March 1974 meeting, approved President Boyd's recommendation of the appointment of May Brodbeck as vice president for academic affairs, effective July 1. A scholar of the methods of science, she had been a distinguished member of the faculty of the Department of Philosophy at the University of Minnesota prior to her appointment as the dean of its graduate school in 1972. She was a person who stood for the highest standards of academic excellence and presented her views very forthrightly. I was pleased that I had introduced her to Sandy one evening at a cocktail party that I hosted at our house for some visiting graduate deans.

Office Organization

Early in my tenure, I came to understand that advisory committees were a necessary part of my life. To be sure, many of the meetings were tedious since I often could predict the outcomes in advance. Nevertheless, meeting with the members required us to rationalize our positions and not infrequently modify them as the result of our discussions.

I assigned individual members of our staff to each of the twenty-six committees advisory to me at the time as vice president for educational development and research or dean of the Graduate College. Only a few were university charter committees, for example, the university Research Council and the Graduate Council. The rest were ad hoc, usually having been created to monitor activities generated by faculty initiatives or our offices that typically could be expected to chart new ground that might well involve the development of new university policies.

Old Capitol's Change in Roles

Plans were under way to restore Old Capitol, Iowa's first capitol building, to its original internal design, eliminating its use as a university administration building. The Senate Chamber, however, would continue to be used as a public meeting space. The Offices of the President and Vice President for Academic Affairs would be moved to Jessup Hall, and mine across the street to Gilmore Hall. I did not resist the plan. On the contrary I welcomed it, since our principal offices were in Old Capitol's basement and were much too small for the activities for which we were responsible. Sponsored programs had already been relocated in a separate building, Jessup Hall, in the light of our increasingly desperate need for space. I wanted to have my several offices under one roof for the sake of efficiency. The move to Gilmore Hall would make that consolidation possible.

Graduate College

During my meeting in the fall with the departmental executive officers and directors of the graduate programs, I warned that the closing out of many training programs would require some significant changes in the block allocations from the Graduate College budget that departments had become accustomed to receiving. I justified the changes on our belief that balance in the breadth and vitality of our graduate programs was a key to a dynamic academy. It was a warning that some programs would face significant reductions in block grant allocations, while others would receive significant increases.

These circumstances provided ample reasons for me to increase the pressure at budget time for larger allocations from university funds for the block allocation program. The departments were aware that the program was unique among graduate schools in the United States. They liked it because, in the final analysis, it gave them the discretion to allocate their awards as they chose according to their unique needs and individual priorities: research assistantships, tuition scholarships, and fellowships.

The Quad Cities Graduate Study Center

In May 1974 the Board of Regents authorized the university to enter into an agreement with the Quad Cities Graduate Study Center to join a consortium that included Augustana College, Iowa State University, Marycrest College, Northern Illinois University, Southern Illinois University, University of Illinois, University of Iowa, University of Northern Iowa, and Western Illinois University to offer courses at the center. The center was to receive its support from the Illinois Board of Higher Education (35 percent), the Iowa State Board of Regents (15 percent), and local community donations (50 percent). The center had been established by members of the chambers of commerce of the Quad Cities and its courses were to be offered to local and area residents. It was seen by the business community there as an important enticement for encouraging potential employers to locate in the area. It continues to function today with little change from its original charter. The University of Iowa offers courses leading to the master's degree in business administration and in social work and various courses in education and nursing. As many as fifteen faculty members may be involved in any given semester, building the teaching into their regular university schedules along with the additional requirement that they must commute to the Quad Cities to classes scheduled at times when the students, most of whom work full time in the area, can conveniently attend.

A Brazilian Encore

My previous stint working at the headquarters of USAID-Brazil resulted in a second invitation to return to Brazil to continue to work with a Brazilian group on the national project on graduate education. This time I was joined by Provost and Dean David Deener of Tulane University and John Hunter, director of the Latin American Studies Center of Michigan State University. We did our work principally at the Federal University of Rio Grande do Sul in Porto Alegre. It was a six-week assignment, during which we developed a detailed plan for graduate education in Brazil, including changes in the university structures for faculties, projections of needs and enrollments, and costs.

A special bonus was that our time there included the period of Carnival, the precursor to our Mardi Gras. Since most offices were, in effect, closed, it was arranged for us to spend three days in the apartment of a local Rio de Janeiro family who would be away during that time. For three days the parades started in the evening and continued to dawn. Glorious music, glorious costumes, glorious camaraderie. And we were there to the glorious end!

I was invited to return to Brazil for yet a third time to participate in a seminar on research administration in Rio from July 9 to 13, 1973. Following the seminar, I spent a week in consultation with officials at the Federal University of Para in Belem.

My paper at the seminar covered a lot of ground, including the organization of U.S. universities for research administration, principles behind their relationships with external funding agencies, levels within the university at which research administrators participate and why, and some of the issues with which research universities deal. Although I addressed the questions that I had been asked to speak about, I concluded after conversations with the attendees that the material was beyond the present levels of experience of most of them. Federally funded programs for higher education in Brazil were only beginning to be developed; many Brazilian universities were loosely organized by separate schools; and the centralized arrangements of universities were in their infancy. Consequently, my paper must have been seemed very removed and abstract from the experiences of the attendees. Nevertheless, the paper came to the attention of the American Council on Education, which published it in 1975 as a monograph entitled "Research Administration in Academic Institutions."

Research

Among the items that I ticked off for the Research Council to consider during the 1973–1974 year were continuing development of a comprehensive human subjects policy; possible revision of the policy on the use of animals in research; review of a patent committee proposal for the establishment of a university research foundation; defending the place of research and creative activity in universities, and the proper level and nature of the support that a university should provide for them from its own resources. I really didn't expect to get definitive answers to the questions from the council, but I was reminding them and myself of the many intangibles that are taken into consideration, by default or otherwise, in making everyday decisions about budget allocations and in stroking the faculty.

Developmental Assignments

The Research Council took a strong position about the need for a sabbatical leave program and in April 1974 drafted a statement of the need:

> [One of the major obligations] of a university is to facilitate the steady scholarly growth and creative renewal of the faculty. . . . It has long been the practice of most major universities to have programs of support for faculty development and scholarship. . . . Lamentably, the University of Iowa is one of four CIC [Council on Institutional Cooperation] institutions not having a sabbatical leave program; moreover, its formal alternative to a sabbatical program — the research assignment program — is grossly underfunded and unworthy to be considered seriously as an alternative. . . . It is the unanimous and urgent conclusion of the Research Council that this deplorable situation at the University of Iowa must be remedied now. . . . During the coming year, therefore, the Research Council proposes to make increasing such support its major project for investigation and action.

This position would prove to be a key ingredient in the significant increase of funds for research assignments, ultimately to be called "developmental assignments" to avoid criticism from state government that they were paid vacations.

Keeping Track

Not surprisingly, we developed a computer program to monitor our progress in seeking and receiving external funding. It was, after all, a source for developing hard data that are difficult to come by in other areas of university endeavors. Increasingly, we used these data to chart our progress. We also developed the capacity to track the outcome of proposals to external funding agencies, even though the time required to learn about outcomes varied from a few months to several years. Doing so gave us the capacity to generate success ratios. We shared this information with the collegiate deans for the faculty within their units, and we used the aggregated ratios as one of our data points in making some of our allocations to departments.

Happily, our capacity to store and retrieve data served us well in another way. In January 1973 President Nixon announced his determination to hold federal spending to $250 billion during fiscal 1972–1973 and $270 billion in fiscal 1973–1974. "Self-imposed" cuts were needed, according to President Nixon, to avoid inflationary deficits and a tax increase, even if it required impounding several billion dollars' worth of appropriations that Congress had already approved. Cuts were made or projected for some of the federal programs in higher education based on the contentions that there was no evidence that the programs were needed, that there may already be an excess of qualified scientists, that there was no evidence that stipends were a determining factor in student career choices, and that the normal process of supply and demand would produce enough trained workers. Among the affected programs were the training and capitation grants from the NIH, the NSF, and the Department of Education. No specific programs were identified, of course, and the outcry locally was muted undoubtedly in part by the view that "surely our program will not be subject to the ax." We reacted with concern, of course, but little was to be done until we could document the impact. Only then could we propose damage control responses.

President Boyd took note of the cuts in his fall 1973 speech to the faculty. On September 6 the Des Moines *Register* carried an article about the speech with the headline: "Boyd Assails Nixon Policy." On October 1 the editor of the *Register* received a letter from Secretary of HEW Caspar Weinberger in which he referred to the speech with the comment that Boyd "strongly criticized the administration's policy of 'cutting back' federal financial support for higher learning." He went on to say, "I am amazed that the 'cut-back' myth continues when, in fact, aid to higher education has increased each year under the present administration." He cited examples in the area of student assistance, including the new program of Basic Education Opportunity Grants based on President Nixon's philosophy that "no qualified student who wants to benefit from postsecondary education should be barred by lack of money," citing primarily programs, new and old, administered by the Office of Education.

The *Register* editor asked President Boyd for comment. I quote from his October 15, 1973, reply to the editor:

Contrary to Mr. Weinberger's letter, the budget proposed by the national administration for fiscal year 1974, if approved, will lead to real — not "mythical" — reductions in federal financial support to the University of Iowa. Mr. Weinberger's analysis is confined to one of several agencies in his department, the Office of Education. At the University of Iowa only 13.3 percent of the funds we receive from HEW is channeled through that agency. It is through the other agencies of HEW, which he does not mention, that the University of Iowa is experiencing the most devastating cutbacks. These include a reduction in educational funds of 48.8 percent for nursing, 50 percent for pharmacy, 28 percent for dentistry, 16.5 percent for medicine, and an abrupt cessation of funds for allied health traineeships for such fields as physical therapy and dental hygiene. Equally severe and continuing reductions for graduate student support are proposed by HEW.

However, we didn't wait for the local programs to march in protest. As soon as the announcement of the impoundments were made, Margery Hoppin and Brian Harvey in sponsored programs began documenting precisely which programs at the university would be affected. By the summer of 1973 they were ready with the list of affected programs by college: Dentistry, eight programs; Medicine, thirty-six programs; Nursing, eight programs; Pharmacy, one program; Liberal Arts, nine programs; and the Graduate College, two programs. Clearly, the health colleges bore the brunt of affected programs.

In the end we were able to draw down state funds to cover our losses as they occurred ($1.5 million in 1974–1975, $1.7 million for 1975–1976, $2.1 million for 1976–1977, and $1.1 million for 1977–1978; total: $6.484 million). No funds were appropriated to cover losses for student employment and support. The silver lining was that these funds became part of the university's recurring budget and acquired a permanency that they would not have had once federal funding expired, as it inevitably would have. It's my recollection that Iowa was the only state that appropriated funds for these federal losses, thanks largely to the outstanding work of the sponsored programs staff.

Not all the myriad federal regulations that were descending on us were ill-advised. For example, our human subject committees and the Research Council had concluded that we should improve our procedures for ensuring that informed consent and associated research protocols were obtained before the proposed research was begun. I reviewed our recommendations with the collegiate deans, some of whom wondered out loud whether we were succumbing with "supine acquiescence" to the feds. I responded with a memo in which I said that "the Research Council and I both believed there was a very strong case for a comprehensive human subjects requirement, and the presence or absence of federal pressure had absolutely nothing to do with our strong advocacy of the proposed policy changes." In fact, the council and I agreed that procedures similar to those required by HEW should be employed in non–HEW-sponsored research, and we ultimately established a committee to deal with those research protocols in a way similar to that required by HEW. This was one of several times when federal requirements nudged us to do what was right.

Computer Technology

The emergence of computers as a relevant educational technology was clearly becoming a reality that could not be ignored. "The Fourth Revolution" — so dubbed by the Carnegie Commission on Higher Education in 1972 when referring to instructional technology — was an increasingly common topic in the conversations of faculty and administrators in higher education across the country. Thanks primarily to the prophetic vision of Gerry Weeg, director of the University Computing Center, we felt that we had no option but to struggle with the revolution's implications during times of great fiscal restraint. Gerry wrote a "dream document," described in detail in chapter 7, which became, with lots of squirming, our computing reality. But the computer was already making itself felt in our budget allocations. The issue was one of priorities and limited financial resources.

Our annual report to the NSF on the progress of the Biological Sciences Development Grant for the 1973–1974 fiscal year was a positive one, in which I announced that the objectives of the NSF for the program had, in my opinion, been achieved. Our initial grant of $5.1 million in 1967 had been supplemented by $1.6 million in 1971 and extended without additional funds to June 30, 1975. Funds for construction accounted to 40 percent of the initial award and had been used to build an addition to the Zoology Building and provide partial support for the construction of the Basic Science Building. Twenty-four new faculty positions had been filled along with supporting equipment and personnel. The departments supported by the award (anatomy, biochemistry, botany, microbiology, pharmacology, physiology, psychology, and zoology) received increasing national recognition. President Bowen's prompting and prodding had paid off.

1974–1975: NEVER THE SAME RIVER

Personnel

Change is a creative force for all, individuals and institutions alike. Academic institutions consistently maintain that, while they welcome change, it should be deliberative to make sure that the time-tested values of the academy are not lost. Perhaps the most dramatic and regular change is brought about by the student body. Each new class brings priorities, beliefs, and values that are somewhat different from those of previous classes. While faculties attempt to tell these new idealistic, bright, and eager students how it is, their new audiences provide feedback that, although subtle, tempers the faculties' views.

Change also occurs constantly at the faculty and staff levels. Young faculty, especially at Iowa, find their wings and move off to other opportunities. Even presidents find greener pastures! Older faculty retire. Fields change, requiring the recruitment of experts in new fields. Day-to-day changes, like growing children, are barely perceptible and without drama but profound year by year.

During the 1974–1975 academic year a number of changes were announced that would affect my areas of activities. Effective January 1, 1975, Robert Hardin resigned as vice president and dean of health affairs to return to the faculty of internal medicine. Bob's assignment change was a personal loss for me since he was a strong advocate of one university, which clearly included the health colleges. He also became a close colleague during the times of student unrest, when he and I pooled our organizational skills, drawn largely from our common military experiences, to establish the central "command post" described in chapter 8.

Gordon Strayer moved, effective January 1, 1975, from the position of director of public information and university relations, to director of health center information and communication, a new position stemming from the growing importance of health issues among our external constituents. All our health colleges were affected. I had come to admire Gordon's work through our many contacts since the university office he headed reported to my office "for rations and quarters," and he, too, had worked closely with those of us in the command post during the student unrest days.

Edward Jennings changed from professor and head of the Department of Business Administration to assistant dean of faculties, effective June 1, 1975. It was a move that would cast the die for Ed, who would ultimately become vice president for business and finance and then move on to become president of the University of Wyoming and later president of Ohio State University. He was a lively and enthusiastic colleague with a devilish twinkle in his eye, fun to work with.

The staff rosters of my offices were, in the main, very stable; a number of my key staff (Deans Jakobsen and Mason, and director and associate director of sponsored programs Margery Hoppin and Brian Harvey), were with me from or near the beginning to the end of my tenure. Nevertheless, and for no single reason, there were changes, especially during this particular year.

At the end of the year John McCrone resigned his position as associate vice president for educational development and research to become dean of the

School of Arts and Sciences and professor of biology at Western Carolina University. (An established arachnologist, John kept a live black widow spider in a glass bell in his office!) By his activities John had continued to define this relatively new position, which recognized the university's need to relate regularly with our congressional delegation and with the major foundations. His work established our office as a source of definitive information about these groups and as an effective channel for queries and messages to them. He was to be followed by William Farrell, who came from Marquette University, where he had been director of foundation support and associate professor of English. In addition to continuing to make the rounds prepared for him by John McCrone, Bill exercised his love for writing by doing occasional pieces for *Research and Graduate News* — thoughtful and pithy. He, too, would move up the administrative ladder, becoming first president of Plymouth State College in New Hampshire and later, and still, chancellor of the University System of New Hampshire. Some days, I had the feeling that I was managing a farm for budding university administrators.

In some ways the most profound change for the university and me came in the middle of the year, when brain cancer forced Gerry Weeg to resign as director of the computer center. Gerry had taken an embryo unit and built it into a major university facility, leading the university, sometimes kicking and screaming, into a computer world that it only dimly understood, most definitely not as a major element to be reckoned with in both teaching and research. The technology descended on us with an overwhelming suddenness for which Gerry clawed to prepare us. He taught us all so much, despite the fact that we frequently were unwilling students. He dreamt for us, cajoled us, and shamed us unrelentingly. Despite his pushing, he was a lovable human being who left a major void in the university when he was forced to leave the scene.

The Vietnam War Ends

On April 30, 1975, the war in Vietnam ended and the Saigon government surrendered unconditionally to the Vietcong government, ending thirty years of warfare. The last nine hundred Americans had been airlifted to U.S. Navy ships in the China Sea. It would close the chapter on a bitter time for the United States, including its universities and their students.

All the selective service draft offices except the one in Des Moines closed their doors for the last time in February 1976. It was an end to an era that had started in 1941 with conscription. The Iowa City office had been housed in the post office building, now the Iowa City Senior Center, and had been the scene of pickets, draft card burnings, speeches, and sit-ins. The closing of the Iowa

City office passed almost unnoticed — an indication of the changes that had taken place since the protests of the late 1960s and early 1970s. Presumably, similar circumstances would not occur again; the use of the draft is unlikely except in extreme national emergencies, given the move to an all-volunteer "professional" military.

Graduate Matters

The future job market for new Ph.D.'s elicited dire predictions. There was a flurry of publications filled with data and warnings about the Ph.D. glut. Many saw the graduate establishments as chained to traditions, such as educating students in the images of their mentors, that were no longer valid. In 1973 the Educational Testing Service in Princeton, New Jersey, published *Scholarship for Society*, which cited three major conflicts: the tension between the thrust for democratization and the need to preserve value; the tension between the mastery of scholarship and the need for public involvement; and the tension between the values of diversity and order.

The diminished opportunities for academic appointments for our new Ph.D.'s dominated both meetings of the graduate faculty during the year. My closing admonition at the May meeting reflects my own personal dilemma about the issue:

> I trust that you will develop materials to be given to prospective students that indicate as clearly as possible what you consider to be their employment opportunities and options when their educational programs have been completed. In doing so, however, I also hope that you will recognize the possibility that a great poet, or historian, or physicist, or zoologist may be among the applicants who seek admission to study in your field on the grounds of a sincere and profound desire to learn more rather than for the purpose of obtaining a job.

Use of Radioactive Materials in Research

The Radiation Protection Office was one of our responsibilities. It was, and is, responsible for the receipt and disposal of radioactive materials used in animal research and in human diagnostic and therapy procedures in our hospitals and clinics. Approximately three hundred faculty and staff used such materials in 1974. In addition, an isolated, underground "cellar" on the Oakdale campus was used for storage of used materials pending appropriate disposition. Almost all of the radioactive materials emitted low levels of radiation and had a short (six months or less) half-life. The waste materials consisted of unused portions of tracer substances, paper, glassware, and other materials used in diagnosis and therapy, and carcasses of animals that had been part of research protocols. These materials had to be disposed of appropriately, which meant shipping them in special containers to federally approved receiving sites, sometimes located hundreds of miles away, an increasingly expensive operation.

In January 1975 the *Daily Iowan* report of seventeen allegations of improper procedures resulted in an investigation by the Nuclear Regulatory Commission (NRC). The Radiation Protection Executive Committee concluded that only two of the allegations had any substance and that, even in those instances, there had been no radiation hazard. In the end we tightened up our management procedures and were given a clean bill of health by the NRC.

The experience nonetheless dramatized a matter that would be of growing concern as the use of radioactive materials and the cost of their disposal grew exponentially. The problem was a common one among research universities. Ultimately, we built a storage facility at Oakdale which included an incinerator for materials that become inert in time, reducing our need to ship the materials to NRC-approved receiving sites, and instituted sophisticated and rigorous handling procedures. It was, and is, our policy not only to meet but exceed NRC management requirements. We are proud of our record that no persons, including the staff of the Radiation Protection Office, have been exposed to hazardous health risks due to radiation.

The Research Foundation

At its January 1975 meeting the Board of Regents approved the formation of University of Iowa Research Foundation (UIRF) through the University of Iowa Foundation, but with an arm's-length relationship to it. It was deemed appropriate also for the UIRF to maintain the arm's-length relationship to the university since some of its activities would involve for-profit entrepreneurial ends, including potential liabilities that did not fit comfortably with a university's mission. Since then the UIRF has developed a moderate but consistently productive portfolio, having spun off by 1997 ten for-profit companies, some of which have the potential for major earnings for the university.

Educational Developments

Computer-based education and its possible implications were familiar topics on campus. On October 19, 1974, the university hosted a meeting of the Upper Midwest HP (Hewlett Packard) User Group. The day's agenda consisted of new applications in a wide variety of fields such as business administration, secondary education, pathology, and dentistry. This summary of my remarks catches the primary dilemma we were facing:

There are two important questions to keep in mind. First, it is obvious that efforts in this area require substantial amounts of money. So the first question is how much can we afford to do? The second question, and the more troublesome one, is: as we strive to maintain excellence in education, to stay abreast of the continuing developments in educational technology, to provide the best learning environments for our students, how much can we afford *not* to do? Hopefully, the answer to the last question will significantly influence our answer to the first.

University House

In preparation for the annual congressional luncheons, the Iowa delegation typically went to Washington the evening before. That allowed time for rehearsing our presentations over dinner and for making visits to congressional offices and agencies for an informal exchange of views during the morning preceding the luncheons. Sometimes we discussed other topics over dinner, including future university needs and options. During our dinner before the February 17, 1975, luncheon, we talked about a vision that we had for a place to foster scholarship, even dreams, unrestricted by daily faculty obligations and stretched by a mix of faculty from a variety of disciplines. We talked about establishing a center for interdisciplinary studies and the possible location of such a center. We thought Eastlawn would be ideal since its use for music practice rooms would cease when the music department moved into its new building. When we came home, we did an unofficial evaluation of the renovations that would be required, reckoning that the project cost would be $704,900.

Our dream was overtaken by the hard realities of pressing space requirements. Nevertheless, the seed was sown for the idea, which, after a long period of incubation, is now a reality in the Obermann Center for Advanced Studies on the Oakdale campus.

1975–1976: GETTING THE WASH OUT

Change

At the end of the year Frank Horton, dean for advanced studies, resigned to become vice president for academic affairs at Southern Illinois University. I felt that it was imperative to have someone in the position by September 1, since my vice presidential duties were so totally consuming that I simply did not have time to direct the day-to-day activities of the Graduate College as well. I was fortunate to recruit Professor Ada Jacox from the faculty of the

College of Nursing for the position on an acting basis until May 31, 1976. Ada made very clear that she would not be a candidate for the regular appointment. She had strong credentials: a doctorate in sociology from Case-Western Reserve University, and a fine research record since coming to Iowa in 1969 that included the directorship of a research program on the alleviation of pain through nursing intervention. She was a member of the Nursing Research and Education Advisory Committee of the NIH, and a member of the editorial review boards of *Nursing Forum* and *Nursing Research*.

Filling the dean for advanced studies position on a permanent basis created questions in the minds of some of the faculty, especially those in the College of Liberal Arts, about the actual need for the position. I was taken aback, to say the least, by a letter out of the blue from Professor Laurence Lafore, then chair of the Department of History, raising questions about the need for a replacement: "We have no grounds for supposing that [the office] performs an indispensable function. . . . We hope that the proper authorities will give very careful consideration to defining and analysis of the duties of the position, . . . and to the possibilities of abolishing the position or perhaps filling it with a junior person, perhaps someone with secretarial rather than professional training. . . . We observe that the salary attached to the position would be sufficient to provide two quite senior faculty members."

Dean Stuit followed up with a memo to President Boyd and Vice President Brodbeck: "You have a copy of Professor Lafore's letter . . . about the position of dean for Advanced Studies. . . . The views expressed by Professor Lafore are rather widely held — at least that's my impression. I believe this matter deserves your careful attention."

To say that I was upset by this brouhaha, which seemed to us not to be widespread despite Dean Stuit's observation, is putting it mildly. To be sure, some of the fault rested at our doorstep. Obviously, we had not communicated fully to the faculty the extent of the new responsibilities of our offices and the increasing amount of time that I was devoting to those in addition to graduate education. I was working long hours seven days a week on a regular basis, and my staff was doing almost as much. My knee-jerk response was to say, "To hell with this place if total dedication isn't enough!" I came close to turning in my keys and walking out. But I took time to renew my perspective. I got together a list of the duties then being discharged by my offices and went over them in great detail with the Graduate Council. Then I responded to Professor Lafore with copies to Dean Stuit, Boyd, and Brodbeck:

> Mindful of the judgments involved in the staff level appropriate for the
> Graduate College, I discussed the position [dean for advanced studies]

at some length with the Graduate Council in the early fall [1975] before we began the search for the person to fill it. Recently [your letter made me] aware that some questions had been raised about the need for the position . . . and I asked the council to consider the question in depth once more.

The council met on February 5 [1976] to review the matter. At that time I presented descriptive material to them, some of which is the enclosed lists of duties. . . . Following the description of the positions and functions by the Graduate College staff, [we] withdrew from the meeting and the council went into executive session to consider the matter. The council reported following the executive session that it was unanimous in the view that the "dean for Advanced Studies was a most important position and that it should be filled with the strongest possible candidate." . . . I trust that this information will be informative to the faculty of the Department of History and will serve to assure it that the Graduate College is dedicated to serving this university with a structure that is justified with the same rigor required of any academic program.

I sent a memo to President Boyd and Dean Brodbeck to the effect that I would not remain in my position if it was determined by them that the position of dean for advanced studies was not required. Hearing nothing further about the matter, I concluded that the issue was not seen as one demanding central administration involvement, and our search for a permanent replacement for Frank Horton as dean for advanced studies moved along quickly. At its April 1976 meeting, the regents approved the appointment of Rudolph Schulz from our Department of Psychology to be the new dean. I had become acquainted with Rudy when he was the chair of the department. I also knew of his work as the editor of *Memory and Cognition* and of his authorship of a book on verbal learning and his many research papers. I was confident that he would be a steadfast keeper of the quality-control button of the Graduate College.

Graduate Matters

Agony over job market prospects and the need for graduate program adjustments to meet those changes continued to be one of the major topics in graduate education circles. There was talk at the national level of "decoupling the production of research from the production of Ph.D.'s" to which I took strong exception. At the meeting of the graduate faculty on December 17, 1975, I discussed a series of related topics, including the basic research function of graduate education, particularly at the Ph.D. level, the need for reconsideration of the master's degree within academic structures, the growing numbers of nontraditional students, and our appropriate response to supply-and-demand forces.

I continued to worry aloud to the graduate faculty about appropriate responses to these issues at our meeting on May 5, 1976, and asserted my belief that we should and could maintain the quality and characteristics of our traditional programs while at the same time experimenting with new forms of graduate education. By repeating that we needed to look for new ways and justifications for what we were doing, it was my hope that enough faculty would heed the message and take appropriate actions to avoid the imposition of new packaging of graduate programs from the top.

In April 1976 we announced the availability of some funds to support qualified minority students in addition to those then available through Special Support Services. Part of the funds covered stipends and tuition for five fellows chosen by the Graduate College Affirmative Action Committee from those nominated by departments. The other part was used to assist departments in improving the competitiveness of offers that they were intending to make to minority students by paying their tuition or by supplementing the stipends that departments were able to offer. We were determined to add reality to our statements endorsing affirmative action.

Research

Our office had been administering the modest "research assignment" program, which all agreed needed to be expanded. The name of the program was changed to "developmental assignments" and the responsibility for it, appropriately in my view, was shifted at the beginning of the 1975–1976 academic year to the Office of Academic Affairs, where it remains. The program differs from the sabbatical since it is not automatically awarded and requires peer judgments of the proposed use of the assignment time. Equally important, it avoids the perception, held by many outside the academy, that it is additional vacation for faculty who are perceived as working few hours and already having ample vacation time.

The University Press

In October 1975 we had to face up to the continuing funding problems of the University Press. We had stopped accepting manuscripts the previous year while we took stock of its status. In addition to the salaries for two persons and other overhead provided directly by the university, an additional $50,000 annually was required. Those funds came from the University of Iowa Foundation and from my office (cost-of-education allowances). By then, we knew that an acceptable long-range solution was required. It was not particularly heartening to know that most university presses across the country were facing similar problems!

I agonized over the matter for weeks because we were living in particularly difficult financial times. In the end I wrote a seven-page memo to President Boyd and Vice Presidents Brodbeck and Chambers weighing the pros and cons of continuing the press, concluding that we should continue it to address the needs not only of scholars but also the interests of a wider educated public.

> [The press] publishes works of high quality in a broad range of fields but also develops a special standing in several where we may attain unique publishing distinction; puts on display, along with the university imprimatur, the scholarly and artistic products arising from those fields in which the university is preeminent; encourages scholarship within the university; meets some of the publishing needs of this region at the same time that it addresses itself to a national constituency of scholars and educated readers; attempts through shrewd editorial and management policy to increase its sales income at the same time that it holds true to its status as a university press; and finally, brings to the university a well-earned reputation for the promotion of scholarship and its dissemination "far and wide."

My conclusions were unanimously endorsed by the Faculty Senate, and we decided to keep the press going, little knowing that our lofty goals would be largely fulfilled, in no small measure, later as the result of the particular support of President James Freedman, who was not yet on board.

The Orthodontic Wire with a Memory

Coincident with the establishment of the University of Iowa Research Foundation came the announcement in April 1976 that the Unitek Corporation had purchased the manufacturing rights to Nitinol wire, the orthodontic application of which was an invention of Professor George Andreason of the Department of Orthodontics. George conceived of the idea that he could use Nitinol, an alloy of nickel and titanium that had been developed by the U.S. Navy, to move and straighten a patient's teeth by using the body heat in the patient's mouth. His clinical trials proved that he was right, and Bill Trease, an attorney on our staff and executive director of UIRF, worked with him for many months in successfully processing the patent application and in monitoring Nitinol's licensed use. Unitek's interest, as well as that of several competing companies, followed. The licensing brought significant returns, which, according to university policy, were shared equally by the inventor, his department, UIRF, and the research office. Successful pursuit of patents, however, is an expensive matter, the outcome of which is not predictable. The success of Nitinol raised the sensitivity of the faculty to the importance of disclosing their ideas in a timely fashion for potential patent evaluation. The result has been a steady increase in the numbers of patents issued to the university.

Audit

"University of Iowa: You must remit $1.27 million by return mail for unallowable costs which you have charged to the federal government for projects that it has supported during the period from 1971 to 1974." That is, of course, a paraphrase of the actual message, but it accurately reflects the unexpected jolt that we got in October 1975 from Kansas City auditors of the Department of Health, Education, and Welfare (HEW). A predictable reaction to the message, when word of it trickled out to the news media, was that some unlawful skullduggery was involved and that there were culprits within the university who should be held accountable. It was the start of a tortuous and expensive time for the university and would involve challenges to the integrity of many university investigators who were supported by federal awards. Ultimately, it would require the imposition within universities of some very expensive and burdensome administrative procedures that continue in some form to this day. Our only consolation was that we were joining forty-two major universities across the nation who were also being criticized by the federal auditors for not following prescribed cost accounting procedures. Here are a few of the details.

President Boyd appeared before the Joint Committee on Education Appropriations of the Iowa legislature on January 26, 1978, at its invitation, as the result of news stories, and explained that the audit issues "are both simple and complicated . . . and reflect the complexity of . . . the federal grant system. . . . The University of Iowa is contesting HEW's position. . . . No one has ever questioned the quantity or quality of the work done. . . . No one has been over paid."

Three areas were found defective and are summarized briefly from the forty-six-page audit report dated April 15, 1976:

The auditors found that the payroll system was "driven by budget estimates rather than expended effort." The university did not have in place a paper trail system for directors of federal projects to report, after the fact, that they and the persons working for them had done the work for which they were paid. Consequently, the auditors asked the university to reimburse $946,344 in salary, fringe benefits, and indirect costs.

Second, the auditors found inappropriate expenditure transfers of $234,882 to and from grants to other accounts because the transfers "were not made due to the applicability of the receiving grants, but rather were made because of fund considerations." In their opinion the university administration accepted requests from its investigators for transfers without adequate written justification, and thus reimbursement was indicated.

Finally, the university was challenged for paying "stipends" to graduate research assistants and postdoctoral fellows from federal research grants. The issue revolved around whether or not payments to graduate students and postdoctoral fellows, which were considered nontaxable under the Internal Revenue Service Code, represented payment for work done on the grant. In this instance they recommended that $312,422 be refunded to the federal government.

The findings shocked the university community because previous federal auditors had found satisfactory the same university systems that were now being deemed inadequate. After an unpleasant meeting of five university staff with over twenty-five federal officials in Kansas City shortly after the informal report was received, it was clear that a consultant accounting firm was needed to assist the university in developing new documentation procedures. The university hired the firm of Peat, Marwick, and Mitchell.

The university conducted a case-by-case review of each of the auditors' disallowances, and on April 23, 1976, an appeal was presented to the Financial Advisory Branch of the National Institutes of Health (NIH), the designated agency to review the university response. Several meetings were then held in Washington, D.C., to discuss efforts the university was making to respond to the auditors' recommendations for better documentation procedures, and to resolve misunderstandings the university perceived in the audit findings about the rules underlying some of the grants. It wasn't until May 5, 1978, that the agency concluded that the Kansas City audit findings should be sustained. On September 12, 1978, the university appealed to the NIH Grant Appeals Board, and two years later, on October 20, 1980, they agreed with the university's position that "student salaries were for services rendered to federally supported projects and as such should not be disallowed." However, they sustained the disallowances of the first two audit findings.

The university and its external advisors still felt strongly that the government conclusions were incorrect, and a decision was made to appeal to the highest level of HEW. At that point we hired a member of a Washington, D.C., law firm, Clare Dalton (who during the case became a Harvard Law School faculty member), to prepare our case. It was a great decision; the day before three voluminous appeal binders were to be delivered to the HEW judges, NIH suggested a meeting to settle, and the university agreed. Finally, on December 3, 1981, a negotiated settlement of $632,000 was reached that covered the period from 1970 through 1980 for all federally funded projects. The obligation accepted by the university resulted in $300,000 of adjustments to the subsequent three years of the university's indirect cost rates, and $332,000 were offset by reducing the indirect cost payments due on three grants current at that time.

In the end the University of Iowa did not write a check to the government. Richard Powers, chief of the Financial Advisory Services Branch, Division of Contracts and Grants, National Institutes of Health wrote the government settlement letter and stated that "neither the audit findings, nor the terms of this settlement, should be construed to imply that the university failed to fulfill the programmatic objectives of grants received from or contracts made with the federal government. Nor do the audit findings or this settlement reflect a determination that the university has engaged in any fraud, deliberate misrepresentation or wrongful appropriation of federal funds."

From the inception of the audit review there was no doubt that the university needed to institute expensive new payroll documentation systems to satisfy the government's standards. First, a monthly "activity report system" was developed to provide an after-the-fact certification that work was done on a federal project. Once our proposed system received prior approval by HEW, training meetings were held with faculty and administrators in each college. Not only was the report necessary to validate federally paid salaries but also cost-shared salaries and effort spent on teaching, research, service, and administration regardless of funding source. The Offices of Academic Affairs and Research were heavily involved in this effort. Faculty were mostly cooperative, but a few who were not on government grants refused to participate. The paperwork generated was a nightmare and strained the university system. Transfer of costs to and from grants and contracts now required extensive written justification and prior approval from many levels of administration. Additional staff were hired at many university levels to handle the increased work.

Universities across the country found these new systems a major source of friction between the government and universities and, within the institutions, between the faculty and administration. A position paper from the American Association of Universities, dated August 7, 1981, asserted that "documentation of faculty effort has placed demands on faculty that are incompatible with the academic environment and academic traditions — demands probably unanticipated by the government officials responsible for those requirements."

Ironically, several federal agencies subsequently recognized that some of the newly interpreted procedures were a hindrance to the researcher. The after-the-fact report was reduced from a monthly to quarterly, and finally a semi-annual system. The NSF pioneered a "prior approval system" that allowed cost transfers between related federal projects and gave institutions authority to make decisions on changing allocations of many of the granted funds without going to NSF for prior approval. Subsequently, the NIH and other agencies granted more decision-making authority to universities to reduce administrative burdens on the faculty researcher.

After all, the publication of important scientific findings, or the graduation of superbly trained students supported by federal dollars, should be the ultimate test that government funds have been well spent. The systems requiring the work to be separated into detailed categories that are often inseparable, such as research and advanced training, have fostered cynicism toward the federal government. Unfortunately, some of the folks in the regulatory arm of the government, at least at that time, felt that checklists calling for a project director's recollection of how he or she spent time in the previous months was the ultimate proof for valid accountability of federal expenditures.

The Price of Partnership

Accepting federal dollars was proving to have unanticipated consequences, hearkening back to Mr. Hancher's earlier concerns. I wrote two "As I See It" pieces for *Research and Graduate News* in January 1976 that reflect the nature of some of the issues of the day. One was entitled "The Price of 'Partnership'!" and dealt with the growing intrusion of federal regulations on our work. Specifically, I discussed proposed changes to Federal Management Circular 73-8 that would reduce the recovery of indirect costs at the same time that our operating costs were being increased by additional government reporting requirements, including monthly time and effort reports for all persons (secretaries, technicians, faculty) paid from federal funds. The other piece, "Living and Making a Living," dealt with increasing demands for data from universities covering such matters as costs per credit hour by level of instruction, typical costs for each degree, the ratio of credit hours to faculty, and the percentage of placement of graduates by discipline. The alleged purpose of such reviews was to focus fund support on programs with the most favorable cost/benefit experiences. It was assumed that those institutions providing advanced education most beneficial to society and hence most deserving of support were those that prepared students at the smallest cost!

Stewardship for the Oakdale Campus

At its January 1976 meeting the Board of Regents approved the 1977 transfer of the tuberculosis and other pulmonary care programs from the Oakdale campus to University Hospitals. This would clear the way for the consolidation of the state Hygienic Laboratory operations from the main campus to

Oakdale. It would also lead to the assignment of space in Oakdale Hall, then Oakdale Hospital, to other university activities, most especially for what is now the Obermann Center for Advanced Studies. Our office was given responsibility for the campus, which involved primarily policy development and oversight. The great plus for the campus was that the physical plant had been developed and maintained for a population that no longer demanded it. Thus, the legislative transfer of the campus to the university had been a very special gift of space and facilities. We sought to make the distance between the campuses invisible by subsidizing regular Cambus (university bussing) services between the two, and by establishing computer, copying, and library services. We were especially eager to identify spaces that could be used on an ad hoc basis for temporary arrangements for research and teaching programs that could not be accommodated otherwise. In the light of my responsibilities for development, assigning the Oakdale campus to me was deemed logical. I loved every minute of it.

In response to a query about Oakdale from one of the members of the Board of Regents, President Boyd responded:

> We consider Oakdale merely to be an extension of our campus and not in any way to represent a multi-university development. This is one reason why we are attempting through the proposed transportation shuttle system and other administrative support mechanisms to integrate the Oakdale campus at an enhanced level with the main campus. . . . The programs that will be located at Oakdale will, accordingly, be interrelated very directly with a host of functions here on the main campus and should not be viewed as isolated programs.

1976–1977: MORE WASH

Celebration

Planned to coincide with the observance of the United States bicentennial, Old Capitol was restored to its original likeness when it opened in 1842 for the Territorial Assembly and later as the seat of state government until 1857. The original balcony was discovered and rebuilt in the House Chamber, replicas of working desks were placed in the House Chamber, and the various offices were furnished with period furniture. Old Capitol was rededicated on July 4, 1976.

The three-day period of special events culminated in a major ceremony on the Pentacrest and was attended by some 6,000 spectators. The climax came when Governor Robert Ray, using its original key and lock, opened

Old Capitol's front door. The festivities included games and bands on what is now Hubbard Field, a special exhibit in the Museum of Natural History, the Great Byron Burford Circus, an "old time" band directed by university symphony conductor James Dixon, and much more. The restoration of Old Capitol to a standard that would insure that it endured to be appreciated and enjoyed for generations to come was, we felt, worthy of this type of public acknowledgment.

Change

Getting the attention of potential new enrollees was a nontrivial concern to us since our sister institutions were doing a better outreach job of capturing the interest of the high-school graduates in the state than we were, especially with respect to merit scholars. So much so that we felt that we had to devise strategies for improving our prospects. Ray Muston, assistant dean of faculties, became an expert on enrollment projections and the intentions of prospective university enrollees.

Early in the fall of 1976, the Joint Committee on University Outreach was appointed with representatives from the Alumni Association, the UI Foundation, and the university, plus the heads of the Alumni Association, the foundation, public information, and me as chair. We took our charge from remarks by President Boyd:

> This is a time in which the number of young people in our population is declining while the need for continuing education is increasing, . . . a time in which critics are challenging the career value of a college and university education and our nation's frontier is shifting from that of limited physical resources to that of unlimited ideas, and the general public is turning increasingly from the trivia of television to the colleges and universities to restore quality to their lives. . . . Public awareness of the university is a critical factor in our future. We are the university of *all* Iowa. This means that we must be understood and appreciated for what we are in all sections of the state. To do this, we must expose Iowans of all ages to our varied programs [through a series of targeted outreach programs]. We must bring an ever-increasing number of people into contact with the existing excellence of the university.

Development

Our relationship in the past with the city of Iowa City had been cordial and supportive. To be sure, there had been differences, which would continue to occur, but sooner or later they got worked out on an ad hoc basis. In December 1976 we arranged conversations with the mayor and the city manager. We described areas of our responsibilities as they might relate to cooperative ventures with Iowa City in "development," and I offered our office as a clearinghouse when the city folks had ideas about ways in which the university could participate in joint ventures. The seed was sown at that meeting for the more structured arrangements for community development that would emerge in the future.

In April 1977 the university received a $375,000 three-year grant from the Andrew W. Mellon Foundation to bring faculty members from independent colleges throughout the state to University House, now firmly established in Oakdale Hall, for work during the summer sessions. During its first year some twenty-five faculty from independent colleges joined their counterparts at Iowa in working on public policy issues at the state, national, and international levels. President Boyd noted that the award "has significantly increased opportunities for . . . faculty development efforts and will greatly strengthen the pluralistic system of higher education to which the University of Iowa is firmly committed."

Membership in MUCIA

On February 9, 1977, I wrote to President John Ryan of Indiana University and chair of the Midwest Universities Consortium on International Activities (MUCIA), requesting that the University of Iowa be considered for membership in the consortium. At the time seven of the Big Ten universities were members, all but ourselves, the University of Michigan, and Northwestern University. MUCIA had been organized out of necessity since very large pools of specialists are required to respond to requests for proposals to participate in international institutional building. An exaggerated example might be "a library specialist who is fluent in French, a specialist in sub-Sahara history, and available for a six-months' assignment from January to July." On July 1, 1977, the university's membership in MUCIA became official.

Our petition was an outgrowth of our increasing interest in international activities, stimulated in no small measure as the result of the programs and leadership emanating from our Office of International Education and Services. The early life of MUCIA had been dominated by a major grant from the Ford Foundation, the consortium having served as the body for disbursing the funds to its members for international programs that the foundation was willing to support. We applied for membership at approximately the time when the funds had been largely expended. Later, some of the members revealed surprise that we would apply when the honey pot was nearly empty.

Our interest, however, was motivated by our desire to become more actively involved in international research projects and institution building. We were admitted and had a kind of beginner's luck because soon after we joined, MUCIA began to compete successfully for a wide gamut of contracts from such agencies as the World Bank and USAID, and such host countries in programs of institution building as Nepal, Indonesia, Malaysia, Ethiopia, and the Caribbean islands. Our faculty and staff had opportunities to join teams of faculty and staff from the other member universities.

Graduate Matters

At the December 16, 1976, meeting of the graduate faculty I mulled aloud about the meaning of "campus" as we faced new demands to accommodate the needs of the private sector, offering employees advanced educational opportunities close to their workplaces. Many universities responded by establishing branch campuses with special programs to fit the needs of students with full-time employment. We did not follow that course; rather, we found ways to deliver some of our existing programs, some with new subtracks, off campus. But our standards for admission and minimum grade-point average remained unchanged.

The graduate faculty, at its meeting on May 10, 1977, confirmed a landmark decision to discontinue the M.A. and Ph.D. programs in Child Behavior and Development. It marked the final dissolution of the Institute for Child Behavior and Development, which left a proud legacy of outstanding faculty, outstanding research, and outstanding graduates who had done pioneering work in learning about child development and translating that learning to educational programs at all levels across the country. The program had been created in the 1920s as the result of the work of a few individuals who sought answers to significant child development questions. Many of those folks had either retired or moved on, and the program had lost its luster. It was now time to recognize that the program had run its course.

The Graduate College responded to national affirmative action mandates by establishing an affirmative action committee. It did so without protest because of its belief that the educational experiences of all students at the university would be enhanced by increasing the cultural diversity of our graduate student body. The committee recommended, and we agreed, that a Graduate Opportunity Scholarship and Fellowship program should be established to provide five one-year fellowships for qualified students new to the university. Nominations were solicited from departments; the outcome was reassuring. The committee had difficulty making a selection from many fine nominations. Happily, departments were able to accommodate more of the applicants through their own resources.

As I observed earlier, we fostered the organization of the Graduate Student Senate with the stipulation that it had to have representatives from a majority of the graduate departments. Maintaining that representation was a constant battle for the students, but they had managed reasonably well. Associate Dean Jakobsen continued as our faithful liaison with the senate. In late October 1976 he reported that a group of students from English and rhetoric planned to sponsor a forum about the potential for unionization of graduate students. They intended to invite representatives from several unions and graduate student representatives from the Universities of Michigan and Wisconsin, both with experience in unionization of graduate students, to discuss the pros and cons of unionization. One of the top items for improvement concerned health insurance. About fifteen students attended the meeting, hardly a groundswell; the issue would continue to bubble for another twenty years until unionization became a reality.

In February 1977 the Graduate Council formulated a statement that was widely distributed, having to do with employment possibilities of our graduates. It said in part:

> A number of recent studies have predicted a substantial decline in future academic employment opportunities for students receiving doctoral degrees. Almost all such forecasts call for sharp drops in academic employment during the 1980s, but are somewhat mixed in predicting demand in non-academic areas. . . . It would seem imprudent to ignore the near uniformity in the predictions of declines in academic demand. . . . The council strongly recommends that departments make every effort to inform prospective students, especially prospective Ph.D. students, of the possible employment outlook.

While there was no direct monitoring of departmental responses, we received little feedback about major recruitment/employment issues following the issuance of the statement.

On May 3, 1977, the *Daily Iowan* ran an article about the Graduate College with the headline "Graduate Program Permeates UI" as part of its series on all the colleges preparatory to the North Central ten-year accreditation review. (There were graduate programs in all the other colleges.) Quoted extensively in the article, I noted that the expectation that professors should "profess" and be judged by their peers was not new. I quoted UI president George McLean, who said in his 1899 inaugural address: "We require our professors be more highly built up in knowledge, and be men [*sic*] who are doing research work and publishing. . . . We want a man who is adding to the stocks of knowledge, and teaching our students not simply by the importation of a stock of knowledge, but teaching them how themselves to be discoverers of knowledge." (Not incidentally, the Graduate College was established the following year and has sought since then to be an instrument for achieving that goal.)

Conflicts of Interest

Conflict of interest was and is a continuing issue that surrounds many investigators who are supported by external entities, frequently by for-profit organizations. Put in a nutshell, the question is, Does the source of the funds in some way influence what the recipient studies and how she or he interprets the results of the research? Fraud or falsification are typically *not* involved. Rather, accusers will argue that, while the investigator is honest and rigorous in the pursuit of her or his research, choices of focus must be made that even subconsciously can be tilted in particular directions at the expense of others.

A case in point was a charge brought in September 1976 by the Center for Science in the Public Interest, a consumer-scientist group. The allegation was that Professors Samuel Fomon and Lloyd Filer, both of the Department of Pediatrics and both consultants to federal agencies, were in conflict-of-interest circumstances by having accepted funds from companies developing and selling infant foods to evaluate those very foods. Both men were highly respected by their peers as outstanding investigators. A full airing of the charges revealed that the funds they received came without any strings attached (they were free to publish their findings, favorable or unfavorable) and were processed through the university system in the regular manner. While the charges were not substantiated, they highlighted the fine line between independence and obligation. The problem has burgeoned as the private sector looks increasingly to university researchers to conduct the basic research necessary for them to continue the development of their products and services.

State Control of Research Funds

In 1977 the legislature created a stir when it introduced a bill (HSB 217) requiring that all federal funds to any state agency, including the institutions under the control of the Board of Regents, must be deposited in the general funds of the state and be available for appropriation as part of the state budget! It may well have been motivated in part by our success in having the state replace our lost federal funding for instruction. It could have been said: "They got in trouble and now they come running to us to rescue them. We have to protect the state from their forays on the state treasury." Happily, the bill got buried before it got to the floor of the House for debate, but it alerted us to be vigilant in explaining ourselves to our constituencies.

Responsibilities

President Boyd called special meetings from time to time to consider pending issues in depth, sometimes in his conference room, sometimes in a "retreat" setting. Retreats to Sandy typically meant places outside of Jessup Hall but not far — the president's house, the Union, Oakdale, once the Amanas, once a home in Stone City, and once, in a major departure from his custom, Ruidoso, New Mexico, at a house I owned there at the time. They typically included his vice presidents and key personal staff. One of the meetings dealt with university planning and organization. Sandy asked me to make some preliminary remarks to lay the groundwork for the discussions. I'm not sure how my "expertise" on such a topic came to be, albeit I frequently made critical remarks about administrative bungling, needless redundancy, and lack of clear task definitions and responsibilities. But I never backed away from opportunities to speak my piece!

Development

Research and Graduate News continued to evolve. It had started out as a vehicle for informing the faculty of specific funding opportunities and deadlines, then grew to include summaries of actions of the Graduate and Research Councils, announcements of Ph.D. dissertation defenses, and major policy announcements of new funding initiatives. During this year, for example, it carried discussions of such topics as "PHS [Public Health Service] and the Young Investigator," "PHS Career Development Awards," "The Federal Government Contracting Process," "Research Abroad I: NSF–International Division," "Cooperative NATO Programs," "National Eye Institute Research," "Neurological and Communicative Disorders and Stroke," and the "National Institute on Aging." It also ran a series on the patenting process in recognition of the growing press to transfer intellectual property to the marketplace; the series included "Something You Should Know about Patents," "Is It Patentable?" and "What an Invention Is *Not*." This was going on at a time when awards from external funding agencies had almost tripled since 1965, from $16.5 million to $44.3 million at the end of the 1976–1977 fiscal year.

In February 1977 the Committee on University Educational Directions was established. Chaired by Professor Stow Persons of the Department of History, the committee published its report, *Educational Directions for the University of Iowa*, in February 1978. The chapter on "Graduate Education and Research" described issues related to the graduate faculty and students, interdisciplinary studies, libraries and computers, and faculty vitality. The presentation consisted largely of descriptive statements of present programs and problems. It was helpful to be reminded of the many verities that the academy takes for granted. While the few recommendations were quite general, one did pique my interest: "The relationship between the Offices of the Graduate College and the Vice President for Educational Development and Research should be periodically examined." The text provided not a word of context for the recommendation to indicate that the relationship was positive, negative, or potentially destructive! However, I didn't spend a great deal of energy puzzling about it because I felt that informed review of the relationship would easily demonstrate the validity of the combined offices. How wrong I was; nearly a decade later President Hunter Rawlings would strike the offices asunder by fiat early in his presidency.

The Silicon Chip

The February 20, 1978, issue of *Time* carried an article on the "miracle chip," the silicon chip with a calculating capacity that made possible the development of microcomputers with computing power equal to the existing computing monsters. Since I felt a singular responsibility for pressing new technologies, having felt like a lone wolf in trying to insert computer technology into the instructional structure of the university, I wrote a memo to the academic docket group urging them to read the article, a copy of which I enclosed. Some excerpts from my memo follow:

> The Persons' committee [referring to the previously mentioned Committee on University Educational Directions] makes no mention of the educational implications of the microprocessor even though it is probable that nothing since the Industrial Revolution will have as significant an effect on the lives of all of us. How can we plan realistically for the future without taking the impact duly into account? . . . How can persons be liberally educated without at least an introductory course which informs them about this technology? What are the curricular implications for computer science? Engineering? Business Administration? What are its implications for our modes of instruction? for libraries? for the organization and management of our educational systems? etc. . . . Some universities will seize the initiative in dealing with the implications of this technology and emerge as the educational leaders of the next decade or so. . . . The big question then is: Where will the University of Iowa be?

I did not expect a dramatic and definitive response to my memo, and there wasn't one. While, in retrospect, my alert was understated, the miracle chip assumed a life of its own. In fact, it has become so ubiquitous in everything we do these days that most of today's action generation would find it hard to imagine a time when it was not fully available.

Graduate Issues

President Emeritus Howard Bowen addressed the graduate faculty at its regular meeting on December 13, 1977. He had an abiding faith in the value of a well-educated citizenry to solve the nation's problems and to open up opportunities for social growth in all its dimensions. The topic of his address was "Advanced Study: Some Thoughts on Future Social Needs for Highly Educated Men and Women." Some of the highlights of his remarks were:

Suppose the nation were to improve its educational system from the cradle to the grave in several ways, for example (1) by expanding early childhood education and day nurseries; (2) by enriching programs and reducing class size in elementary and secondary schools; (3) by providing compensatory programs for the underprivileged and work-study arrangements for teenagers and young men and women; (4) by coordinating work and study of adults and providing financial aid suited to the special needs of adults. These programs could, of course, be carried out only over a period of years and over time would require at least a million additional teachers and other professional workers.

Suppose the nation were to push scientific research and technological development to deal aggressively with problems such as energy supply, conservation of land, and other natural resources, preservation of natural beauty, and abatement of pollution. If these things were done, the need for scientists, engineers, and administrators would increase by hundreds of thousands.

Suppose the nation were to embark on a determined effort to deal with urban problems including land planning, transportation, housing, utility development, crime abatement, legal services for low-income people, public health improvement, etc.; a great variety of professionals would be needed.

Suppose that under a national system of health insurance, medical, dental, and psychiatric services were made available to everyone to the same extent that they are available to upper income people; vast increases in the number of health professionals would be needed.

Suppose the nation became more involved in economic and social development abroad and in the education of foreign nationals; an increase in virtually all kinds of professional people would be needed.

Suppose serious efforts were made to promote the arts — including applied arts such as architecture, household direction, and design of products; hundred of thousands of humanists and artists would be needed.

. . . In the short run the political outlook for meeting the social needs I have mentioned and for creating the professional and administrative jobs they would generate is less than promising. . . . [But his belief in the importance of education remained steadfast.] I firmly believe that persons with the perspectives of science and scholarship in a wide variety of fields could contribute enormously in public affairs, and that universities should help facilitate their flow into business and government partly by helping them to see new opportunities, partly by helping them to introduce themselves to a new and largely untapped source of talent.

I am still struck by how well he anticipated the mantra of the 1996 national election campaign, which sought to demean the role of government in solving our social problems, and how strongly he indicted the restricted visions of those who aspire to lead and are leading this country.

On June 2, 1978, President Boyd wrote a memo to the vice president for academic affairs and the liberal arts and graduate college deans. It apparently was generated following a meeting, presumably with these three and perhaps others, about international education and highlights some of the substantive programs that already were in place to add international dimensions to students' thinking and values.

It is extremely important for the university to be concerned about the international dimensions of all of its programs because of the inescapability of the fact that we live in an international as well as a national society. . . . The Global Studies Program offers the possibility of a rallying point for international concerns which would, over time, involve diverse faculty and diverse students. . . . Comparative Studies offer considerable potential for this university but is not broadly staffed. . . . The foreign language requirement offers the opportunity of immersion in another culture which is important. So also does the literature requirement permit immersion in another culture. . . . Visiting foreign faculty is another extremely important approach.

Nevertheless, international education began and continues to be a shoehorn effort on this campus. Not surprisingly, the full impact of the implications of "one world" are still not well understood and appreciated.

Research

While federal dollars available to support research were not growing, our faculty steadily became more competitive. Federal support for research received by the university for the previous year grew 20 percent (to $29 million), accompanied by a 16 percent increase in applications forwarded. That, too, was good news, since the outflow from the pipeline is dependent on the inflow. The old law "nothing in, nothing out" applies. The bad news was that the complexity of research had increased, requiring increasingly more complex instrumentation, which in turn required more specialized space. No external funds were available to meet those needs, and universities, including the University of Iowa, had few resources to divert to these purposes. It would take over ten years — university cultures change with deliberateness — before university planning would take these new realities into account in the renovation and construction of new space.

Use of Animals in Research

A significant portion of research funding that was coming from the National Institutes of Health was associated with research involving animals (about $14 million in 1978–1979). Animal welfare was of increasing interest and concern, and the responsibility for setting standards and insuring compliance with them is vested in the U.S. Department of Agriculture. The USDA conducts unannounced inspections, one of which occurred at Iowa in the spring of 1979. We were found to be in noncompliance in eleven of the twelve animal facilities. Most of the citations were minor and easily corrected. In one instance cage cleanliness was related to a cage washer that was not operable and costly to repair. Another major item related to cage size, stemming largely from recently raised federal standards. Failure to come into compliance in a timely manner could result in cutting off all research funding from federal sources in support of animal research and possibly losing our institutional license, which would prevent us from conducting animal research regardless of source of funding. Obviously, changes had to be made quickly, with the first of several phases costing nearly $500,000.

This has been a tortuous saga that continues to have significant implications for the viability of the university's research enterprise, which has relied heavily on animal models. However, the tight centralized control and supervision now exercised on the use of animals in teaching and research did not always exist. Prior to the 1970s it was largely left in the hands of the individual researchers. However, in the early 1970s the Public Health Service issued its first policy on the humane care and use of animals.

Since all research using animals that was supported by federal agencies was subject to these regulations, I asked Brian Harvey, then associate director of sponsored programs, to monitor their developments. Here is Brian's accounting from a 1995 interview:

> In the 1970s we began to see the regulations that dealt with environment, ethical issues, and humane care of laboratory animals. In the late 1970s the U.S. Department of Agriculture [USDA] showed up accusing the university of mishandling animals and charging our oversight committee with failure to do its job properly. At that time the Animal Care Unit, now a university-wide facility, was a service unit in the College of Medicine, whose faculty conducted 90 percent of the research requiring animals. However, we had animal facilities all over the campus in departments and colleges where there was animal research going on: psychology, zoology, dental science. There was also some activity in engineering and bioengineering.
>
> Then the USDA inspector showed up, demanding to see the highest ranking official in charge, who was Sprie. The inspector was authorized to do all kinds of things that included levying fines and penalties and closing down all of the animal research on campus. He could have notified every funding agency from which we were receiving support that the university was out of compliance and that all research funding must be withdrawn. At that time we were receiving about $35 million in research grants. He could also have directed that the animals be terminated on the spot, which meant euthanizing them.
>
> Spriestersbach had to agree to come up with $500,000 in twenty-four hours to renovate the animal units and provide adequate caging for the animals. Not only did he have to come up with the funds but the USDA inspector had to see the requisitions all filled out and signed to prevent these awful penalties from being imposed. The upshot of all of this was that we immediately ordered many new animal cages. When they arrived they just sat at Oakdale for months because there wasn't any place to put them.
>
> Since we were under these USDA orders, a comprehensive review of the university's animal resources was begun. At the same time that we were reviewing our program, the government was increasing animal care requirements to the point that we didn't know what standards to use in

planning for changes in our animal management. Now not only was the Animal Care and Use Committee required to inspect the facilities but they were required to review as well the research protocols that called for the use of animals.

Very soon we dedicated ourselves to gaining accreditation by the American Association of Accreditation of Laboratory Animals [AAALAC]. That's the best that you can get. Finally, just a year ago [March 30, 1994] we received AAALAC accreditation. It took fifteen years to get it. It was a major milestone and naturally something that was very pleasing to everyone who worked on it.

Paul Cooper, university veterinarian, carries on the story:

When I first came here as veterinarian, we ran the hotel, but we were not really persons with whom the researchers were interested in having any communication. Our place was not to question or to help with their research, which has obviously changed with the laws. Now we even get some respect, as well as the opportunity to advise them about the models that they need to use in research, and the care and treatment of those models.

I try to look at the way that the laws have changed the thinking and why people are so responsive now and I think that it has actually evolved from a point of fear to a point of understanding. We're not staying in compliance because we're afraid of the law. We're staying in compliance because it's the best way of doing it.

Today, the Animal Care Unit controls the procurement of animals, caging, and housing systems; it provides care on a fee-for-service basis. It also provides appropriate training in humane practices of animal care and use, as well as training in research and teaching methods that minimize the animals' distress and the number of animals required to obtain valid results. In fact, without any regulations the researchers themselves are motivated to adhere to these practices. The use of animals in their research is expensive and imposes special burdens on them. If they conclude that they must use animals, they know that good science must involve healthy animals. No researcher that I know of would prefer to use animals in her or his research if their use can possibly be avoided.

More Federal Rules and Regulations

But back to 1979. Animal care wasn't the only issue about which we were watched by the feds. By accepting federal funds, we had become beholden to many federal agencies, requiring the development of special records that had to be maintained by investigators and administrators, certifications that had to be processed and signed, and on and on. In May 1979 I asked Brian Harvey to draw up a list of the various agencies that had a direct effect on us. Here is his list; even I was taken aback by the magnitude of it:

Occupational Safety and Health Administration [OSHA]: requiring compliance with the Occupational Safety and Health Act of 1970.

U.S. Department of Agriculture: requiring that we submit an annual report designating the number of animals by species which involve experimentation with no pain, pain with drugs, and pain — no drugs.

Food and Drug Administration: involving standards for investigational new drugs, good laboratory practices for nonclinical studies, radiation emission standards, regulations affecting clinical laboratories and institutional review boards for human subjects.

Drug Enforcement Administration: requirements for recording and security of drugs within the university.

DHEW: concerning compliance with Section 504 of the Rehabilitation Act of 1973.

DHEW: concerning conditions for qualifying for Medicare: infection control, standards of hospital radiology services, and general hospital safety.

DHEW: concerning the use of human subjects in research.

NIH: requiring adherence to guidelines involving research using recombinant DNA molecules and Care and Use of Laboratory Animals.

National Cancer Institute: regarding safety standards for research using oncogenic viruses and for research using chemical carcinogens.

Center for Disease Control: concerning regulation of human etiological agents.

EPA: concerning enforcement of the Safe Drinking Water Act and meeting criteria for identifying hazardous wastes.

Nuclear Regulatory Commission: concerning the use of radioactive materials under an NRC license.

The environmental impact of these requirements, and many more that required actions by other university offices, added significantly to our administrative financial burdens. Of course, we were not alone in our attempts to cope with this growing external force. *Change Magazine* (February 1978) estimated the cost to higher education institutions of federally mandated programs to be $2 billion annually. The *Chronicle of Higher Education* also did a series of articles about mandated programs of review and their costs.

Development

Thanks to Bill Farrell's efforts, we were pleased to get a major award from the Northwest Area Foundation in September 1978 to support the university's Legislative Environmental Advisory Group (LEAG). It drew its members from our Institute of Urban and Regional Research, faculty and administrators of our three state universities, members of both houses of the Iowa General Assembly, and various state agencies. LEAG's efforts paid off with an award of $52,000 from the Northwest Area Foundation, which was matched by an appropriation of $67,000 from the legislature. LEAG's efforts provided a model for the value of constructive dialogues between the units of the state for planning and actions in the state's interest.

Subsequently LEAG projects — conducted by faculty from geography, law, preventive medicine, and urban and regional planning — included "Iowa's Agriculture Land Use, Cropland Production Base, and Prime Agriculture Land"; "The Impact of Rural Non-Farm Residential Development on the Provisions of Local Public Services"; "Eliminating Legal Constraints to Solar Energy Development"; "An Examination of the Effectiveness of County Zoning to Preserve Prime Agricultural Land in Iowa"; "Urban Revitalization"; and "Evaluation of Alternative Definitions of Flood Plains." LEAG worked actively with the legislators on these projects and received many plaudits for the assistance that it was able to give them.

1979–1980: MORE COPING WITH SHIFTING SANDS

Graduate Issues

On September 18, 1979, my remarks at the first meeting of the Graduate Council touched on some agenda items that I predicted would surface throughout the year: efficient use of energy and environmental problems relating to energy consumption, issues surrounding our aging faculty and the need to create opportunities for new minds in the academy, ways to maintain high levels of scholarly activity in the face of declining graduate enrollments, and preparation of students working for advanced degrees for change — specialization versus generalization. I wondered about the significance of the flip of resident/nonresident ratios of our graduate students from 55:45 to 45:55, and solicited help from the council in interpreting the trends.

Combined Graduate Program

In 1976 NIH awarded funds to the university to support the UI Medical Scientist Training Program. It enabled students to work for the M.D. and

Ph.D. degrees simultaneously. Funds came from the private sector and from the Graduate College in addition to NIH. In 1980 fifteen students were enrolled in the program, combining course work in a selected basic science department with the M.D. curriculum. Admission qualifications were high and only a very few applicants were admitted each year. When the students graduated with the two degrees, they were highly sought after for research positions. We were proud to be able to work so easily with the departments in the College of Medicine to foster this prestigious program.

Status of Graduate Students

The April 17, 1980, *Daily Iowan* carried an editorial entitled "Student Labor Is Slave Labor." It cited advantages to unionization that it asserted had occurred at the University of Wisconsin-Madison, which did have a union. It called for uniform salaries based on the amount of work done, improved working conditions, and an admission by the university "that it is neither handing out welfare nor granting awards, but paying for labor." It's my recollection that the editorial wasn't taken very seriously because it was not seen as representing the views of the majority of graduate students, coupled with the memories of the faculty who had also worked for pittances as graduate students as a necessary part of the upbringing of budding new professors. Shades of things to come in 1996, when the majority of graduate students finally voted to unionize.

We were concerned about the status of the students from another angle. The performance of entering graduate students remained high. Scores on the GRE, for example, were running above the national trends. Our new criteria for allocating funds to support graduate students was sending a message to the faculty, since priority in the allocations was being given to those requests that demonstrated that research assistant assignments were being used to maximize educational benefits to the students as well as to enhance faculty productivity in research and creative scholarship. Systematic program reviews were also having a positive impact.

Research

At the first Research Council meeting of the year on September 21, 1979, I spoke of some of the disquieting items that were before us: Proposed legislation requiring federally financed researchers to state the practical application of their work before it could begin, and prior approval before publication of federally supported research; issues relating to the rights under the Freedom of Information Act to raw data in the hands of the grantees of federal funds; and required cost sharing. I reported on our just completed survey of research equipment needs in the biological sciences: cost $2.5 million; and the appointment of a task force to review the occupational health responsibilities of the university concerning biohazards, radioactive materials, animal care, and occupational health and safety. I noted that we were at the fourth-draft stage of a proposed policy on rights and responsibilities of individuals related to university-sponsored educational materials (persons employed expressly to develop materials that would prove to be salable). But despite the litany of sticky problems, I suggested that we should take heart in the steady growth in gifts, grants, and contracts, with annual increases of 17 percent in 1976–1977, 20 percent in 1977–1978, and 29 percent in 1978–1979. Our success ratios (funding versus applications) was 40 percent and greater, well above the national average.

The disposal of the eighty tons of radioactive waste produced annually in connection with treatments at the University Hospitals and in biological research was a problem that took on major proportions. For years we had been trucking the waste to licensed disposal dumps. The number of nationally certified dumps had decreased and hauling costs skyrocketed since the dump sites were typically far removed from Iowa. We sought ways to reduce disposal costs.

Most of the waste had relatively insignificant radioactivity. And, for most of it, the radioactivity deteriorated over several months, reducing it to inert material. After considering many options and consulting broadly inside and outside the university, we determined that the best solution was to build a storage facility where materials could be sorted and stored safely until the radioactive levels had dropped to zero, then incinerated. Short of discontinuing radioisotope use in health treatments and research, we could find no other acceptable alternative. We began to plan for that option, which would require major capital funds. We also began to plan an information program for members of the university and the surrounding community about the proposed solution to allay their concerns over incinerating "radioactive" materials. A number of meetings with the community were ultimately held and the majority of attendees found them adequately reassuring.

On February 1, 1980, I wrote a memo to departmental executive officers entitled "Central research support facilities." It was the outgrowth of increasing clamor from investigators for funds to support equipment and facilities that they had acquired, perhaps through external funding, but could no longer afford to maintain or replace. Some facilities were poorly utilized or not available to researchers other than the principal investigator. For example, at the time there were over twenty transmission electron microscopes on campus. It seemed obvious that we didn't need them all nor could we afford to maintain them at state-of-the-art levels, especially when that art was changing almost daily. The memo announced that our office would accept nominations for units to be designated as university facilities that would receive some central support.

The project went forward and the number of such units peaked at eleven. A university brochure describing all the services was distributed not only within the university but to potential outside users who could be accommodated on a time-available basis. The program became a model in the United States at a time when unnecessary duplication of equipment and facilities was being pinpointed concurrent with insistent demands for ever more sophisticated and expensive research equipment.

Development

On August 24, 1979, Margery Hoppin, director of our Division of Sponsored Programs, in writing a memo to me justifying the need for a research coordinator in that office, revealed the changes we were experiencing relating to external funding sources, particularly those of the federal government:

> Federal dollars alone have increased from $41.3 million in fiscal year 1975 to $59 million in 1979. The number of proposals to external agencies have increased from 911 to 1,342 in the same time period. . . . One half of the time of one of our professional staff has had to be diverted to dealing with DNA, biohazards, animal care and laboratory safety matters. New constraints on human subjects have made it necessary to divert another staff member half time to coordinate the human subjects review functions. . . . A number of important functions are not being offered . . . due to special restrictions from granting agencies, timing problems, change of investigators, lack of understanding of faculty and administrative staff about the spending rules and the increasing use of contracts. These require that this office negotiate these contracts and, along with the Business Office, review the clauses carefully before recommending that the business manager sign them.

The new position was created. In some ways the problem was one of our doing because we were devoting major amounts of our time to encouraging faculty in every way we could think of to increase their chances to obtain external funds in support of their scholarly activity.

"Effort" reporting was a continuing contentious issue among faculty and staff who had external funding. Federal regulations required that all applicants for federal research grants, when preparing the applications, estimate the amount of contributed time as well as time to be paid by the grant. Having received the award, they were required to track the actual amount of contributed time during the conduct of the research. The contributed amounts were then consolidated by the university for data required in negotiating our indirect cost rates. One consequence of the requirement, in addition to completion of yet more forms by the researchers, was that the reconciliation between what had appeared in the application to demonstrate high levels of interest and dedication through contributed time and what was actually contributed during the conduct of the research might not match closely. If so, justifications of the discrepancies were sometimes required. The requirement was more fuel for the fire about unnecessary paperwork.

In March 1980 Randy Bezanson, vice president for finance and university services, estimated that, excluding one-time start-up costs, the annual operating cost to his offices for these new reporting requirements would exceed $200,000, funds that would not be available to support the teaching and research functions of the university. But Randy and I knew that we were caught between a rock and a hard place. The funds from external sources had become too large and too well integrated into the life of the university to be dismissed easily. At the same time the university needed major additional funding for academic programs. Nevertheless, we felt that we had no options but to keep demonstrating why it was that we constantly insisted that our offices needed more funds with which to operate.

Despite our problems, technology inexorably marched on. The *Daily Iowan* on May 12, 1980, carried an article with the headline "UI Computer Appetite Increasing." Bobby Brown, the director of the Computer-Assisted Instruction Laboratory, noted that the College of Business Administration led all university units in the use of computer systems, followed by political science and the departments in the College of Engineering. At the time we had seventy terminals distributed throughout academic buildings and Burge Residence Hall. We considered the latter to be a real innovation since it allowed students to access the system at their convenience. Already students were complaining about the difficulty of getting on the systems, particularly because, as one student said, many who did get on "don't know what they're doing." The possibility of truly distributed computing systems and of individual units was only dimly anticipated by most users.

A jarring note on the scene was the continuing litigation involving my removal of Howard Dockery as director of the Weeg Computing Center (discussed in chapter 7). A second suit was brought against one of the center's staff, Philip Dyloff, and me (since, in the final analysis, I was responsible for all that happened at the center), accusing Dyloff of making accusations against Dockery that were "willfully, maliciously and knowingly made for the purpose of having [Dockery] removed as director [of the center] with full knowledge that such accusations would damage and defame the character and reputation of [Dockery] as well as any subsequent business opportunities he might have." Counsel on both sides began preparations for the trial to come.

I appointed James Johnson to be the acting director of the Weeg Computing Center; under his leadership, the staff quickly began to feel more secure after the recent turmoil related to the leadership change at the center. Jim produced a document which, in detail, set out the principles and objectives of the center, and identified the responsibilities of various subunits. He pressed for a balance between a structured and an informal organization with the capacity for change during times of a rapidly changing technology. I was impressed and pleased with the wholehearted way in which the bright and talented staff threw themselves into the challenges ahead. I felt at ease to turn to other university matters despite the pending Dockery litigation. I had a clear conscience, outstanding legal counsel, and faith in the legal system.

Remembering Carl Seashore

On April 18, 1980, I welcomed the Society of Experimental Psychologists to their annual meeting, held that year on our campus. In my remarks I noted that Carl Seashore had been a longtime member of the society and that he had had a profound effect on the Department of Philosophy and Psychology, as it was known when he came, and on the Graduate College, of which he was dean for some thirty years. I noted that "perhaps his greatest contribution was his insistence that, even in applied areas, the scientific laboratory approach to processes was fundamental. That approach is still seen in the curricula of this university concerned with the education of students in speech, music, audiology, speech pathology, the gifted, the mentally disabled — all areas in which Seashore became personally involved in the early years of their development." Seashore set the course for graduate education at the University of Iowa and established standards of performance for it in a host of other ways. In my opinion the impact of his tenure has been largely forgotten and too little appreciated.

1980–1981: MAJOR PASSAGES

Personnel Changes

In December 1980 May Brodbeck resigned as vice president for academic affairs and dean of faculties, effective June 30, 1981, to return to the faculty of the Department of Philosophy following a year as a fellow at the Center for Advanced Study of the Behavioral Sciences at Stanford. A distinguished scholar, May brought high standards of intellectual performance with her to Iowa. All her academic decisions were colored by those standards. In addition she increased the sensitivity of the academy to the status of women and sought in every possible way consistent with her academic standards to advance their participation in the life of the university. She and Boyd also established the Ida Beam Visiting Scholar program, which continues to bring prominent scholars to the campus for short periods for lecturing and scholarly exchanges. Tragically, May's untimely death in August 1983 deprived us of a superb faculty member. Her legacy of excellence, however, continues.

We had hardly gotten accustomed to May's departure when, on March 12, 1981, President Boyd announced his resignation. Effective August 31, he would accept the presidency of the Field Museum of Natural History in Chicago. He would be president emeritus of the university, retaining his tenure at the College of Law on indefinite leave. For most of us his announcement came as a big surprise. He had not talked about the possibility very far in advance even with those of us who worked with him daily. He explained to the press that he had been at the university for a total of twenty-seven years and that Iowa needed a new top executive. Despite that assertion I am not aware of any calls for a leadership change.

President Boyd clearly had been the right person for the times at Iowa. He had survived the "dirty word" episode (a public meeting in Shambaugh Auditorium, Main Library, in which he had quietly endured being taunted by a foul-mouthed student from the audience) and calls from legislators to clean out the troublemakers at the university. He had championed the rights of all, including women and minorities; he had been open to suggestions for change; he had shown flexibility in adjusting to new times and priorities; and, most of all, he had been a steadying influence during chaotic academic times. In my case, he tolerated my tirades while at the same time giving me full credit for those of my initiatives that were deserving. In retrospect I have come to realize that I could not have had a better boss.

The search for May Brodbeck's successor was suspended until Boyd's successor could be named. That was clearly appropriate since presidents must have close and compatible working relationships with the number two officer of the university. For the interim Kenneth Moll, who had been associate dean of faculties since 1976, was nominated by Boyd to become acting vice president and dean effective July 1, 1981.

In early May 1981 S. J. Brownlee was elected president of the Board of Regents, succeeding Mary Louise Peterson. "S. J.," as he was called, had received a B.A. in economics from Iowa and was a member of Phi Beta Kappa. Naturally, I took note of the change but little realized how important it would be to me in just a couple of months. Again, another stroke of luck for me!

Graduate Matters

In May 1981 President Boyd surprised me by announcing that the D. C. Spriestersbach Dissertation Prize, carrying a stipend of $2,500, had been established to be awarded annually for the best dissertation in one of four broad disciplinary areas: humanities and fine arts, physical sciences, biological science, and social sciences — with the competition in each area to occur once every four years to coincide with a similar program of the Council of Graduate Schools. Our selection would become the university's nominee for the national prize. The first award went to Mark Knuepfer, who had worked with Professor Michael Brody of pharmacology on the possible role that the brain might have on high blood pressure. To date we have had three national winners and three finalists in other years. (No other school has had three and only three schools have had two national winners: Yale, Michigan, and UC/Berkeley. Not bad company!) A copy of each winning dissertation is specially bound and placed in a prominent place in the Graduate College conference room to serve as tangible evidence — as "gold standards" — of the outstanding work of which graduate students are capable and to which all others should aspire.

The announcement came as a complete surprise to me. On reflection I couldn't imagine a more satisfying way to recognize my tenure as graduate dean and my dedication to quality in graduate education. The action was one more indication of President Boyd's sensitivity to such matters.

Professors and Economic Development

Although the amount of external funding that we competed successfully for grew, there was a consensus that those sources of funding would be capped sooner or later. The state till was running short. Private enterprises were making decisions based on quick turnarounds for their investments. Less and less of their capital was being invested in development, a circumstance that all agreed would result in the well of new ideas running dry sooner or later. Under these circumstances it was natural for universities and the private sector to explore possible common interests. But how to tap them without warping the researchers' judgments about the most productive scholarly work for each of them to pursue? Nevertheless, some of the great private universities —

Harvard, MIT, Stanford — were openly exploring possible areas of common interest with the private business sector.

In September 1980 we held a conference on campus with twelve executives of Iowa industries to establish channels of communication so that we could explore our common interests. At the conference Boyd identified the Office of the Vice President for Educational Development and Research as the "comprehensive contact point between Iowa commerce and the university." He noted that we were anxious to build an ongoing relationship with commerce. There were murmurs of concern by faculty who saw possible dangers in the loss of the university's mission to serve the interests of *all* of the state's citizens. However, we felt that we had no option but to formalize old hand-shake arrangements and establish new ones with our colleagues in the business sector.

As we proceeded we discovered that many informal arrangements had been made between individual faculty and staff members and the private sector that were not documented according to our consulting policy. Funds, usually modest in these informal arrangements, were provided by private sources to support a particular research effort. In the process no accommodation was made for the associated indirect costs — usually as the result of a lack of understanding of university policies and procedures. In effect, the university was subsidizing these costs to the benefit of the private sector. Gradually, we began to ferret out these instances and require that those involved follow university policies and procedures.

Outreach

In October 1980 we announced receipt of a Mellon Foundation grant to support faculty at the University of Iowa and the four-year independent colleges to conduct joint research, especially of a multidisciplinary nature, at University House (now the Obermann Center for Advanced Studies). We were pleased that the grant enabled us to relate in such a meaningful way to the faculties of the four-year colleges and to expand the programs of University House.

The last meeting of the Joint Committee on University Outreach was held on March 21, 1981. An important part of our outreach program was the slide show that Dean Charlie Mason put together, which he entitled "University of Iowa Update." A natural outgrowth of his annual visits to the four-year colleges of Iowa where he met with seniors planning to go on for advanced degrees, Charlie started making the presentations in 1976. It was a twenty-five-minute program that fit easily into the programs of Rotary, Kiwanis, Lions, Optimists, and Sertoma service clubs as well as high-school honors convocations and service club wives' banquets. (He made 534 presentations over seventeen years to approximately 26,000 Iowans.) The reception to his program was overwhelmingly positive, and its contribution to the good name of the university has not been adequately appreciated.

The work of the committee had been significant, in part because it raised our awareness of the need to explain ourselves more effectively to our several publics, and to identify the messages on which we should concentrate. We became more convinced than ever that we could not assume that those publics understood what we did and why our work was as important to their welfare as to ours.

Continuing Development of University Computer Services

The computer technology revolution occurred all around us. Gerry Weeg's legacy clearly had an enduring impact on my thinking. At the same time I had an uneasy feeling that I was alone in trying to think through how the technology would manifest itself at the university and how we should be preparing to integrate it into what we did. Computers would cost money that no one had and would complicate our already trying fiscal circumstances. The lethargy that I perceived should not have surprised me since the deans had their hands full coping with traditional needs without seeking new complexities. Our administrative units provided dedicated services with what they had to work with and shuddered at the prospect of extending themselves further.

But I knew that the ostrich strategy would not do. Our office organized a "Word Processing Seminar" on March 20, 1981. We invited two leading students of the technology to conduct a day-long conference. Both had national reputations as leaders in this new development. Twenty-two of our administrators and staff attended the seminar. At the end of the day our visitors shared with us some of their predictions about the future of information systems: Word-processing machines with optical scanners will eliminate the need for keying into the machines manually; equipment will have a voice component; there will be a personal computer for each desk in offices; the cost of computer equipment will decline at the rate of 25 percent annually; libraries will be viewed as storage/retrieval systems with all information stored on video disks.

They closed with these final words of advice: "No solution will work forever. Be open and willing to revise on a continuing basis. Coordination, guidance, and counseling through experts is the key to the effective functioning of an information management system." Their predictions in retrospect were squarely on the mark. Looking back now they seem trite; then they were revolutionary — so all-encompassing that most of the audience, while not scoffing, went back to their desks and proceeded to do what they had been doing.

Nevertheless, I was heartened to have the visitors confirm my dimly perceived vision of the future and determined to continue to carry the torch for immersing the technology in our academic life.

Research

In a variety of ways, our office sought out faculty with ideas for research and creative work whose dreams required resources. We invited new faculty to our conference room for box lunches during which they described their research plans and the resources they would require. We maintained an open-door policy for all faculty who wanted to talk about their research goals and needs and were determined to help them find sources of support either within or outside of the university. Marge Hoppin entered into these exercises willingly but never let me forget that such a function was most unusual for the staff of sponsored programs of other universities and that her staff performed these evangelical functions in addition to the myriad of other administrative functions involved in processing applications for external funding and tracking the awards that were received. The absence of funds to support worthy scholarly efforts could be demoralizing; we felt that we were constantly in danger of losing opportunities for advancing the quality of our research. Nevertheless, we believed that, one way or another, sooner or later, the necessary resources would be found.

The 1980–1981 year provides a good slice of institutional life that belies the view of the academy as a stodgy, self-protective enclave that flaunts the needs and concerns of those who support it.

1981–1982: SWITCHING HORSES, NOT ONE BUT TWO!

Research

Questions continued to arise, typically from relatively few students and an occasional faculty member, about the propriety of the university's acceptance of funds for research from the Department of Defense. These questions usually came about when we released the summaries of the funds that had been received according to source. In fiscal 1981 we received $1.3 million in research and fellowship funds from federal defense agencies (out of $67 million from all sources), placing us near the bottom of the Big Ten in the amount of defense funds received. The funds supported basic research in chemistry, physics, engineering, and pharmacy. Our position remained the same: basic knowledge in any field and supported by any source can be applied for unpredictable purposes. Since no one can predict such outcomes, we left the propriety question to be answered at the departmental level, making the fact that funds were applied for and received a matter of public record.

A troubling development during the year was an attempt by the Commerce Department of the Reagan administration to restrict the free exchange of scholars, students, and research findings between this country and certain foreign governments, particularly China. It was done through revisions in the Export Administration Regulations. The definition of "export" included one of our scholars' talking to a foreign colleague. Faculty were called upon to report on the activities of visiting scholars, including their attendance at various open national meetings; foreign graduate students were expected to be restricted from access to specific areas of technological development; and international collaboration between our scholars and those of certain countries was to be restricted. Not surprisingly, the academic community responded with vigorous dissent, refusing to file required reports and report on foreign colleagues. In the end the academic community's resistance caused the federal government to ease off and finally to end its efforts.

Personnel Changes

President Boyd's resignation, effective August 31, had kept a search committee busy for several months screening candidates for his replacement. In the end it recommended seven candidates to the Board of Regents for consideration and interviews. At its July 31 meeting the board chose James O. Freedman to be our next president and awarded him an appointment as Professor of Law and University of Iowa Foundation Distinguished Professor. Jim had an undergraduate degree from Harvard and a law degree from Yale. After serving for a year as a law clerk for Thurgood Marshall, then a federal judge in the U.S. 2d District Court of Appeals, he joined the faculty of the University of Pennsylvania Law School in 1964, becoming its dean in 1977. He had an established reputation as teacher, scholar, and administrator. He was well known to many of the members of our law faculty, having spent the summer of 1970 at Iowa as a visiting professor. His appointment was effective April 1, 1982, allowing him time to make an orderly departure from Penn.

Immediately following the board's action on Boyd's replacement, it needed to deal with the appointment of an acting president during the seven-month interim between Boyd's leaving and Freedman's arrival. A phone call from President Brownlee came to me immediately following the board's selection of Jim, asking me if I would be that person. Of course, we all knew that there would have to be such a person, but I don't recall any corridor chatter about whom that person might be. I suppose we assumed that it would be one of the lieutenants in the current administration of which I obviously was a part. But my speculation stopped there and I went about the business of the day. Consequently, the unexpected call came as I sat at my desk in my office in Gilmore Hall. It was short and to the point. S. J. made the offer, named a salary figure, and I accepted. But there was no celebration, since none was called for. The responsibilities that I had just accepted were reason enough to be sober. I immediately told the staff that was around, accepted their congratulations, and sat down with them to begin planning how we would manage for the interim. The ensuing months were made easier by S. J., with whom I had many conversations, always businesslike but friendly and constructive. Again, I couldn't have had a better boss.

President-elect Freedman came to campus several times before his official arrival. I took him to a basketball game and tried to introduce him to the campus and its people in every way that his time would allow. In addition, I sent him loads of material announcing new programs and activities. I suspect I overburdened the mails, but I didn't want to pass up any opportunity to help him hit the ground running on April 1.

Personnel Changes

News release from the Office of Public Information, August 1, 1981: "The name is pronounced SPREE-sters-bock." I had long since gotten used to responding to mangled pronunciations of the name. At one point years ago I had even proposed, in front of my paternal grandmother, to change my name to "Bach." Her vehement reaction put that notion to rest! In any event I was grateful that, at long last, folks would know how to pronounce my name, already a tangible benefit from being named the acting president.

I chose not to name a person to act as vice president and dean during the relatively short interim. I retained the titles and continued to discharge most of my regular duties in addition to those of the presidency. My colleagues agreed, so far as I know without grumbling, to join me in running a little faster to get the wash out. I also chose not to move into the president's office in Jessup Hall. Instead, I continued to do my work from my regular office, installing a direct phone line to the president's office so that longtime presidential secretary and good friend, Mary Parden, could direct calls to me as if I were in the office next to hers. I continued with the Monday morning meetings of the docket group, but in the Danner Conference Room in Gilmore Hall instead of in the president's conference room in Jessup Hall. While these arrangements were convenient for me, by using my regular office and conference room I was reminding myself and others that I was subbing until the next president of the university was in place.

Understandably, the news media were curious about me as a university leader and more particularly about my intentions for the seven months that I would be in charge. The thrust of my responses was that I would try to carry the university forward as I found it, maintaining the momentum that we had under Sandy Boyd's leadership. I also wanted to do what I could to prepare the university for the changes that would inevitably and properly come with the advent of the new administration. At every opportunity I preached that change should be viewed positively, as a source of revitalization for new challenges that would certainly present themselves.

At the request of the Faculty Senate I continued the practice of giving the annual fall presidential address to the faculty; it took place on September 3, 1981. In the talk I announced that my goal for the seven months was to keep the university "humming and moving forward" so that it "doesn't miss a beat." I noted that, while there would be a change of leadership style when Mr. Freedman took over, "the verities from which the university derives its purpose and its strength will continue to be valid. Nevertheless, perhaps no organization, agency, or institution in our society can less endure inaction, deferred decision-making, delay, or tentative commitment to function than a university."

During the fall address I announced an appointment. I named Jim Johnson as a special presidential assistant to evaluate "the many complex and vexing questions" relating to computerized information systems. I felt that this was a matter that could not wait in the light of the phenomenal growth in the use of computers across the country, and that it had to be taken into account in any ongoing planning that we were doing. At long last I was in a position to place the matter at the forefront of university planning. Subsequently, the Board of Regents approved Jim's appointment as director of the Office of Information Technology, effective July 1, 1982. It was a prophetic move that would ultimately lead to the establishment of the central position of associate vice president for research and director of information technology services to orchestrate what has become a ubiquitous and necessary core to our teaching, research, and administrative functions.

Interim President

One of the important roles that I saw for myself during the seven months was to provide a contact point for President-elect Freedman while he was still at the University of Pennsylvania. I didn't burden him with the day-to-day decisions and paperwork. When the Rose Bowl became a part of our schedule, we saw to it that he and his family were invited to attend and to appear wherever it seemed appropriate. In early March 1982 Jim made one of his several get-acquainted visits to the campus (although, as I have noted, he had spent time at the university previously as a visiting professor in the College of Law). I was able to take him to his first Big Ten basketball game — the last such game to be held in the Field House. In the fall he would have the pleasure of leading the opening ceremony of the Carver-Hawkeye Sports Arena. I enjoyed being the point of contact for him during the seven months. From my point of view the transition went very smoothly; I felt no tensions at all as we shifted from one "real" president to the next.

While I did not seek decision-making opportunities during my interim presidency, I did make decisions, some of them controversial, when I felt that they could not be deferred. One had to do with the use of the ROTC color guard at football games.

Starting many years ago, that honor had gone to students enrolled in ROTC. Tradition called for the guard to be armed with rifles. In 1973, during the era of student unrest, President Boyd had suspended the practice of the color presentation as one means of reducing possible disruptions by students who were upset by U.S. involvement in the Vietnam War. When representations were made to me by the ROTC units wanting to reinstate the practice in the fall of 1981, I agreed. I felt that the time was ripe for restoring the tradition, much to the consternation of some of my advisors, who felt that there might be loud protests. The Board in Control of Athletics concurred with my decision. We made one concession: the guard was to be "armed" with sabers. I got a number of phone calls and notes when the change was made, all complimentary. While there were several *Daily Iowan* editorials condemning the change, there were no organized disruptions. Most students didn't seem to care one way or the other.

The *Daily Iowan* caught up with me to do a story about my feelings after I had been on the job for a month as the acting president. Here are some of my fairly candid comments as published in the October 5 issue:

> Sweet-sour. . . . I have agreed to be acting president in addition to my other duties so it's been a very busy month. . . . No insurmountable problems although I run out of hours of the day and energy. . . . The support and understanding have been very heart warming. . . . I've learned some details that it wasn't necessary for me to know before so I've been learning during this period. . . . I will be relieved when President Freedman comes in April not because I'm having a bad time and not because I'm doing a bad job but presidents of universities have very major responsibilities to do all sorts of things. They have to give their lives on a 24-hour basis. Long ago when I flirted with the possibility of being a university president and had the opportunity to be considered for such a position, I chose to remove myself from that arena. . . . I chose not to live in that kind of a fishbowl. I like to have personal choices and I think university presidents have very few.

Bette, my wife, and I chose not to live in the president's home on Church Street during the seven months. As did the Boyds, we preferred our own home. We did, of course, do the necessary entertaining there — student and faculty groups, committees, visiting notables, and supporters.

We did host one major family party on Church Street, though. Most of my family live in Minnesota, where I grew up and went to college (then Winona State Teachers College). I came to Iowa as a graduate student at the time that the Golden Gophers were one of the leading football teams in the country and was torn by school loyalties until the Gophers played football that fall of 1939 in Iowa City and Iowa's Iron Men beat them. I switched loyalties that day. On October 24, 1981, we played Minnesota in Iowa City. We invited the immediate family and the aunts, uncles, and first cousins to see the game from the press box. Essentially, all of them, some fifty, accepted the invitation! Some, including my parents, stayed in the president's home, some at our house, and a few with friends. The family felt that we had outdone ourselves by "allowing" Minnesota to beat Iowa that day! All in all it proved to be a memorable weekend for everyone.

Coping with Changing Realities

Governor Ray's Conference on Iowa Economic Opportunities took place on November 9–11, 1981. It focused on energy, natural resources, capital formation, transportation, and education. Bill Farrell was chair of the planning for the conference. His role was an outgrowth of his leadership in organizing and encouraging the work of LEAG.

President Reagan had called for a 12 percent reduction in the budgets of domestic programs, even in the face of high levels of inflation. Major slashes were proposed in student assistance programs, along with proposed caps on the recovery of indirect costs. NIH proposed to reduce the number of investigator-initiated awards from 5,000 to 4,100. Priorities were being established by the chairs of key congressional committees rather than as the result of open congressional hearings and debates. In the end support for research held its own, but student assistance programs had to absorb troubling reductions.

The Rose Bowl 1982

While our lobbying for federal funds was sometimes unsuccessful, we were doing better on the football field. In fact, we were the Big Ten representative to the Rose Bowl game in Pasadena in 1982, ending the season tied with Ohio State for first place in the Big Ten. Two of our wins that season stand out in my memory: those with Nebraska and Michigan. Iowa hosted Nebraska that year. A gentle query came down from Governor Ray's office about the possibility of hosting the Nebraska governor's party at 102 Church Street for brunch before the game. We were pleased to oblige. The Nebraska group came late with considerable loud bravado and backslapping. "May the best team win! Ha! Ha!" The party also sat in the press box with us during the game, continuing, early on at least, to exude the same hail fellow spirit. That changed as the game progressed. We won! We were a bit smug, feeling that poetic justice reigned after all.

We played Michigan at Ann Arbor, our sixth game in an eleven-game season. It was a crucial game for each team. We won nine to seven. It was my custom when we did not attend out-of-town games, which we rarely did, to send — win or lose — a telegram to the team. Mary Parden, longtime assistant to presidents, had a talent for composing short, witty telegrams. We sent the usual wire after the Michigan game, and even though I was attending an AAU meeting of presidents in Austin, Texas, at the time, Mary connected me with Hayden Fry to deliver another word of congratulations, since the outcome determined which team would go to the Rose Bowl.

It was a special honor for me to be president of the university during that Rose Bowl year. I got many congratulatory messages on behalf of the team and the university. One that I particularly treasure came from Governor Ray:

> With all the excitement and jubilation over the Hawkeyes finally making it back to the Rose Bowl, I just wanted you to know that it is a good feeling to be governor at this time, and I hope it is a good feeling for you to be acting president of this great university. It is never easy to be filling in such an important position as president of a major university, waiting for someone else to come to take the reins, but you have done such a good job and I am grateful for it. I wanted to let you know that and to congratulate you for having a winning football team while you are president of this university.

It isn't only the football team that is busy during a Rose Bowl appearance. Their accompanying presidents are busy too, as I soon found out. It was Iowa's first appearance since 1959, and the first in the last fourteen years when a university other than Ohio State or Michigan had represented the Big Ten. Well-established obligations included a mix of activities sponsored by the Pasadena Tournament of Roses Committee, with its own traditional protocol for this event, and by the Big Ten. Short speeches from the presidents of the universities represented were expected. I had a program of activities from early morning to late at night — the Los Angeles Breakfast Club breakfast, the Kiwanis Rose Bowl Kickoff Luncheon attended by some 3,000 people, the Big Ten Club Dinner for Champions in 1981, featuring Bob Hope among others, the Tournament of Roses Committee reception followed by a black tie dinner, the All Iowa Bash, the Rose Bowl Parade, and the game. Sandwiched in was the trip to Disneyland for Iowa Day.

The grand marshal of the parade that year was Jimmy Stewart. He, his wife, Gloria, President William Gerberding and his wife, Ruth, of the University of Washington, and Bette and I stood at the head of a reception line that seemed to go on for hours before the Tournament of Roses banquet. Tired hands and feet provided a level of camaraderie that we carried over to the dinner table, where we were seated with the chairman of the Tournament of Roses and his wife. The Stewarts were charming, humble people. Accomplished actor and speaker, Jimmy still needed to review his notes, as did I, before we gave our short remarks after the dinner.

We estimated that we had 30,000 Iowa fans assembled in Los Angeles/ Pasadena for the event. We knew that, to a degree, we would be responsible for them if they got into difficulties. We did our usual planning. Billy Barnes, then dean of the College of Business Administration, was our special representative with the law enforcement agencies in the area. He went out in advance to make contacts and establish lines of communication. We arranged an Iowa headquarters at the Century Plaza Hotel with duty officers around the clock from the official party to deal with any and all inquiries, emergency or otherwise.

Adding to the complexities of the logistics was a late-in-the-day decision by President Reagan to stay at the same hotel at the same time. That meant that he occupied the presidential suite, which was on the same floor as the suite reserved for the university president. All persons not associated with the Reagan group who wanted admission to the floor had to have security clearance and had to get off the elevator one floor below to be checked before walking up the stairs to the floor where we were staying. The consequence was that the only persons who got up to our suite were Presidents Bowen, Boyd, and Freedman and their wives. We couldn't have close friends drop by for a late night, shoes-off chat before going to bed.

One of the positives that came from having President Reagan in the hotel was that his office also had a headquarters located just across the hall from ours. One slow evening, early in President Reagan's stay, Charlie Mason, the duty officer for the night, wandered across the hall to visit with the president's duty officer, a lady. Charlie soon determined that she could arrange a short meeting with President Reagan. After much scurrying through the night, we assembled Governor Ray, Mr. Freedman, and myself and went up to the Reagan suite for a photograph of us all giving an Iowa sweater to the president. Later, each of us received in the mail an autographed picture of the event.

January 1 was rainy and cold. We had to be ready at 4:30 A.M. to get in place to review the parade. While the people riding on the floats provided human interest, the skimpy costumes worn by some caused us to shiver even more, even though we were bundled up and encased in rain gear. It was the start of what turned out to be a gloomy day for Iowa. We lost the game twenty-eight to zero! Aside from that, the event went off without any major problems. The next day, we returned to Iowa City to find our cars encrusted with several inches of ice — a crushing reality after several days in never-never land!

Presidential Duties

Despite my extended account of the activities surrounding the football season — which fortuitously turned out to be quite special — my days were fully occupied with academic duties and concerns. The winter commencement, held on December 19 in Hancher Auditorium on a stage richly adorned with poinsettias, saluted 1,200 graduates. As dean, I had participated in all the graduation ceremonies during my tenure. This was the one and only time I was in a new role, giving the traditional charge to the graduates and conferring the degrees. While all the commencements have been moving occasions for me, this one took on a special significance. I led the academic procession, I "charged" the graduates, and, for the moment, I was the symbolic leader of a great institution.

On January 26, 1982, I gave the traditional presidential address to the Joint Service Clubs of Iowa City luncheon. I entitled it "W(h)ither Higher Education?" I was doing my bit to send a message of distress on behalf of the higher education enterprise. Here are some excerpts:

> Higher education has, over the years, accumulated an impressive cluster of purposes: scholarship; personal development; the preservation and advancement of knowledge and culture; the preparation of leaders, of skilled and professional personnel, and of informed participants in a democracy; the economic advancement of self and nation; and finally, extended service to society. In discharging these responsibilities, the university is today the major institution in our society concerned with nurturing, questioning, and advancing our way of life.
>
> But higher education can contribute to the public good only if it receives public financial support. Today, the strength of that support is unclear. The budget ax has fallen, and higher education — not improperly — has taken its share of the blows. In the process, however, its continuing vitality is being placed at risk. Thus one of our current priority issues re-

lates to our willingness to risk the future of our educational programs for what appears to be some current savings.

Whither higher education? It is one of America's greatest resources. It educates our citizens, enriches our communities, conducts a major segment of our research, and contributes to the nation's well being in countless other ways. Fulfillment of its mission is indispensable to America's continued vitality and justifies a major capital investment. I hope that you will agree with me that we cannot afford to let higher education — including the University of Iowa — wither.

During my seven months as president of the university, I couldn't have remained silent if I had wanted to. Academic, legislative, service, and support groups of every hue were meeting and asking for statements from the academic leadership of the state. Frequently, I was a spokesperson:

Governor's Conference, "Building Blocks to Progress" (11/81): "It is high time that those of us in leadership positions take the necessary steps to devise effective ways in which to bring our awesome intellectual resources to bear on a new future, rather than attempting to be comforting to those who continue to believe that the present nightmare will soon be over, allowing us all to 'go home again.'"

Alumni Association Board (11/81): "We must . . . maintain and increase the high regard and support received by the university . . . from our many constituencies."

Parents Association (11/81): "If investment in higher education is not continued, . . . education is in danger of 'eating the seed corn.'"

College of Business Administration Convocation (12/81): "If we remain passive, uncommitted, and uneducated, we will lose the opportunity to create our future. Instead, we will . . . *inherit* it."

Joint Service Clubs of Iowa City (1/82): "W(h)ither Higher Education?" "There are no panaceas, and only through compromise, consideration of the common good, and sacrifice will we create our list of what must be accomplished and when."

18th Annual Iowa Congressional Luncheon (3/82): "Many of the 'savings' in education, research and health passed this year or proposed for next year are not really savings at all. They are simply shifts in costs from the federal to the state and local levels. . . . I hope we can reverse this trend in cost-shifting."

Fyi interview (3/82): "The major challenge of the University of Iowa for the 80s is to remain a high quality university. To do so will not only require money but guts."

Daily Iowan interview (4/82): "We got the wash out! . . . The university has advanced with confidence, with enthusiasm and hope."

Passing the Torch

On President Freedman's first day in his Jessup Hall office, we had a little ceremony during which I turned over the proverbial key to the university. Again, I left Jessup Hall that day with mixed feelings. On the one hand, I was happy that my special responsibilities were over; on the other, I was sorry that this time had ended. In retrospect, I had the opportunity to serve the university in a unique role for a short, action-packed time. I hope that the actions that I took during those days continue to serve it well.

Carl E. Seashore, dean of the Graduate College, 1908–1936 and 1942–1946. The architect of graduate education at Iowa. Courtesy of the University of Iowa Archives.

Virgil M. Hancher, president of the University of Iowa, 1940–1964. Courtesy of the University of Iowa Photographic Service.

Howard R. Bowen, president of the University of Iowa, 1964–1969, and its visionary planner. Courtesy of the University of Iowa Photographic Service.

Willard L. Boyd, president of the University of Iowa, 1969–1981, and "Sandy" to all. Courtesy of the University of Iowa Photographic Service.

D. C. Spriestersbach, acting president of the University of Iowa, September 1981–
April 1982; vice president for educational development and dean of the Graduate College,
1965–1989. Courtesy of the University of Iowa Archives.

James O. Freedman, president of the University of Iowa, 1982–1987. Courtesy of the University of Iowa Photographic Service.

Richard D. Remington, acting president of the University of Iowa, July 1987–
August 1988, and vice president for academic affairs, 1982–1988. He was Freedman's first
major appointment. Courtesy of the University of Iowa Photographic Service.

Hunter R. Rawlings III, president of the University of Iowa, 1988–1995.
Courtesy of the University of Iowa Photographic Service.

Gilmore Hall. Original location of the College of Law, now home to educational development and research and the Graduate College, viewed from what was then North Capitol Street. Courtesy of the University of Iowa Photographic Service.

*Old Capitol. The capitol of
the state of Iowa from 1846 to
1857 and home of the president,
vice president for academic
affairs, and vice president for
educational development and
dean of the Graduate College
until 1974. Courtesy of the
University of Iowa Photographic
Service.*

*Governor Robert Ray (center) opens the doors to the
newly restored Old Capitol on July 3, 1976, for Mary
Louise Petersen, president of the Board of Regents,
and University of Iowa president Willard Boyd, who
holds the original skeleton key used to unlock the
doors. Courtesy of the* Cedar Rapids Gazette, *photo
by Tom Merryman, July 4, 1976.*

Gerard P. Weeg, director of the university computer center from 1964 to 1974 and architect for computing on the campus. Courtesy of the University of Iowa Archives.

John P. Dolch, director of the computer center during its beginning days of vacuum tube technology. Courtesy of the University of Iowa Archives.

Security forces prepared to maintain law and order during student protests. Courtesy of the Iowa City Press-Citizen *collection at the State Historical Society of Iowa, Iowa City.*

Students blocking the intersection of Clinton Street and Iowa Avenue. Courtesy of the Iowa City Press-Citizen *collection at the State Historical Society of Iowa, Iowa City.*

Originally designed to be the Laser Center, now the Iowa Advanced Technologies Laboratories. Courtesy of the University of Iowa Photographic Service.

U.S. President Ronald Reagan, Acting President Spriestersbach, President-designate Freedman, and Governor Ray during a presentation in the presidential suite at the Century Plaza Hotel in Los Angeles before the 1982 Rose Bowl game between the University of Iowa and the University of Washington. Courtesy of the University of Iowa Photographic Service.

Presidents Bowen, Freedman, Spriestersbach, and Boyd before the 1982 Rose Bowl game in Pasadena, California. Courtesy of the University of Iowa Photographic Service.

Expressing admiration

S.J. Brownlee (left), President of the State Board of Regents, presents D.C. Spriestersbach with a package containing a bound resolution from the Board. The resolution reads: "Be it resolved that the Board of Regents of the State of Iowa expresses its great admiration and appreciation to Duane C. Spriestersbach for his dedicated leadership in advancing the University through his service as President of The University of Iowa during the interim period September 1, 1981-April 1, 1982."

S. J. Brownlee, president of the State Board of Regents, presenting D. C. Spriestersbach a resolution of thanks for his leadership as acting president, 1982. Courtesy of Tom Jorgensen, University Relations Publications, University of Iowa.

President Freedman with Vice President Spriestersbach, July 15, 1986, cutting the cake to celebrate reaching one billion dollars in cumulative external funds awarded to the faculty and staff of the University of Iowa since 1962. Courtesy of Tom Jorgensen, University Relations Publications, University of Iowa.

4. THE FREEDMAN YEARS
1982–1987

1982–1983: ANOTHER BEGINNING

James O. Freedman was inaugurated as the sixteenth president of the University of Iowa on October 25, 1982. He gave a stirring address entitled "A Covenant with Quality." He touched on several themes in his address: education for citizenship, liberal education, interdisciplinary education, and international education, concluding his address:

> In the beginning and in the end, university education is an experiment. Our nation and our state have staked much on the success of that experiment. Whether that experiment succeeds in the future, as it has in the past, will depend, finally, upon our commitment to reaffirming a covenant with quality. Justice Oliver Wendell Holmes, Jr., once wrote, "I have always thought that not place nor power nor popularity makes the success that one desires, but the trembling hope that one has come near to an ideal." I embark upon my tenure as president of the University of Iowa with the trembling hope that in the years ahead this university will come near to the ideal of reaffirming a covenant with quality so that it may achieve excellence in everything that it undertakes.

Those remarks established the stamp that would characterize Freedman's decisions. I found the blueprint to be an appealing charter — all the more so because its contents were totally consistent with the person that I had come to know in the six months that he had been on the job. First, he was a dedicated scholar; he read widely, thought deeply, and enjoyed learning about others' ideas. He was a gentleman in every sense of the word, affable but somewhat shy. He could hold his own, but he did not seek out jawboning circumstances. In my case he gave me my head and supported my initiatives. I found him a joy to work for and with.

President Freedman had been in office only a week when he asked me to organize a seminar on institutional planning. This first meeting dealt with enrollment projections; it was an activity that would continue on a fairly regular basis to introduce the new president to issues and to teaching and research programs.

Graduate Matters

Every five to ten years in recent times, individual scholars and national educational organizations attempt to assess the quality of graduate programs in U.S. universities. It is a nearly impossible task since the parameters of "quality" are open to debate. Certainly, there is no unanimity among observers as to what they should be. Nevertheless, institutions and their programs acquire reputations, good, bad, or average. Those reputations tend to become the coin of the realm and influence decisions made by professors considering positions and students considering graduate work. In 1978 the Conference Board of Associated Research Councils began to do another of the series of evaluations. I was a member of the panel that directed the study. In early 1983 the conference board published "An Assessment of Research Doctorate Programs in the United States." Twenty-eight graduate programs at Iowa were rated; overall, we tended to fall in the middle of the eleven CIC institutions. A few of our programs, notably in the biological sciences, were given high marks. The subsequent commentary tended to depend on the place of one's program among the pack. The effort was worthwhile, in my opinion, because it caused faculty members to reevaluate their own programs in the light of the criteria that had been addressed.

The Graduate College issued a long-range planning report covering the period from 1982 to 1987. It was a somber document because the times were somber. The national climate was characterized by an economic recession. High interest rates coupled with a decline in productivity and double-digit inflation had thwarted attempts to chart a course of economic recovery. We proposed to support strong programs and discontinue others, at the same time supporting the establishment of new programs that were designed to meet new needs (primarily through interfaces with existing programs), and continue to maintain and strengthen the scholarly work of the faculty. A rather prosaic set of objectives, to be sure, but ones that we tried, rather successfully in my opinion, to put into operation as we made resource allocations day to day.

Research

The teaching/research symbiosis is a continuing topic for review among college and universities faculties. On May 12, 1983, the *Daily Iowan* carried an article entitled "Faculty Research Vital to Growth," quoting several deans. We all spoke about the necessary relationship between research and intellectual growth for effective teaching. The relationship is not well understood by our critics, who frequently assume that a teacher masters a package of knowledge and then teaches it with impunity for the rest of his or her teaching career. Even a cursory glance at the pace of change and technological advancement these days makes clear that intellectual growth is imperative for survival of our citizenry.

Limiting Research Purposes

Déjà vu! In the spring of 1983 the radical student organization, the New Wave, challenged the university's acceptance of funds from the Department of Defense to support research "related to the development of weapons systems." The group secured two thousand signatures of students on a petition to that effect. After extended debate, the Student Senate failed to support the petition by a vote of fourteen to eleven. The group then organized a rally on the Pentacrest, attended by 150 persons, that included a "die in." The majority of the student body clearly ignored the effort.

But the issue remained the same. The university prohibits the conduct of secret research. That being said, the decision to do research on selected topics continued to be left to the individual investigator, who functions within the context of his or her peers. The students who would listen had no answer to my question: "Who should be the deciding authority?" I knew of no benign university figure who could or would accept the role of predicting in advance the social value of proposed faculty research. We made no changes in university policies as a result of the petition and demonstration. Abstracts of all supported research were available for public review, and although there was an established process for challenge, no challenges were ever filed.

Classified Research

The issue of should we — or did we — do classified research at the University of Iowa also surfaces through many of the years of this history. Classified research was prohibited when I came into central administration, and I supported the prohibition with deep convictions. Over the years I restated the policy many times and supported fine-tuning its statement to remove any possible ambiguities.

The *Manual of Rules and Regulations* of the Graduate College did not deal specifically with the classification issue as applied to student work until 1955, when the following appears: "If classified research projects result in a regular thesis which is subject to examination in the regular way and cleared for publication, the State University of Iowa has no objection to such research." This statement continued until the major revision in 1966, when it was dropped.

The present *Rules and Regulations* specify that two copies of the dissertation must be deposited in the Graduate College and that dissertations will be microfilmed and "made available on a permanent basis." This policy, by implication, is consistent with the prohibition of classified research at Iowa.

There are cogent philosophical reasons for the prohibition in academic institutions. Julia Mears, who served from 1981 to 1992 in the position of assistant to the president on legal matters, put it very well in a 1995 interview:

> Secret research is antithetical to the purpose of the university, which is to spread knowledge. That principle . . . is emblematic of the way that public institutions need to think. We were being exhorted by well-meaning people to refuse to do military research because military research was wrong. On the other hand we were being exhorted to do military research by people who believed military research was right because defense of the country was honorable. Rather than decide on that basis, whether military research was right or wrong, the university came up with a way of thinking about the problem that was derived from the university's own purposes. . . . A university is for the creation and dissemination of knowledge. Therefore, to the extent that military research is secret, it can't be done. Not because it's military, but because it's secret. . . . What universities needed to do, or what any public institution needed to do, was find a way to think about the question that derived from the universities' reasons for being, as opposed to the personal opinions of the people in charge, no matter whether you agree with them or not.

Frequently, there is a kind of knee-jerk conclusion that only the military establishment would want to support classified research. Not so. Pharmaceutical companies, for example, find it advantageous to provide contract funds to university researchers to study the effects of drugs on diseases and behavior. Yet they live in a very competitive world and need every time advantage that they can get. It's not surprising, then, that they frequently seek to require prepublication review of completed research that they have supported or to place publication restrictions on the findings from the supported work. The staff in the Division of Sponsored Programs was constantly on the alert to prevent the inclusion of such requirements in contracts. In a few instances that meant that the proposal to fund the research was withdrawn.

There is, of course, another type of restriction that any researcher may place on her or his work during the time that it is being done: Withholding hypotheses, experimental designs, and results until the researcher is ready to go public, because premature release can lead to erroneous conclusions and actions, and because others can preempt the topic and experimental design before the researcher is ready for peer scrutiny. However, researchers are not compromised by disclosing the fields and purposes of the inquiry, and external funding sources, if any. Furthermore, if any students are doing collaborative work with the researcher as part of a thesis or dissertation requirement, it must be fully reported and made available in the university library. There are, or course, no publication requirements on the part of faculty researchers, although that is rarely an issue since peer review and approval of one's work is part of the system for peer recognition and academic advancement.

More Partnering

President Freedman led the small Iowa contingent to Washington on March 3, 1983, for the annual congressional luncheon. In his prepared remarks, after warning that there was a finite limit to the amount of financial obligations that could be shifted from the federal government to the academic community, he spoke about the same concern:

> Perhaps the most worrisome issue on the federal scene . . . is one that has nothing to do with funding. I am speaking of the constraints on communication that the federal government is imposing through International Traffic in Arms Regulations and the Export Administration Regulations. As presently implemented, these rules have the ominous capacity to classify unclassified research after the fact.
>
> Embargoes on communication have no place in American universities. Secrecy imposed on research, scientific interchange, and teacher-student dialogue will save us little abroad and cost us much at home. Openness is an essential quality of the academy, and it must be preserved.

It was the theme of educational leaders everywhere. Federal attempts to impose restrictions quietly disappeared.

Development

At the beginning of the 1982–1983 fiscal year Vice President Bezanson and I gave Jim Johnson, our new director of the Office of Information Technology, a joint statement of his new responsibilities. It was a major step in bringing the interrelated information systems of the university under one roof. From today's perspective that may seem to be a trivial accomplishment. However, in those days the need for such coordination was not fully appreciated by administrators up and down the line. We were well past the central black boxes for computational research and administration. Terminals for office use had sprung up; the library was looking into ways to manage its information resources; academic records were available at administrators' desks; and more.

It had been a long march to this stage, but we felt confident that we now knew what its general direction should be.

On April 1, 1983, the Office of Information Technology announced a program whereby faculty and staff, in addition to the students who already had the privilege, could also purchase computers and associated peripherals at the Weeg Computing Center for personal use at significant discounts. Johnson said in making that announcement that "most faculty and staff do professional work at home. We are interested in assisting them in the acquisition of reliable equipment which is compatible with the university system. We believe it will mean an increase in productivity." This was another indication of the speed with which the computer invasion of the university was taking place.

In June 1983 we announced the establishment of the Video Production Fund to support the development of video materials. The primary criterion used in proposal evaluation was the extent to which the project enhanced the quality of instruction and research of a department. Some months previously, I had been given the task of making recommendations for upgrading our video facilities. After broad consultation we concluded that the university should have a modern facility and that it should be capable of producing materials of a standard that could be used by commercial professional channels. Obviously, there was a big price tag. We had already recruited a video engineer, who developed the specifications for the equipment that would be needed. The bill came to several hundred thousand dollars. We phased in the upgrade over time and managed to achieve a reasonable state-of-the-art facility. We were then in the position to accept faculty proposals (for example, an introductory tour of the university libraries for rhetoric students, or vignettes of the behavior of children for a course in psychology on child abuse), which our Video Advisory Committee reviewed three times a year. Many of the products were intriguing and helped to raise the awareness of the faculty to another resource for enhancing instruction and, hopefully, learning.

In early fall Professor Edward Haug, of our Mechanical Engineering Department, came to tell me about a new computer software program that he and his colleagues had developed that could create simulated "movies" of proposed mechanical systems rather than creating the physical prototypes. The program, which would later become known as the Dynamic Analysis and Design System, or DADS, could save millions of dollars from the expense of building and testing prototypes. His visit was an alert to what he predicted would come and introduced a series of developments that ultimately would involve the transfer of intellectual property to the private sector. After a tortuous journey involving reviews and plans, it would emerge as the for-profit company Computer-Aided Design Software, Inc. (CADSI), now ensconced in its own building on the Oakdale campus. The national driving simulator, also on the Oakdale campus, draws on the same body of software programs, demonstrating yet again how necessary it is to respond to new and creative ideas even though they may, at the time, be out of step with established programs and routines.

Reflections on Technology Transfer

Technology transfer is a topic like the story of the blind men describing an elephant; one's point of view depends greatly on the vantage point from which the transfers were viewed. Bill Trease, then the executive director of the UI Research Foundation, remembers:

> We saw some companies develop from patents that we licensed: CADSI from work of Ed Haug and his colleagues in Engineering; Neurotron from Randy Rozier, then an orthopedics resident; and Integrated DNA Technology, Inc., from the work of Joe Walder, then a faculty member in Biochemistry and now president and CEO [chief executive officer] of the company.
>
> The invention that made the most money for us for many years was one developed by Dr. George Andreason in the College of Dentistry. He found that he could use Nitinol, the wire with a memory, as a substitute for the old stainless steel wires that were used in the straightening of teeth.
>
> We filed a patent application, of course, and licensed the invention to a company called UniTech Corporation. It became the best product out there at the time.

We wanted to be sure that the teaching and research of the students wasn't being improperly warped by outside interests involved in the transfer of ideas to the marketplace. To make sure that didn't happen, I appointed a committee to review the academic programs of faculty who were involved. The committee would render a report following each review, offering suggestions for procedural changes from time to time, but I don't recall that we ever had problems in getting appropriate resolution to any issues that the committee raised.

Associated with the technology transfer issues was the matter of attracting companies to the area to take advantage of our patents. Ray Muston picks up the story. He had come to the university to serve as assistant dean in the College of Education. Then he served a period in the Office of Academic Affairs to provide leadership for our outreach programs. From there he became president of the Iowa City Area Development group (ICAD) for five years before returning to his faculty position in the College of Education. Here are some of his reflections from his five years with ICAD:

When I got involved with executives in private industry, I found out that one of the things they were very concerned about was new products and new technology that might be coming out of the university that could compete successfully in the marketplace. They had all these images of the university being this great storehouse of ideas and, if we would just let go of them, they could get rich.

On the flip side, many people in the university thought these market-driven hucksters didn't understand the complexity of the research. It was interesting to get the two together and realize there was a middle ground in there somewhere that did make some sense. There were a lot of extremes that didn't.

Bruce Wheaton has been involved, in one way or another, with the Office of the Vice President for Research since 1981. In 1984 he became director of the Technology Innovation Center, moving in 1989 to become director of the University Research Park and executive director of the University Research Foundation. He has been much involved in the development of the operating philosophy of the center and the park, in the process plowing new ground for the transfer of intellectual property and assisting young companies with the realities of the marketplace. Here are some of his recollections:

There were really three things going on in the early part of the eighties with respect to corporate sponsorship: one was the change in the patent law in 1980, which allowed universities, for the first time in a uniform, convenient, and predictable way to take ownership assignment of intellectual property that resulted from federally funded research. That meant companies would be more attentive to universities because they could enter into exclusive licenses.

The second thing was that at least two important technologies, biotechnology and microelectronics, began to increase radically their rate of acceleration. The buzzword at the time was that corporations wanted a window on university research, which meant that they wanted to be sure that they were keeping abreast of this rapidly changing field, which they had judged already to be at least potentially commercially important.

The third factor that got mixed into the increasing level of interaction between corporation and universities was the economic considerations generally associated with the broad downturn of the economy in the early to the mid-eighties. This had the direct correlative effect of increasing the level of public pressure on universities to be responsive to corporate needs and to do something to make the economy better.

I don't think most big universities fundamentally changed their mission in response to the tech transfer development. It changed their rhetoric, a little bit. But the policies that were in place then are still in place now; they're interpreted in roughly the same way.

David Vernon, professor of law, has served through the years as an ad hoc advisor to Iowa's presidents and central administration officers, dean of the College of Law, and twice as acting vice president for academic affairs. Here is his 1995 response to my questions about technology transfer:

> My recollection is that there was a lot of resistance at establishing a center at Oakdale for developing industries. It was viewed as being nonacademic, and some on campus were not very happy about what they viewed as the promotionalization of the institution.
>
> My view is different from that of most people. I was quite enthusiastic about that part of it. But it was all part of a more general view that the university was an important component of the economic development of the state. Sometimes I still think that priorities get a little confused, not on campus but outside, with several of the state officials viewing this as our primary role, while I share the view of many others that this is an academic institution dedicated to teaching students and helping the inquiring mind develop. It seems to me that it causes an identity crisis for universities to be viewed as merely economic development agencies. But I thought that the way it was done here, despite the fussing, was pretty well controlled, and, in retrospect, it helped the faculty. But it was all part of a general movement away from universities being solely academic academies.

In the meantime the university was being nickeled and dimed into higher levels of cost sharing by the federal agencies from which we received funds. In addition, funding of federal grant programs were being reduced. Our awards for the 1982–1983 fiscal year were $66 million, down from $70 million the previous year. (Funds for equipment and facilities were particularly at risk.) Yet the costs of research were increasing at alarming rates and the expectations, even demands, of quality faculty that we were recruiting grew enormously. Specially designed laboratories and expensive equipment were becoming the standard resources if we wished to secure the people that we sought. We scrambled when and where we could. A case in point was the announcement by NSF of "Young Investigator Awards." It was a great program, providing substantial support to persons who were no more than seven years beyond their doctorates. Universities were asked to solicit matching support from industry. We made a heroic effort, but we were only minimally successful.

Research

The University of Iowa Research Foundation is charged to take all prudent actions to protect the university's interests in the transfer of intellectual property to the private sector. The first big test of its charter came during the 1983–1984 academic year, when we proposed to establish a for-profit company to advance the application of computer software developed by Professor Edward Haug and his colleagues. In fact, it would become a cause célèbre for the New Wave student organization that would dog us during the entire year.

In May 1983 the UIRF Board authorized the formation of a for-profit corporation to market the Dynamic Analysis and Design System, described earlier. It became clear that the DADS software had wide potential applications for the development of any and all mechanical systems with moving parts.

In September 1983 CADSI was incorporated and the paperwork was completed to transfer the DADS software material to it in accordance with university policies concerning the rights of the university and the inventors in sharing royalties and other earnings. I was chosen to be the pro tem president of the company while a business plan was developed, capital raised, and a full-time chief executive officer hired. This plan was duly reported to the Board of Regents. The publicity associated with these several transactions put the spotlight on Professor Haug, the principal developer of the software. In July 1983 he was awarded a grant from the Department of Defense to explore the "promising techniques" of the DADS system. In August he was awarded another grant from DOD (Tank Automotive Command) to evaluate "vehicle dynamic performance." Those awards caused questions, again primarily from New Wave members, about the appropriateness of "weapons" research by anyone associated with the university. The questions brought a renewal of demands to examine the university's policies for doing research, especially that which might be used in military weapon development.

The Research Council again conducted a detailed review of the appropriate university research policies, recommending in the end that they remain essentially as they were: The policies vested in the individual faculty members and their peers' decisions about the objectives of all research including "the advancement of knowledge through research and scholarship; the preservation and dissemination of knowledge; and the advancement of the public welfare."

The September 30, 1983, issue of *fyi* published a short statement by me entitled "The Dilemmas of Research and Inquiry." In it I tried to state in simple terms what I thought was the crux of the matter. Here is an excerpt:

> It is my conviction that the faculty should be free to do whatever research it wants to do. We have but one requirement: whatever research is done must be in the public domain.
>
> Universities are open institutions. . . . If we were doing research which we didn't want to tell anyone else about or transmit in our teaching, . . . the university would become an entirely different kind of institution.
>
> There is, some feel, a dilemma about making judgments concerning the uses to which new information will be put. The extreme position is that we should not do any kind of research at all because we might learn something which could be used in a harmful way. That is the dilemma. . . . What are good purposes and bad purposes? Who makes the judgments?

The New Wave was not convinced. Its members repeatedly challenged President Freedman and me to debate the appropriateness of allowing the university to do "weapons" research. I spent many hours meeting with them to little avail in an effort to explain the system. But I refused to engage in a public debate with them on the subject because I wasn't convinced that the merits of their argument deserved that kind of public attention. That was, in retrospect, probably a strategic mistake since we had nothing to hide, and their rhetoric would, in my opinion, have done much to discredit them. In the absence of such an open review, repeated stories, typically initiated by the New Wave, kept the spotlight on our every move or lack thereof. They were fed by the long but typical time for start-up companies such as CADSI to find capital and a CEO.

The students raised questions about Ed Haug's potential conflict of interest in doing and directing continuing university research on the software system while, at the same time, being so intimately involved in marketing the software. We acknowledged the conflict possibility and established the committee that I referred to earlier to monitor the use of research assistants in the basic study of the system and to insure that there weren't subtle ways in which the students might be diverted from other research interests to concentrate on research that would advance the development of DADS. In this we had enthusiastic support from Ed Haug himself.

Nevertheless, the newspaper headlines tell another story: "Critics Doubt CADSI Profit Projections"; "Ethics of CADSI Prompt Debates"; "Regents Concerned about CADSI Plans"; "UI Denies Debate on Defense Research"; and "Tactics to Halt Research Studied." On March 1, 1984, the *Daily Iowan* included a graph showing that funds in support of research from the DOD had risen from $.5 million in 1968 to $2.5 million in 1983. The accusation was made that the military was moving into a funding vacuum and "taking over" as funds from other federal agencies were cut back, this despite our receiving $66.7 million from all external agencies during the 1983 fiscal year; 3.75 percent was hardly a takeover.

The matter came to a head during the March 1984 meeting of the regents. We reported that we were close to securing the necessary financing for the company and that when the transaction was completed we would seek board authorization to transfer title of the software program to the company in return for company stock. One of the regents worried that the investors might use the university's reputation in selling stock to small investors and that, if the company did not succeed, the university's reputation would be sullied. However, the majority of the board supported our plan and, in the end, approved the transfer. Vice President Ellis and I took the heat, as appropriate, during the several public discussions with the board. We agreed that we were damned if we did and damned if we didn't. There were growing public expectations that the universities should "do something" to bolster the economy without involving ourselves in the nitty gritty of profit-making businesses. Admittedly, we were walking a fine line.

Nevertheless, we proceeded with the plan. Ultimately, we found investors and hired a CEO. The company built a building in the University Research Park and continues to develop and expand the software that created such a fracas in the first place. Perhaps of more importance were the policies and procedures by which CADSI was established and developed with university assistance. They have served well in support of subsequent technology transfer efforts.

Development

President Freedman gave his fall speech, entitled "A Proposal for the Future of the University of Iowa," to the faculty on September 13, 1983. Proposing the creation of a university endowment, he hoped to accomplish three goals: "a substantial number of professorships," "a substantial number of outstanding doctoral students," and the establishment of an interdisciplinary Center for Advanced Studies. He called for setting "in excess of $100 million" as the goal of the drive. While the UI Foundation had been increasingly successful in expanding gifts to the university for enrichment purposes, this was the first time that we undertook an endowment drive. The faculty and the foundation gave the proposal their enthusiastic support. The public phase of the drive, called "Iowa Endowment 2000: A Covenant with Quality," was launched in

1986. Later, the goal was expanded to $150 million and now has passed $250 million. Clearly, this major initiative will have lasting significant benefits to the university.

President Freedman also established the Presidential Lecture series. It was created to provide an opportunity each year for a distinguished faculty member to present significant aspects of his or her work to the university community and "thereby stimulate intellectual communication among the many disciplines that comprise the university." Sherman Paul, Carver Distinguished Professor of English, was selected to inaugurate the series.

In the fall of 1983 we continued to develop the plan for students, faculty, and staff to purchase computers from the Weeg Computing Center. As I have noted, selling products by the university is a sensitive matter since it raises questions about possible unfair competition between the university and private retail outlets. We already had computer clusters located at selected locations around the campus. The linking of university buildings in a communication net with Weeg was only in the talking stage. However, there were some faculty and staff who felt that it was only a question of time before computer purchases by students would be as commonplace as the purchase of books! On a trial basis we chose to mount a pilot program for fifteen freshmen and sophomores living in Westlawn Residence Hall. The engineering and business students were also well launched into the computer era by this time, but this program would be our first test of their use by a group of liberal arts students. Today, those first steps seem timid and quaint, but in the academic year to come they were seen as bold indeed.

President Freedman revealed his keen interest in "internationalizing" the campus early in his tenure. He gave a speech to the business community in which he called attention to the enormous development potential of the Pacific Rim countries. He sought to learn about our various international programs and activities. This was heady stuff for our "internationalists," myself among them. Old proposals were dusted off and refurbished and new proposals advanced. Governor Branstad appointed President Freedman to chair the Governor's Task Force on Foreign Language Studies and International Education, which made its recommendations in June 1983. In July 1983 the Advisory Committee on International Activities completed a review entitled "Recommendations for Strengthening International Education at the University of Iowa" in response to President Freedman's request to evaluate the status of international education at the University of Iowa and make recommendations for improving and strengthening it. Its first and foremost recommendation was that an associate vice president for international education be appointed in the Office of the Vice President for Academic Affairs. It was a recommendation that I supported strongly since our interests and activities had broadened greatly from the early days of my tenure, when I sought to provide a more active and unified support program for our international students, then largely enrolled in the Graduate College. But the times were not quite right then for an associate vice president. Only in 1997, some fourteen years later, was the position created, through the interests and efforts of many in the intervening years.

Advancing international studies and research continued at the February 1984 regents meeting, when they approved the university's recommendation that a Center for International and Comparative Studies (CICS) should be established. There had been a Council on International and Comparative Studies since 1981. During the ensuing years internationally related activities had grown to the point that a more formal structure was called for, namely, the center. Its functions were to coordinate the existing interdisciplinary international programs (for example, global studies, Asian studies, development studies, women in development, and African studies) and facilitate obtaining external funds for the enhancement of international studies programs. These programs continue today under the umbrella of International Programs.

International concerns were not our only focus; the pressure on the regents universities to offer specific ways in which they could advance the economy of the state had been building for several years. We felt that one way we could do that would be to provide space for small start-up companies at low rents and under circumstances whereby university services could be made available for a fee. Thus was born the notion of the Technology Innovation Center. The space and support services were available on the Oakdale campus. We applied to the Iowa High Technology Council for financial assistance to start the project and were pleased when the council awarded us funding for two years starting on July 1, 1984. The center continues to provide support — currently, it has fourteen tenants; twelve have "graduated" to off-campus locations — with a ratio of success to failure of about three to one, good by any standard.

1984–1985: DOG DAYS — HEAR THE CORN GROW

In January 1985 Jim Johnson informed me that he would be resigning as director of Information Technology May 1 to accept the position of vice chancellor for computing at the University of Houston. It was a moment that I had been anticipating with dread; I knew Jim was ultimately destined for even more significant leadership positions.

In 1978 Jim had taken over leadership of the Weeg Computer Center, then in great disarray, restoring the morale of the staff and giving them vision and direction. Then he had moved on to provide leadership in helping all of us think through the implications of the technology revolution that was sweeping us up, ready or not. In doing so he had earned the respect of the entire university community. It would prove extremely difficult to find someone to take his place.

Graduate Matters

We were delighted to learn that David Lasocki, a doctoral student in the School of Music, who had received the D. C. Spriestersbach Dissertation Prize in 1983 for his Ph.D. dissertation on "Professional Recorder Players in England, 1540–1740," would also receive the distinguished dissertation award from the Council of Graduate Schools of the United States. It was our first hit for the national award, and we were especially pleased that it was in the area of the humanities and arts, fields that had been strong at Iowa almost from the beginning of its graduate programs.

We shared with President Freedman the extensive spreadsheets we had developed on graduate student characteristics and departmental practices (ratio of applications/acceptance, mean GRE scores, degree productivity, ratio of grant applications/awards, etc.). He was fascinated by the wealth of information that they provided about our programs, revealing, as they did, clear differences in academic standards, selectivity, degree productivity, etc. He was convinced by the data that there was imperative justification for including funds for doctoral fellowships in the Iowa 2000 campaign, and he sought our help in articulating how such funds would make a difference in the quality of our graduate programs and the level of scholarly activity of the university generally.

Research

The issue of the use of animals in research began demanding special attention during the year. The university had always taken the problem seriously, but the priority for allocating resources for animal care had clearly lagged. This year we continued our program to upgrade our facilities and tighten our review procedures. Faculty and staff were committed to openness as the best way to deal with a very emotionally charged matter.

Also during the year President Reagan initiated the controversial "Star Wars" program, with the goal to provide an invincible shield over the United States as a protection from incoming missiles, presumably from the Soviet Union. The plan created a furor in part because of its huge cost and doubts about its effectiveness when in place. It was also objected to as another ratcheting up of the Cold War. We were startled in June 1985 when the Department of Defense announced that a consortium had been formed to investigate and study innovations in space science and to conduct "novel experiments in space." The University of Iowa was listed as a member of the consortium.

Apparently, the story stemmed from a letter that General James Abrahamson, director of the Strategic Defense Initiative Organization, had sent to the senators of fourteen states in which researchers at university or government laboratories were located, announcing that the investigators were about to receive funding for their research applications. The timing of the letter was immediately suspect since it arrived on the senators' desks just before a crucial vote on limiting the funding of the SDI program. MIT president Paul Gray used his commencement address to blast the DOD move, asserting that MIT was being used as a "political instrument." Iowa's participation consisted of a funded proposal from two members of our physics faculty to conduct "Laboratory Experiments in Support of the Strategic Defense Initiative." The unclassified research dealt with plasma and ionized gas. The local news flurry died down when it became clear that Iowa was not part of any SDI consortium, the research was unclassified, and the application for the funds had been processed through regular university channels.

In September 1984 President Freedman approved a modest policy change concerning the provisions in the *Operations Manual* dealing with the suitability of research done at the university. It was an outgrowth of the press during the previous year for access to materials in the Office of Sponsored Programs having to do with applications to external agencies for funds and the reports resulting from the research supported. The changes made clear that anyone in the university community (faculty, staff, and students) could request information about specific funded research projects, and it established time limits for making the final reports available to inspection. There was, however, no ban, as originally requested by the New Wave, on specific areas of research such as that supported by the Department of Defense.

We were ecstatic when we totaled the numbers on external funds that the faculty and staff had generated during the year that ended June 30, 1984. We had experienced a 25 percent increase in funding and processed over 1,600 applications, up from 1,575 the previous year, and were especially proud that our faculty had been successful in seven out of seven applications for shared equipment grants (over $1 million). Our efforts were paying off; we had done everything we could think of to congratulate the faculty on their efforts and to publicize funding opportunities to target groups, for example, the social science faculty, the internationalists, and those new to the university. We provided a compilation of the names of our faculty who volunteered information about their current service as advisors to federal, state, and private agencies, or as editors of professional journals, so that potential applicants to external funding agencies might visit with their faculty colleagues who served on the appropriate advisory boards concerning the agencies' priorities and review procedures. We offered seminars on writing grant proposals, preparation of proposal budgets, and orientation to the services that we were prepared to offer to the faculty. Grantsmanship, for better or for worse, had become an expected and necessary part of the lives of the faculty.

The University and Economic Development

The pressure on the universities to contribute to the state's economic development expanded, and the demands grew significantly louder. The state now had the lottery and offered to use some of its earnings to prime the economic pump, even for the universities, if we could come up with convincing proposals and plans. Expectations were high. At this point it's timely to step aside for a moment to consider the whole story.

Statewide economic development was a hot topic during the 1980s. The issue was how to get the state out of its economic doldrums. State institutions were not immune from the concern, most especially the regents universities. It was not unthinkable, for example, for the legislature to reason that the universities included many smart people with specialized laboratories seeking answers to a wide variety of questions relating to natural phenomena. Surely, these faculties had made discoveries that had value in the marketplace. Legislators made these beliefs known to us with repeated requests for information and for appearances before committees that were plotting strategies for lifting the economy of the state.

Here is a recap of selected newspaper headlines: "Regents to Explore Business, University Ties"; "CADSI Gets Funding from Outside Firm"; "Tech Center to Aid Local Growth"; "CADSI Endures after One Year"; "Foundation to 'Spin Off' CADSI"; "UI Asks for $20 Million Slice of Lottery"; "UI Proposes $27 Million Research Development Program"; "Lottery Bill Expected to Pass Senate"; "Higher Education and Economic Growth: Challenges and Opportunities"; "Referrals Keep UI Tech Center in Contact with Corporate World"; and "High Tech: Razzle Dazzle or Hope for the Future?" Elsewhere in this history I have recounted the establishment of the UI Research Foundation and the Technology Innovation Center, and the development of Neurotron, CADSI, and the Laser Center, all the result of our efforts to transfer university intellectual property to the private sector. This section fills out that story.

On July 10, 1984, President Freedman responded to an inquiry by state representative Lowell Norland regarding the transfer of knowledge from the University of Iowa and the other regents' institutions to the state's industrial and productive base:

It is standing university practice to encourage faculty members to disclose ideas that may lead to inventions and patents. In selected instances the University of Iowa Research Foundation pursues these disclosures to obtain patents that may then be licensed to the private sector for development. One recent effort has led to the development of a corporation for profit that is contracting with an Iowa firm to produce the item created by the invention. We have sought to do the same thing in a second instance but have been hampered by the absence of venture capital available to support the effort. Nevertheless, we continue to believe that some of the ideas of our faculty will find themselves transformed to the benefit of the Iowa economy.

The University of Iowa has just received approval from the Board of Regents to create a Technology Innovation Center which we hope will prove helpful in transferring knowledge to private industry. The center is an "incubation" facility, with an associated support program, which is designed to encourage the growth of technology-based industries in Iowa. The university will lease a cluster of minimally-furnished laboratories and offices on the Oakdale campus to businesses seeking to develop and market products based on new and advanced technologies. They will be rented at reasonable rates for a limited period of time.

The university is also proud of the fact that many employment opportunities for Iowans are created through the success of faculty members in applying for federal, corporate, and foundation funds for their research and demonstration projects. During the 1982–83 academic year, the university's faculty attracted $66 million in grants, of which $23 million was used for salaries and wages on research projects. This figure translated into 815 full-time-equivalent salaries, plus a large number of hourly employees. During the past five years, university faculty members have competed successfully for more than $220 million in external grant funds to support this research. Approximately half of these funds were used for salaries and wages.

On November 12, 1984, state representative Charles Poncy wrote to President Freedman as follows:

I am writing to ask that you share information with the House of Representatives Education Appropriations Subcommittee about research institutes within your institution, especially in those vital areas in which the transfer of technological advances and other information will promote the economy of Iowa and the creation of jobs. A better informed General Assembly will be better equipped to provide further assistance to regents institutions in promoting economic growth in Iowa through research activities.

On January 24, 1985, we developed a document for the legislature entitled "Proposed Contributions by the University of Iowa to the Economic Development of the State of Iowa: Building from Strength." We opened the document with the statement: "The University of Iowa is eager to participate in the economic development of the state. While there is no quick solution to the economic problems of the state, the role of the university in developing solutions is clear; we must increase the research capabilities of the university and we must work diligently to transfer the results of our research to the private sector." The proposal called for $27 million, with $20 million coming from the state, presumably from lottery proceeds, and $7 million from private sources. It would be used for the following: $4.5 million to develop the interdisciplinary laser science and engineering program; $5 million to expand the university's biotechnology capabilities; $8.9 million to increase the university's capabilities in manufacturing technology, productivity, and product-oriented research; $3.8 million to expand the university's cancer center capabilities; $2.684 million to increase the university's capabilities in the international development field; and $2.1 million for shared facilities required for the execution of new initiatives.

We followed up on our proposal by holding a high-tech workshop in the campus union on January 25 and 26, 1985. It was presented by the governmental relations committee of the Faculty Senate to bring together academic and legislative leaders to "discuss high technology research at the UI and how it can be translated into economic development for the state of Iowa."

Not surprisingly, there were components of the university that worried about balance. As I have already indicated, the *Daily Iowan* carried a story on February 1, 1985, with the headline, "UI High Tech Research Bid May Snub Humanities." President Freedman responded with the comment: "We won't be a university if we in any way dilute our commitment to the liberal arts, the intellectual core of education." I added my two cents' worth: "For this university to deserve the faith of this state over time, it must remain a balanced institution. However, everything doesn't march in a parallel way. If I have an opportunity to advance engineering and science today, you can bet that I'll try to help the arts and humanities tomorrow."

The chronology of the efforts of our office to foster economic development is revealing: 1974–1975, incorporation of the UI Research Foundation; 1980, development of the central University Research Facilities begun; 1982, funding of the biocatalysis group; 1982, incorporation of Neurotron; 1982–1983, initiation of task force planning for the emerging revolution in communication technology; 1983, incorporation of CADSI; 1984, establishment of the Technology Innovation Center; 1984, participant in founding of the Iowa City Area Development Group, Inc.; 1984–1985, participant in initial groundwork of the Iowa City–Cedar Rapids corridor group; and 1986, membership on East Central Iowa Development Council.

Dorsey (Dan) Ellis, formerly professor of law and vice president for finance and university services, now dean of the Law School, Washington University, St. Louis, reflects on these times:

> One of the things that I tried to use to explain what the university was contributing was to ask some folks in the Economics Department to do an analysis of the impact on dollars spent at the University of Iowa. Their analysis showed that every dollar contributed to the University of Iowa generated $3.54 in economic activity in the state of Iowa.
>
> I then took that and applied it to what was happening in terms of the dollars that our students were bringing here. Not just the tuition dollars they were paying, not just in fees, but the Financial Aid office's budget for what it would cost a student to go to school here, and used that and applied that to the multiplier. Then we also pointed out the ways in which the strengths of our faculty in their ability to bring in grant money, both from the federal government and from private sources, contracts with corporations, etc., how that contributed to the Iowa economy and through this $3.54 turnover.

More on International Activities

President Freedman's interest in internationalizing the university never rested. Progress had been made: the establishment of the Center for International and Comparative Studies, creation of the Councils on Foreign Language Instruction and International Education, the establishment of the Presidential Scholarships for Study Abroad, and increase in cooperative and exchange agreements with institutions around the world. He said in a faculty address that "in a global community that has drawn us closer and closer to the other nations of the world, meeting the demands for international competence is a fundamental responsibility of higher education. The University of Iowa can be proud that the faculties of its individual colleges have moved creatively to meet that responsibility."

The nitty-gritty of new academic initiatives rarely starts in administrative offices. Rather, it begins in the minds of faculty with visions of what might be. Clearly, that was the case with the Center for International and Comparative Studies. The visionaries were primarily junior faculty who had had experiences abroad and who saw the value those experiences could have for any and all who ventured beyond their parochial pasts. There was a threesome who visited my office frequently to tell me about their dreams: Joel Barkan (political science), Paul Greenough (history), and Mike McNulty (geography). I always knew what the topic would be when I saw any of their names on my appointment schedule. I found their ideas exciting, but I knew that there would be dollar signs at the end. They were stimulating people, full of energy, and not to be resisted. They followed through effectively with the seed funding that I gave them until gradually a group of faculty had been assembled and a program of interdisciplinary educational programs was in the wings. President Freedman's international interest and funds from the Stanley Foundation in Muscatine combined to give the movement additional substance. Happily, the programs are well established today within the university structure.

President Freedman took the initiative personally to approach the Ford Foundation with a plan to introduce Russian, Chinese, and Japanese into the secondary schools. He proposed that university students who applied and were accepted for funding as part of the program would agree to study one of these three languages intensively during their last two years of college, during which time they would receive financial support. During those years the students would have one summer of intensive language support and a second year of study in the country whose language the student was studying. In return, the student would agree to teach at the elementary or secondary level for a minimum of one year for each year of support received. School districts (initially West Des Moines, Des Moines, Cedar Rapids, Marshalltown, and Urbandale) agreed to hire the students once their education had been completed. It was a bold plan designed to get some movement where before there had been largely talk. The Ford Foundation agreed to support the plan.

1985–1986: THE WORLD CONTINUES TO BE MUCH WITH US

Personnel Changes

With the establishment of the Windhover Press, a fine arts press, by Kim Merker of the Department of English, interest grew in the book arts. Kim had been instrumental in recruiting Timothy Barrett to head our papermaking program and William Anthony, a master bookbinder and conservator, to university libraries. The activities of these people brought about the establishment of the Center for the Book in June 1986. President Freedman noted: "We see interdisciplinary studies frequently in the sciences. Here we see it between people whose interests are art, writing, literature, journalism, printing, paper making, graphics and other disciplines. It is an enterprise not only in the production of the book, but in its history and of the role that books, both mass-produced and elegantly produced, have played in society." I was thrilled to have had a role in supporting Kim in his early efforts and to be able to bask in the outgrowth of his efforts. I felt that it was another jewel in the resources that one expects to find in a distinguished university.

In March 1986 President Freedman announced that he had appointed a committee to search for a successor for me when I reached mandatory retirement age in 1987. I suppose that could have been a signal to me that I was now a "lame duck," but that didn't seem to be the case. There were still plenty of challenges that couldn't wait, and life went on pretty much as usual. Nor did I think much about what I would do when I no longer sat at my Gilmore Hall desk; I had never plotted out my future life before, and there didn't seem to be any reason to start now.

Graduate Matters

Unhappily the quality of our graduate programs, in themselves, was not an adequate enticement to attract the very best graduate students to enroll in them. While relatively competitive, the Teaching-Research Fellowship Program — in which the Graduate College joined forces with academic departments to provide support for four years, including a dissertation fellowship year — did not put Iowa in a leadership position. We had to do better. Thus, under the able leadership of Rudy Schulz, dean for advanced studies, was born the Iowa Fellowship Program, which provided twenty four-year fellowships to nationally outstanding applicants the first year, building to 108 fellows when fully implemented. From the outset Vice President for Academic Affairs Richard Remington was a staunch supporter of its goals.

The Graduate College again combined its resources with those of the participating departments to provide stipends, including summer session support, plus tuition scholarships for the successful applicants. Departments made nominations to the Graduate College, from which the very top nominees were selected. It was a program that ranked well with even the most prestigious private universities. The program was mounted during a time when the university was faced with cutbacks in state funding (reversions of 3.85 percent) but was made possible through a program of internal reallocations that enabled the Office of Academic Affairs to redistribute funds to the highest priority programs. The Fellows Program was considered to be one of them.

Development

On August 9, 1985, Governor Branstad paid a visit to our Technology Innovation Center and lauded it as a cornerstone to economic development in Iowa. During the governor's visit President Freedman noted that the university would be presenting a plan to the Board of Regents soon for the development of a research park on the Oakdale campus. At the same meeting he stated that the Technology Innovation Center (TIC) had four tenants and that CADSI had just hired a president. (As I have recounted earlier, getting CADSI up and running had been a tortuous journey!)

On August 21, 1985, I sent a memo to the president and vice presidents, urging that we include considerations of the technology in our strategic planning, noting that it would become increasingly difficult to separate its administrative and academic applications. Déjà vu. I felt the continual need to keep this emerging technology in the forefront of our planning and resource allocation lest we be forced to "pay double" in the future when we found that we had no recourse but to catch up with our peer institutions.

On September 11, 1985, Vice President Remington sent a memo to the collegiate deans, proposing to fund new academic initiatives by a systematic reallocation of resources. His proposal was driven by the assumption that we could not look forward realistically in the foreseeable future to growth in state appropriations. In his scheme every college would operate at an initial allocation level below that of the preceding year. Thus, in preparing their budgets for the 1986–1987 year, the colleges were asked to base them on 99 percent of the previous year, continuing similar reductions for three years. He proposed to use the pool of money created to strengthen undergraduate education, attract increased numbers of outstanding doctoral students, provide improved salaries for our most able faculty members, allocate seed money to promising areas of research, and develop a limited number of new academic programs. It was a bold plan from which some of the programs of my office would benefit — the Iowa Fellows Program and increases in seed money for promising scholarly proposals from the faculty, to name two. While the plan may have generated a grumble or two, the general response was to buckle up and go with it since we all knew that, as an institution, we couldn't stand still.

On September 17, 1985, President Freedman gave his fall address to the faculty. He titled it: "Moving to the Measure of the Scholar's Thought." His purpose was "to articulate, for ourselves as well as for those outside the university, what it means to be a university professor." Here is a sample of what he said:

What do professors accomplish, and what is the value of their work? What are the costs of professing, and what are its rewards? And what does it mean to say that a university moves to the measure of a scholar's thought?

. . . The life of a university professor is a difficult, lonely, and dedicated life. It is a life of privilege, to be sure — the privilege of autonomy in the classroom, the privilege of broad control over the use of one's time, the privilege of free inquiry, the privilege of tenure. But for those privileges, a professor pays exacting costs, in ways that are rarely visible to those who are not academics.

. . . As long as new knowledge is being created and old knowledge is changing shape, a professor cannot simply prepare a course once and then repeat it year after year. As long as new students enroll each semester, a professor cannot coast through the course on last year's notes.

A cost of professing is the struggle to compress a host of protean and unruly tasks into a day that is always too short. Another cost is the knowledge that one that can never be paid in full — is the responsibility of creating new knowledge, whether in the library, the laboratory, or the studio.

A further cost of professing — the last in my list — is the obligation to repay society's heavy investment in the protection of independent thought.

Distinction in teaching and scholarship is the source of our vitality as an institution. Nothing else, not even the most lavish favors granted by Mammon, has value except as a means to that end.

It was, in my opinion, a brilliant statement and should be required reading for all faculty since the question he asked is a recurring one. Many of us have answered it diffidently, if at all.

State Economic Development

The state approved the lottery in 1985. For the fiscal year ending on June 30, 1986, the estimated earnings were projected to amount to $28 million. The perils of using the money to meet operating needs were apparent since lottery funds would fluctuate over time. But there was no dearth of suggestions for spending the funds otherwise. The Board of Regents put their ideas into the pot along with many others. In its first submission, the University of Iowa presented recommendations that included the establishment of endowed professorships. The virtue of the endowments was that we could use the state funds to attract augmenting private gifts, and the endowments, properly funded, would be self-perpetuating. To be sure, the concept of "endowments" required some explaining in Des Moines before it was accepted as a legitimate receptacle for lottery funding. It was the first time that many of the legislators had considered what an endowment was and how it was managed.

Our final proposal, considerably pared down from our initial proposal, sought funds to extend the university's already significant capabilities in laser science, biotechnology, cancer research, hydraulics, and international development. We also sought funds to create new research and development centers in manufacturing productivity, biomedical engineering, and VLSI (very large scale integrated) circuit design. We proposed that the state fund $8.125 million and that the university and private sources match the amount for a total of $16.25 million. The proposals had to be put together with essentially no time for broad consultation throughout the university. I got enormous help from my ad hoc SWAT team, a tremendous group who worked days, nights, and weekends to help me put together a persuasive case for our share of the lottery dollars.

All this was happening at a time when the state's economy was in a slump and the university was making a valiant effort to respond with a wide range of activities to encourage and facilitate economic development. Earlier, in 1984, the university, represented by Randy Bezanson and me, had participated with representatives of the city and the Greater Iowa City Chamber of Commerce to draw up some bylaws for the Iowa City Area Development, Inc., group. TIC had been established, as I noted earlier, and we wholeheartedly accepted the challenge to do our part, mindful, at the same time, that the university's primary missions were teaching and research.

In January 1986 President Freedman appointed a task force to search for new ways the university could contribute to the development of the state. He said that the decision to establish the advisory committee "rests on the simple premise that the destiny of the university is intertwined with the destinies of the citizens of Iowa." Dean George Daly of the College of Business Administration served as chair of the task force. The seventeen-member group, called the Task Force on University Strategies for the Future Development of the State, held a series of meetings throughout the state, seeking ways in which university research might help agriculture, new businesses, and industries. It was a noble effort. While there was little of a concrete nature that came of the dedicated efforts of the task force, it did help to establish the sincere intention of the university to be helpful in dealing with the state's economic slump.

On January 30, 1986, President Freedman gave the annual address to the Joint Service Clubs of the Iowa City Area. His topic was "The University of Iowa in 1986 and Beyond." It was another of his powerful, tightly reasoned statements in which he made the case for maintaining a strong university even in times of economic stringency. He built his talk on a Chinese proverb, "The schools of a country are its future in miniature," arguing that it was the responsibility of our generation "to make certain that this university has the resources to seize the opportunities that will determine this state's future," and that it was and is the responsibility of all of us "to uphold a covenant with quality." It was the right message for our troubled economic times.

1986 –1987: UNEXPECTED PASSAGE

Personnel Changes

We were startled when President Freedman announced that he would resign to accept the position of president of Dartmouth College on July 19, 1987. He had come here on April 1, 1982, for what seemed to have been five short years. Perhaps the opportunity to move to Dartmouth was one of a very few that could have tempted him so early in his tenure here. He had grown up in New Hampshire almost in the shadow of Dartmouth, but not of it. It seemed as though it was a story of "local boy makes good." In any event, most of us understood his decision as a highly personal one.

President Freedman clearly left his mark on the University of Iowa, even though his time here was relatively short. He had been the leading advocate for the establishment of the $25 million laser facility, about which more will be said in chapter 9; he set the course to strengthen liberal, interdisciplinary, and international education, and to establish centers of excellence. An articulate spokesman for the university's efforts to attract top undergraduate and graduate students, he helped establish the Undergraduate Scholar Assistant Program and the Iowa Fellows Program. He was a driving force behind the initiation of the Iowa Endowment 2000 program. Working with the Stanley Foundation, he helped put in place a $2 million gift from the Stanley family to establish the Center for Asian and Pacific Studies and with the Ford Foundation to win the half-million-dollar grant to establish the Critical Language Program to train teachers of Chinese, Japanese, and Russian for Iowa high schools that was described earlier. The UI Distinguished Teacher awards, recognizing outstanding teaching in Iowa high schools and community colleges, were his creation. He appointed the special task force to study the role of the university in the future economic strategies of the state, and he was very supportive of our efforts to establish the Technology Innovation Center and to use state lottery proceeds to support areas of emerging knowledge. A strong supporter of men's and women's intercollegiate athletics, he joked that he was the only university president to take the football team to a postseason bowl game every year during his presidency. Perhaps most important, however, he kept reminding us of the special place and responsibility that the academy had in the lives of the people of this state and this country. I wrote him a note on June 2, 1987, which included the following: "Your vision of university excellence and your expressions of that excellence in strategies and actions will not be forgotten. Rather, remembering them will keep me restive to the end."

President Freedman would be succeeded temporarily by Vice President for Academic Affairs Richard Remington, who would serve as interim president until Freedman's successor was chosen. The headline in the June 1987 *Spectator* read: "Experienced Hands Hold the Health of the University." It was a play on Dick's distinguished reputation in public health. Dick had served as dean of the School of Public Health at the University of Michigan and on a blue-ribbon committee of the National Academy of Sciences charged with making public health policy recommendations. He also served as a member of a panel of the National Institutes of Health that urged Americans to lower blood cholesterol levels to help them maintain better health. He was the first major appointee made by President Freedman after he came to Iowa. One of Dick's accomplishments that came as a surprise to those of us who knew him in his academic role was that he was an accomplished musician who played a tuba in a jazz band that was in national demand.

The New Wave created a campus stir on February 26 and 27, 1987, when they organized a rally, first on the Pentacrest and then in front of Westlawn, protesting the presence of CIA recruiters who were doing interviews at West-lawn under the sponsorship of the business and liberal arts placement office. Some of the Pentacrest protesters moved into Jessup Hall, and twenty-five ultimately occupied Vice President Remington's office. They refused to leave when warned, were arrested for criminal trespass, carried out by the police, and taken to the police headquarters for booking. The recruiters were able to complete their interviews and leave without further incident. It was a mild event in comparison with the days of student unrest in the late 1960s and early 1970s!

Retirement, Albeit Premature

In anticipation of my retirement at the end of this year, President Freedman made clear that an appropriate occasion would be organized in recognition of that day. He appointed a committee, of which he made me aware, chaired by Rudy Schulz, dean of advanced studies, that included eleven other persons from across the campus with whom I had worked closely over the years. They held regular meetings in the Danner Conference Room in Gilmore Hall (next to my office). Of course, I didn't try to learn what they discussed in their meetings, nor did I want to know, but many of the meetings involved raucous laughter. Had I been unduly sensitive I might have concluded that they were gleefully planning my demise!

The day of the celebration of my retirement was April 30, 1987. It started with an afternoon symposium entitled "Society's Changing Expectations of the University," moderated by President Freeman. It was held in the Levitt Auditorium in the Boyd Law Building and proved to be a stimulating and classy afternoon.

The evening banquet was just as classy. Sandy Boyd served as the toastmaster. In addition, the head table included Frank Horton, then president of the University of Oklahoma, President Freedman, Casey Mahon, Rudy Schulz, and spouses as well as Bette and me. Howard Bowen, Ed Jennings, and Ernie Boyer were all in the audience. It's not often that one is blessed with six university presidents or presidents emeriti in attendance on such an occasion!

President Freedman surprised all but one or two people in the room that night, and most especially me, by announcing that an endowed professorship was being established in my honor — "The D. C. Spriestersbach Professorship in the Liberal Arts." I was flabbergasted; I think I just sat with a vacant look, since I didn't know how I could possibly respond in a way that was appropriate to my deep sense of being so honored. Later, as I thought about the designation "liberal arts," I was immensely pleased since I had come to the university as a new graduate student to study in theater arts and had never forgotten that itch or my appreciation for arts generally.

After an extensive series of consultations, Gerhard Loewenberg, dean of the College of Liberal Arts, appointed Edward Lawler, professor in the Department of Sociology, to the Spriestersbach Professorship. Lawler held it from 1990 until 1993, and is now at Cornell University, serving as dean of the School of Industrial and Labor Relations.

Since Ed's departure, the professorship has remained unfilled. I made inquiries about its status, first to Dean Aiken of the College of Liberal Arts and then to Jon Whitmore, university provost. I did so because I knew that the appointment carried with it not only a salary augmentation but a package of research support, including funds for a research assistant; some yet-to-be-chosen faculty member was missing out. On January 29, 1997, Mr. Whitmore replied to the effect that the university in previous years had created professorships beyond its ability to fund in the long haul, and that the professorship in my name was now without ongoing funding. Subsequent to that reply, I received word that the professorship is to be restarted and funded in perpetuity.

The final event went off without a hitch. Some 450 people attended. I was greatly pleased to see that many were from "town," since I had tried very hard to reach out to that segment of Iowa City during my seven months as acting president. Their presence was a demonstration of their appreciation for my efforts.

Even before the celebration, however, it had been announced that I would not retire at the end of the year but would stay on yet another year (which grew to two!) during the interim between President Freedman's departure and the appointment of a new president. I acknowledged that fact at the party and made very clear that, for me, there would not be another observance of my "retirement." In my view nothing could match that one, and I didn't want a subsequent event to mar its memory!

Research

On July 15, 1986, we had a celebration in the Senate Chamber of Old Capitol with punch and a big cake that President Freedman cut. It was to observe that since 1965, when we started keeping the appropriate records, we had obtained over $1 billion in gifts, grants, and contracts from public and private sources, and had reached a new one-year record high, $89.44 million, during the 1985–1986 fiscal year. The record was set by approximately 550 faculty and staff principal investigators. With that record we ranked twenty-second as a recipient of NIH funding and thirty-first among universities receiving federal research and development money. We achieved those standings despite the fact that we were an institution of only moderate size. (The size of the pool of faculty available as potential researchers makes a difference.) I noted that without these funds the university would be different and clearly wouldn't be as good. "The real driving force behind this [achievement] is the intellectual drive of the faculty."

On April 27, 1987, I spoke before a meeting of the National Council for Urban Economic Development to an audience composed largely of persons other than university faculty members. I felt compelled that day to explain how the university research enterprise worked, since it was assumed by those outside of the academy that we operated like corporations. Here are some excerpts from my remarks:

> Research conducted at a university is a unique enterprise in that it allows researchers to pursue their *individual* interests, not those set by a corporate board or a governmental agency. Vice presidents in charge of research at universities are advocates for the projects to which faculty members devote themselves. University vice presidents for research do not give faculty assignments to do particular research tasks. As I have said at practically

every opportunity during my tenure as vice president *for* Educational Development and Research, the fact that my title contains the preposition
"for" and not "of" is both significant and purposeful.

Although it is the faculty who develop research protocols, individual
faculty members are not allowed to make their own arrangements for external support of their work. This is so because scholars are residents of an
academic community which has community policies and procedures to
which they must adhere in their work.

After citing ways in which we had sought and were seeking to mesh with
interests in the public and private sectors, I closed by making two assertions:

No business/industrial firms will be interested in association with any
university unless the association proves to be advantageous to those firms.
They must conclude that they risk losing out unless they keep in close
touch with the world-class work of Professor Jones. If that level of intellectual activity is not going on in a university, all the brave talk about establishing significant links with business enterprises will be just so much
hot air. I need not remind you that world class faculty are not knocking
at the doors of any university. Rather they are courted by institutional resources — salaries, equipment, laboratories, bright graduate students and
accomplished colleagues. . . . The primary mission of the university is to
educate students for a wide array of employment opportunities. The more
adequate that education, the greater the potential of the students to contribute to the business sector and ultimately to society's welfare.

Development

The drive for "economic development" intensified. Legislative hearings in
Des Moines on the topic occurred with regularity; phone calls from individual legislators inquiring about specific projects and rates of progress were fre-
quent; university-sponsored seminars on campus with leaders from the private sector were common; and lottery dollars were dangled before us, daring
us to be positive and innovative in ways in which the university might participate in the common effort to jump-start the economy of the state. While my
staff and I were not consumed by the zeitgeist, it was certainly a major factor
in determining how we spent our time and efforts during those weeks and
months.

This is the context, then, in which the concept for building a world-class
laser center at Iowa was born. That much-maligned effort is treated in chap-

ter 9. However, the other happenings during these days that are reported here should be viewed with the recognition that the cloud or umbrella of "economic development" was omnipresent.

In August 1986 we got word that the Iowa Department of Economic Development had awarded $3.25 million to the University of Iowa from lottery funds for six endowed chairs at the University of Iowa: three positions in laser science and engineering, one position in biocatalysis, one position in hydraulics, and one in manufacturing productivity. The funds were to be matched with university/private funds. Bruce Wheaton, director of the Technology Innovation Center, summarized our strategy for applying for and winning the funds: "The university's strategy . . . is based on the assumption that academic strength leads to economic growth . . . creating a 'grand magnet' for both intellectual and economic activity."

Clearly, the strategy was not a quick fix solution. Using the funds for endowed chairs had been a hard sell in Des Moines and would never be repeated. In that round Iowa State University, University of Northern Iowa, and Westmar College were awarded a total of $1.1 million. In the next round of awards the legislature earmarked $3.75 million for agricultural biotechnology projects at Iowa State University. Consequently, our proposals for that second round included primarily requests for funds to establish several institutes and other facilities (biotechnology, computer graphics, production of tissue culture media and hybridomas, plasma processing laboratory, biomedical engineering institute, drug delivery technology, DNA regional facility, center for research in groundwater quality, and a center for financial services). A positive outcome for our requests was highly uncertain. Ultimately, however, we received an additional $1.3 million for four of our proposed projects.

The continuing press by state government for us to foster economic development efforts caused Bruce Wheaton and me to ask for an afternoon of reflection by the central administration for guidance about priorities and efforts directed to economic development. After the meeting we wrote a memo to file to use as our hook when we got pushed and pulled to do more to advance economic development, and particularly more vis-à-vis economic development:

> The principal objectives of the University of Iowa are to teach and to conduct research. The development of Iowa's economy is a benefit that can follow from pursuit of these cardinal objectives. Since the university recognizes the importance of such benefits, it will continue to identify opportunities that will allow it to maximize those which follow naturally from the execution of its mission.

The UI will act on these opportunities only when they are consonant with the academic mission and available funds. . . .

External funding, both state and federal, will be sought to support these activities, but not before the activities have been given appropriate review to verify relevance to the UI mission and their functional merit.

Auf Wiedersehen

We have no options but to adjust, one way or the other, to changes. The life of the university went much as usual during President Freedman's last months, particularly following the announcement that Dick Remington would serve in the interim. There were several events to recognize President Freedman's tenure here, along with a professorship named in his honor; then he was gone.

5. THE REMINGTON INTERIM
1987–1988

Personnel Changes

Richard D. Remington became interim president on July 1, 1987. He said the period of his presidency would not be a time for "shifting into neutral" but a time for action, for recruiting women and minorities to administrative and faculty positions, and for recruiting minority students. He was pleased to announce at his first news conference that Susan D. Allen, the director of the Center for Laser Studies at the University of Southern California, would join the Department of Chemistry in the fall as a full professor. Not only was Susan a welcome addition to the female faculty but she was also a key addition to the faculty buildup that would be required for the new Laser Center. He ended his news conference by saying that, no, he was not a candidate for the university presidency.

During his fall speech to the faculty Dick said the university was in "a season of change." He felt that we were getting ready for new presidential leadership through our preparations for the decennial review of the university by the North Central Association, by the fund for innovation created by internal allocations (3 percent of the 1987–1988 academic budget), major progress in the Iowa 2000 fund campaign, and affirmative action developments both for faculty and students. He continued the dialogue about the teaching/research balance: "In an environment that emphasizes the development of new knowledge, students learn more than the content of the courses they take. They also learn a way of life. They learn the ethic of learning. They learn an enthusiastic commitment to the advancement of knowledge. That is why undergraduate education in a research university starts with such a great advantage."

In an interesting twist from recent months, Dick, joined by the other presidents of the regents universities, found himself defending research as a vital university function. Some of the members of the Iowa House Education Subcommittee raised questions about the amount of emphasis recently placed on job creation by the universities. At the hearing Marvin Pomerantz, president of the Board of Regents, asserted that the universities should concentrate on educational excellence rather than economic development. "That would do more for economic development and job creation than any other single thing we could do." How easily the tide of opinion turns! The year before we were frantically trying to respond to prodding from Des Moines for evidence of what we were doing to foster economic development directly; this year the emphasis had shifted to educational excellence.

On May 13, 1988, the Board of Regents chose Hunter R. Rawlings III to be the seventeenth president of the university. He would take office on August 1, succeeding Dick Remington. From 1970 to 1980 Rawlings had worked his way up the ranks in classics at the University of Colorado at Boulder. In 1980 he was appointed vice chancellor for instruction at Boulder and, in 1984, vice president for academic affairs and research and dean of the Graduate School.

While Remington had initially announced that he was not a candidate for the position of president, he did in fact allow his name to be placed in nomination for it. In a nasty turn of protocol he was called out of the commencement ceremonies in Carver-Hawkeye Arena and informed that he was not to get the job; after receiving the news he had to return to complete his duties at the ceremonies. The inexplicable lack of sensitivity in timing by the president of the Board of Regents left a deep wound from which it would take Dick a long time to recover. Immediately following the announcement of Rawlings's appointment, Dick resigned as vice president for academic affairs. He was given a one-year developmental assignment to join the University of Texas School of Public Health in Houston, following which he would return to a regular faculty position at Iowa. David Vernon of the College of Law agreed to serve as acting vice president for academic affairs and dean of faculties effective August 1, 1987. It was the second time David had held the position and under similar circumstances. As he did the first time, David made very clear that he would hold the position only until a permanent vice president had been chosen by Rawlings.

The search for my replacement had, in effect, been put on hold following President Freedman's unexpected resignation. It became clear that the one-year extension to my tenure as dean and vice president would not cover the time until a new president was in place and could choose my replacement. In March 1988 the Board of Regents then approved a second one-year extension to my term. While I was beginning to experience a bit of lame duck aura, I agreed to keep on until June 30, 1989, which did, in fact, become my termination date.

A Home for International Programs

Early in July 1987, our international activities were consolidated in the "Old Law Commons" building, now known as the International Center. Jim

Freedman, Dick Remington, and I saw this as a positive move for our international efforts. Some of the involved staff were less enthusiastic since they were presently housed, albeit in temporary facilities, in the Jefferson Building in the heart of downtown Iowa City. However, we took the view that, at long last, international education and its associated activities could be appropriately housed in a building that would do justice to the visions that we shared with the international staff.

Research

On July 13, 1987, we held a press conference in the laboratory of biology professor Barbara Stay to announce that the faculty had attracted $100 million in gifts, grants, and contracts during 1986–1987, up 13 percent from the previous year. Given the increasing competitive pressure for the available funds, the record was especially impressive. We ranked fourth in the Big Ten in federal research funding per faculty member, after Wisconsin, Michigan, and Northwestern. We held the news conference in Barbara's lab because she had been one of the successful competitors, having received $224,000 from the National Institutes of Health to study the process of reproduction in tropical cockroaches to provide impetus for the development of insect control devices. There had been no glass ceiling for Barbara!

Development

The University Press was among the university units that were prospering. Paul Zimmer, as editor of the press, met our expectations and more, having published over fifty books since his arrival in 1985. In early 1988 the unit moved into the Kuhl House, built circa 1840 from the same Devonian-age limestone as the foundation and lower floor of Old Capitol. Paul was thrilled by the ambiance of the place; the move appeared to be the capstone of the revitalization of the press.

Reflection

Dick Remington's interim was the second such presidency in the decade. During my term I had pressed the theme: "Don't miss a beat." But, inevitably, beats are missed. Major issues are quietly put on hold; major new initiatives are forgone, the effects subtle. For the sake of the university, Dick's replacement would need to restart its motors quickly to chart an exciting academic course.

6. MY RAWLINGS YEAR
1988–1989

Shortly after he took office, President Hunter R. Rawlings III announced at a meeting of the collegiate deans and vice presidents his intention to split the Office of Vice President for Educational Development and Research and Dean of the Graduate College into the Offices of Research and Graduate College, to be effective when I left office, July 1, 1989. To my knowledge the decision was made without consulting anyone in the administration. Certainly, I had no prior knowledge of his intent. Nor did he comment further about his decision when one of the deans asked, in effect, "Why fix it if the present arrangement is working well?" Other than that unanswered question, no discussion followed his announcement. I was at the meeting but, feeling that it would not be appropriate, said nothing. Needless to say, I didn't agree with his decision.

The generic issue of the relatedness of the two offices had been frequently discussed at national meetings during my tenure. The AAU universities were about evenly split between those with combined offices and those with separate offices. It was a common observation among my peers on the national level that, in those instances where the two offices were split, the graduate office suffered from lack of prestige and resources. During the last several years of my tenure, the University of Illinois did an in-depth review of its combined arrangement and concluded that it should continue. Since my retirement, the University of Minnesota has done a similar review and concluded that the two offices should be combined after years of being separate. The news release explaining that two persons would be appointed to replace me quoted President Rawlings as saying, "Relocating the deanship in the academic affairs office is part of an effort to strengthen and more fully integrate academic administration at the university."

Obviously, his position was contrary to our experience. The working relationship between my office and that of academic affairs had always been very close. In fact, from the very start of my tenure President Bowen had made it very clear that the graduate dean reported to the vice president for academic affairs in the same way as the rest of the collegiate deans. So far as I am aware, none of my previous bosses had ever raised a question about the lack of such a relationship. The wags speculated that my office was too powerful for President Rawlings's comfort. I was amused by that thought since most of my duties had been assigned, not sought.

In any event, after I left, the offices were split — budgetarily and physically. Since then, significant investments have been made in the renovations of Gilmore Hall to accommodate the two offices, and major staff increases have also been made to support each of them. It remains to be seen whether the new arrangement will continue to be viable for the long term. One thing is undeniable: the necessary and intimate relationship between graduate education and research. Two leaders or one: that is the question.

Upon my departure, Rex Montgomery, associate dean for academic affairs in the College of Medicine, was appointed acting vice president for research and Leodis Davis, acting associate vice president for academic affairs, was appointed as acting dean of the Graduate College. Even with the new arrangements it would be several years before regular heads of these two offices would be appointed.

President Rawlings also announced that he was recommending to the regents the appointment of Peter Nathan, a clinical psychologist, as vice president for academic affairs. At the time Nathan was on leave from his faculty position at Rutgers University while working at the MacArthur Foundation as a program officer. Nathan would replace David Vernon, who had been serving in the vice presidency position in an acting capacity. Ken Moll, the associate vice president for academic affairs, had already announced that he would be resigning effective June 30, 1989. Thus, there would be few holdovers when Nathan came in with his own broom.

My year working with Hunter Rawlings, the final year of my twenty-five-year administrative period, was qualitatively different from my previous years in central administration. For reasons that I have never been able to identify, I was no longer called upon to offer academic strategies and new ideas, or to respond to those generated by his office. I suddenly felt passed by. Out of that context I wrote him a letter in response to a call inviting me to a "final" retirement party before I left office. I hedged over the invitation and explained why. I noted that the past few months had been difficult for me because I seemed to have been cut out of any of the usual staff consultation and planning. I had been left, I said, with feelings of being a nonperson, feelings unique in my entire forty-one years of academic life. Consequently, I was puzzled about my being invited to a retirement party. On reflection, the party may have served a function similar to that of a funeral, a public demonstration of my demise from university administration!

But I did go to the party; it was to acknowledge Ken Moll's leaving as well as mine. There was no exchange about my letter or why I eventually dreaded to attend. From my perspective the event had the spontaneity of a wake! Such a denouement left me feeling sad and in an emotional funk for several years.

Graduate Matters

During the year our offices continued to function much as they had in the past. Under the leadership of Rudy Schulz, dean for advanced studies, we had put together the Graduate College Strategic Plan as part of the universitywide strategic planning process. In the May 1989 report we noted that our goals, in order of priority, were to increase the quality and diversity of our graduate students; maintain and strengthen the graduate degree programs of high quality; maintain and enhance the symbiotic and synergistic relation between research and graduate education through support of faculty scholarship, research, and vitality; foster interdisciplinary graduate activities, scholarship, research, and degree programs; and promote better public understanding of the mission, scope, and significance of graduate education and research. In retrospect the goals may seem idealistic at best, but they were real objectives for us. We had made progress in many of them. It was clear, however, that they were enduring goals to be pressed at every opportunity.

To some considerable extent, the list of goals reflected my personal philosophy about graduate education and was heavily influenced by what I knew about one of my predecessors. My graduate education at Iowa had been steeped in the philosophy of Carl Seashore. My mentor, Wendell Johnson, professor of speech pathology and audiology, psychology, and first chair of the newly established Department of Speech Pathology and Audiology, did his graduate work at Iowa during Seashore's tenure in office. Johnson reflected often on Seashore's philosophy of graduate education, for which he had the greatest respect. Johnson believed that the student was the heart of the matter: build a program of study around the student's interests and aptitudes by seeking out the appropriate members of the faculty wherever they might be in the university without regard to colleges and departments. That attitude was consistent with Seashore's press for the interdisciplinary approach for the university as a whole.

I was awed by the opportunity to follow in the footsteps of Seashore: scholar, administrator, and innovator. One of the things that I knew about him was that he didn't just let things happen; he took actions to shape events when he felt action was necessary. That posture became a credo for me, and I would like to think that during my tenure as graduate dean my colleagues and I didn't just let things happen either, but stepped out to introduce new ways and new opportunities for graduate education at Iowa. In everything that we proposed and did we were conscious of another of Seashore's credos: the Graduate College is composed of the faculty of the entire university and thus is the ultimate expression of the *academy* of scholars at the University of Iowa.

Research

On July 7, 1988, I sent the usual memo, this time my final one, to central administrators and deans, summarizing the gifts and contracts generated during the past six years. During the 1987–1988 fiscal year we had received a record $115 million, 14 percent greater than the previous year. In addition, we had processed $198 million in applications, a 19 percent increase over the previous year. That augured well for awards during the 1988–1989 year, since the volume of applications in the pipeline is positively related to the amount of the awards ultimately received.

Yet I knew that there were big limits to the credit our office could claim for the growth. True, we had worked hard to provide administrative channels with streamlined reviews and processing mechanisms, but for what? To assist the faculty to compete successfully for funds to support their teaching, research, and development projects, for which there were no available state-appropriated moneys. In doing so, they put themselves on the line for the most intensive reviews by their peers. Without their dedicated efforts to move out and be counted, to go the extra mile, we would not have had impressive growth charts to pass along to the press.

As I left the office I reflected on the change that had taken place in my twenty-five years in the office: from $16.5 million in funds accepted in 1964–1965 to this year's record of $115 million; what a difference twenty-five years make!

Development

Research parks affiliated with universities were springing up across the country, the North Carolina Research Triangle being an early and well-known model. Thanks to the Oakdale campus, the university had the necessary open space, a 160-acre tract in addition to the Technology Innovation Center, which was already housed in campus buildings there. President Rawlings's good experience with a research park at the University of Colorado made him comfortable with the prospect of establishing one at Iowa. Criteria were established for potential tenants, the principal ones being that no academic funds would be diverted to any of the enterprises and that there would be a complementarity between some of the expertise sought by the tenants and the research interests of the university faculty. An advisory committee that included faculty members was established to monitor the development.

Society's benchmarks are the result of individual visions and dreams. The same force results in academic initiatives as well. A prime example is the driver simulation facility on the Oakdale campus. Again Ed Haug, professor of mechanical engineering, appears on the scene. I was among the first to hear about his dream in the fall of 1988. It was so exciting to me that I agreed to arrange for him to make a presentation to the central administration decision-makers in our conference room. Another computer graphic system from the same genre that gave birth to CADSI was being proposed to simulate driving conditions for testing drivers and real automobiles. What Ed proposed would be state of the art, world class. The consensus was that seeking the funds for it was worth a try.

Up to this time the University of Michigan was considered to have the best highway-safety institute in the country. It would take many presentations and much political lobbying of the federal establishment to convince it to invest large sums of money in such a research project — where? Iowa? But Ed was undaunted and the lobbying process was begun. It would take some seven years of maneuvering before the final federal and state funding decisions were in place to start the planning for the facility now officially called the National Advanced Driving Simulator. It will be a reality approximately ten years after that first presentation in the Danner Conference Room in 1988. What is perfectly clear is that nothing would have happened if Ed hadn't gone the extra mile to press his vision.

President Rawlings referred an article from the May 10, 1989, issue of the *New York Times* entitled "Some Top Universities in Squeeze between Research and Academics" to several of us for comment. The article focused on private universities that were in the process of eliminating some fields, even departments, of study in an attempt to keep tuition levels from increasing, while at the same time redistributing some operating funds to existing programs, primarily at the undergraduate level. My response read:

> There is no question in my mind that during my time in this business there has been a shift from teaching to research. When I started teaching here it was common to have a load of twelve semester hours; now the norm is six. In my early days tenured faculty were constantly in the classroom. Today those who are get written up for their dedication to teaching! I would not argue for returning to the good old days but I would argue for return to a better balance between teaching and research.
>
> However, such a return can hardly be expected to occur among our faculty in the sciences and engineering who are successful in obtaining external funding for their work. They and we have become deeply depen-

dent on the funds they generate. Consequently we constantly give them signals of approbation through salary increases, promotions and publicity, and we make heroic internal allocations of funds, obviously at the expense of other programs largely in the humanities and arts, to make sure that they continue to do their "things" effectively.

Well, we've made little progress in biting that reallocation bullet. And the issue of teaching/research balance continues to reverberate not only within the university but throughout the state. In fact, as I write (1998), President Coleman's administration has made headlines by its pledge to get more senior faculty in the classrooms for more teaching hours.

When I left office I was already an emeritus professor in the Department of Otolaryngology — Head and Neck Surgery and in the Department of Speech Pathology and Audiology. Both departments invited me to hang my hat in their units when I moved from Gilmore Hall. I was grateful for their invitations but chose neither. I had become especially attached to the Oakdale campus during the years when it had been one of my responsibilities. Having spent the last twenty-five years of my professional life in higher education administration, I felt I would be most apt to reflect on those years rather than my earlier ones. So I chose Oakdale, where I am still happily officed.

The Summer 1989 issue of the *Spectator* carried a final article about my retirement. Its title was "User Friendly: Longtime Research Champion Supports the Arts, Science." Here are a couple of my observations taken from that interview:

> One of the roles that our office has been able to play over the years is to provide a kind of balance wheel effect, so that when there were significant external opportunities for the sciences and engineering and few for the humanities and arts, resources could be dedicated to them from internal funds. . . .
>
> The Office of Educational Development and Research has been built on the philosophy that we are here to respond to the aspirations of the faculty, to be facilitative, to be "user friendly," and to do everything we can to help them learn about opportunities for expanded support for their work. . . .
>
> These have been interesting years because this academy, as all good academies, is filled with people with lots of ideas, imagination and high motivations. To be bombarded with all of these ideas all of the time — it's very heady.

Very heady indeed.

7. THE COMPUTER INVASION

Today's World at Iowa

As of October 1997, almost 40 percent of incoming freshmen brought a computer to campus with them. If they don't have their own, they can use a computer at one of the twenty-six student computing areas, called Instructional Technology Centers (ITCs). Connected to the campus network and a file server for backup and print control, the ITCs include dot matrix and laser printers. Special equipment, such as scanners, Zip drives, CD-making units, etc., are available at select ITCs. The student computing fees (currently $49 to $165 per semester for full-time students based on the college in which the student is registered) go toward equipping these areas.

In addition, students have free e-mail accounts, with almost 98 percent of the incoming freshman registered for one. Electronic communication is widely used to communicate with professors as well as peers. All the computers in the ITCs have access to the World Wide Web. Many classes make use of the Web to find information, and many faculty members use it as part of their teaching.

Finally, students have access to several midrange computers for programming or statistical analyses. They also have access to a computer that has sixteen processors on which they can do multiprocessing. Problems too large for this system can be given time on a super computer at one of the NSF sites. Students can also access the IBM 3030, which is the university's mainframe system. Computers have clearly become an integral part of teaching and learning at the University of Iowa. But it was not always thus!

The computer truly invaded the University of Iowa, and there wasn't a consensus about how it should be seen — friend or foe! The members of the academy were split; some welcomed it with open arms and great anticipation; others saw it as an intrusion to be shunted to the side, ignored, even opposed, since it could be a drain on precious resources. This is a recounting of my perceptions about its accommodation and ultimately of its centrality at the University of Iowa.

The Early Beginnings

On March 15, 1964, John Weaver, then vice president for research and dean of the Graduate College, wrote to a professor named Gerard P. Weeg, who was at Iowa State while on sabbatical leave from Michigan State, finalizing the details for Gerry's appointment as director of the computer center and professor of mathematics at Iowa. It was a significant moment in the history of the University of Iowa; we had now identified the "general" who would lead the computer invasion in a style reminiscent of that of General George Patton!

Gerry was not to be denied. Little did I know when I was appointed in February 1965 that he would become one of my charges and that he would turn out to be similar to a precocious, impatient, talented visionary offspring who, many days, seemed bent on saving us from ourselves. Even so, I sensed from the beginning of our relationship that we were fortunate to have this man in our midst.

The computer center had been established in 1958, largely as the result of efforts by Professors E. F. Lindquist, education, and James Van Allen, physics and astronomy, to provide support for their programs in test construction and evaluation and in space physics. At the time its budget came largely from grants and contracts. When I became responsible for the center in 1965, the total contribution of the university to the operation of the center was only $46,000, out of the center's total budget of $256,000; the balance came from user fees.

Here are Professor Van Allen's recollections of the beginnings:

Beginning in 1952, I was planning on using an inexpensive technique for making physical observations at high altitudes (about 100 km) by launching small rockets carrying various sensors and detectors from balloons at altitudes of about 15 km in order to obviate the drag on the rocket in the dense lower atmosphere. One of the challenges was assessing the arrow-stability of such rockets fired from rest at approximately 15 km. I developed the appropriate differential equation and put the problem of solving it numerically to Joseph Kasper and Ernest Ray, two graduate students. We located the original Vannevar Bush mechanical differential (analog) analyzer in Cleveland where it had been transferred from MIT. Kasper inspected it but judged it too massive to move here, although we could have acquired it at no cost. But he adopted the general scheme — shafts, discs, rolling wheels, etc. — and built a working model here. This worked beautifully and was the basis for his 1955 M.S. thesis, "Construction and Application of a Mechanical Differential Analyzer."

More or less simultaneously, Ray was interested in the trajectories of cosmic rays in the Earth's magnetic field. His 1955 Ph.D. thesis and published paper were primarily analytical, not numerical. Soon thereafter, Ray, by then an assistant professor, guided Kasper's 1958 Ph.D. thesis and, in 1959, published a paper using a digital computer for the first time in our program. A quote from his paper: "However, in pursuing other and more elaborate goals, the author recently computed some 2,000 trajectories of charged particles in the field of a magnetic dipole with the use of an IBM Type 704 computer." The computer in question was located at the General Motors Technical Center in Detroit and made available to us by my arrangements with Dr. R. E. Herman, a former colleague of mine. This research by Kasper was, I believe, the first work done in our department (and perhaps in this university) using a high-speed digital computer. Kasper, later a physics professor at Cornell College for many years, is properly regarded as the pioneer in introducing us to the computer age.

All of our early 1958–60 satellite data (Explorers I, III, IV, and VII, and Pioneers III and IV) as well as all of our rocket flight data (1952–57) were handled in a primitive analog manner by displaying them on rolls of paper using pen-and-ink oscillographs (or in some cases on photographic paper using photo-oscillographs). Since 1960, we have had essential dependence on digital computers for handling our data from many, many satellites, planetary spacecraft, etc.

Early financing and use of such computers was shared with Iowa Testing Services but after some point (probably early 1960s) we had our own dedicated computers. Later the UCC [University Computing Center] was developed as the central computing facility for the campus and we were among its important customers. However, we continued to have our own Univac 418, for example, and became increasingly convinced that we could meet our needs much less expensively and more efficiently with our own dedicated system rather than relying on the UCC. This conviction led to the only significant policy disagreement that I ever had with you [Spriestersbach] over the years and was symbolized by a rather tense meeting of the Computer Committee in the late 1970s.

As of 1997, we have dozens of dedicated and general purpose high-performance computers and work stations throughout our research laboratories and, so far as I know, very little use of the University Computing Center.

The "policy disagreement" that Jim refers to was, in retrospect, the tip of the centralized vs. distributed computing iceberg. In the 1970s the computer explosion/revolution surrounded us. Computer hardware was relatively expensive. System compatibilities and wide-scale networking were still in the future. The core issue then centered around providing adequate computer service to the most — with limited resources. And for most the answer was to maintain a central computer resource and avoid incompatible distributed systems. Furthermore, we anticipated that if university units were allowed to purchase their own systems, they were apt to be ill-informed in their acquisitions and unprepared to service them. The result would be that we would have a modern-day computer Tower of Babel.

Then the Department of Physics and Astronomy came along with its computer expertise, its own funding, and its own somewhat exotic data reduction and manipulation needs. In the 1970s its wish to go its own way was seen by many to be potentially destructive of the policy, supported by the majority of members of the several computer advisory committees, to concentrate on centralized facilities only. In the end the department won the argument, and properly so. We would have saved a lot of wear and tear of individual psyches if we had recognized that exceptions to the rule are legitimate if the circumstances are truly exceptional, as they were in this case.

It's startling to realize how humble our proud beginnings were. They are eloquently described in a newspaper article, "Computer Center's Growth Continues," found in the July 22, 1965, issue of the *Daily Iowan*:

> [In 1958] the university leased an IBM 650 computer capable of storing 20,000 words and recalling any one of them in a few seconds. Researchers said with pride that in five seconds the 650 could do a problem that would take a week to solve using a desk calculator. [Four computer generations later in December 1964 the 7044 was installed which] can store 32,000 words in its memory bank and recall any word in two millionths of a second. . . . Computer use is growing so fast that Director Weeg believes multiprogramming equipment will be needed in the near future. This equipment could provide input and output terminal points at such locations as the Physics Department, the College of Engineering, the College of Medicine, the College of Business Administration, and the College of Education. Students at these terminals will be able to feed information into these computers from the classroom and get answers back in a matter of seconds. The multiprogramming of the equipment would allow 30 or 40 programs to be sent to the central processor simultaneously.

The central processor at the computer center was the only computer resource available at the time. Accessed primarily by IBM cards that were brought to the center already key punched, or key punched by center operators from the data supplied to them, the center then processed them into hard copy print-outs available for pick up, hopefully the next day. Thus, distributed terminals were a real step forward.

In 1968 the UCC had joined with eleven four-year colleges in Iowa and Illinois to form the Regional Computer Network (RCN). The purpose of the consortium was to determine together how best to provide computing for the instructional and research needs of the colleges. The RCN was a remote computer terminal network with card reader and line printer terminals on each of the eleven campuses. In 1970 UCC developed a proposal to design, program, and implement two major systems at the RCN schools: registration and business-office record keeping. It was an outreach program that was very well received.

Part of the center's budget problem was an outgrowth of the changing nature of the uses made of the central computer facilities. In the beginning, as I noted earlier, the principal users had been the Department of Physics and the Measurement Research Center (MRC), both of which brought their own funds to the table. In the 1964–1965 fiscal year together they had accounted for 61 percent of the center's income. The other major source of funding had come from the Graduate College (30 percent). By 1969 the business from MRC began to decrease and would ultimately disappear as it developed its own computing capabilities. At the same time computer technology was changing and improving almost daily. More and more educators were sensing its relevance to their teaching and research. How to cope? To what degree should the UCC attempt to meet its budget needs by seeking commercial accounts?

On July 17, 1969, then President Bowen wrote to me after we had conferred about the center's problems: "I am in accord with the proposal that the center take on commercial contracts to replace those with MRC which have recently been lost and to make the center economically viable. As in the past, such commercial contracts should be entered into only under the following conditions." He then went on to specify the conditions: acquire only the equipment needed for the university; commercial contracts entered into only to use surplus time; commercial contracts should have educational significance and should be conducted in such as way as to minimize abrasive relationships with competitors; commercial rates should be at full cost; and, where possible, nonprofit institutions should be served. Finally, he urged that the computer center take on enough outside work to avoid deficits.

In mid-June 1970 the university hosted a national meeting with support from the National Science Foundation on "Computers in the Undergraduate Curricula." Over seven hundred persons attended and some eighty presentations were made. The nub of the conference had to do with the degree of centrality of the computer in undergraduate instruction; did it make a positive difference or didn't it? In my remarks I noted that about one thousand of the nation's twenty-five hundred colleges now had computers available for instruction, suggesting that many educational leaders had clearly concluded that the computer was a significant, even necessary, ingredient in college education. I waxed philosophical: "The final question facing educators is whether computers and the 're-oriented curricula' can make a noticeable change in the 'misery quotient of society.'" That question remains unanswered to this day, but it's clear that the marriage, for better or for worse, is not one subject to divorce.

Very early in these developments, the supporting costs for the emerging technology became a difficult issue. For example, Gerry Weeg pointed out in 1970 that the College of Engineering was moving ahead aggressively to acquire computer-associated equipment. Who was to pay for the costs of operating it, the college or the computer center (which meant, in the end, the Graduate College)? There were no budget provisions for such costs in any existing university budgets at the time. Who would/should have the responsibility for belling this cat? It took several years for a budgeting/funding pattern to emerge.

Internal Outreach

Prompted by good "instructors," especially Gerry Weeg, we announced that we would sequester some of the Graduate College funds that had been allocated in recent years to academic computer users and make them available for new and innovative ideas requiring computers. We established committees to review the proposals. We dedicated $90,000 (out of $202,000 available in our office for computer support) for the program in the view that the more turned on the faculty became with the computer's capacity to enhance instruction, the easier it would be to justify expanding budgets for new equipment and support services. However, the special allocations lasted only two years. Budget cutbacks for the entire university forced us to return to the original departmental allocation scheme.

The External Constituent Dilemma

Our computing capacity had now developed to the point where folks outside of the university were beginning to take note. On January 21, 1971, Gerry Weeg wrote to me: "The Rock Island Arsenal has assumed the role of one of the principal users of the UCC. Authorities at the arsenal have indicated a desire to increase the level of their operation with the computer center. Shall this increase be encouraged or not; or shall all relations with the arsenal be terminated?"

Attached to the memo were projections in considerable detail for the income and expenses of the center. It had been determined with great care that none of the work that the center did for the arsenal was classified. With its business we could plan for regular equipment upgrades and increases in the level of service provided to the university. Without its business the center would have to claw to stand still, which really meant falling back.

On February 6, 1971, the University Computer Committee held an extended meeting on the matter. The committee finally approved a motion (four to three) that "the UCC not renew any contract with the Rock Island Arsenal, even if the alternative is restricting the use of available facilities." The committee recognized that mixed moral and technical considerations affected the vote. We ignored the vote because operational realities required that we continue doing business with the arsenal, a decision that would have repercussions later on, when a couple of the members of the Iowa legislature asked for justification of the practice.

The issue of nonuniversity business was presented to President Boyd. He responded to me on February 9. "I think, as a matter of policy, it is unwise to rely upon an outside user to finance major expansion of the computer center, let alone use existing available time. Therefore, I believe that in the future the university must seek to support the computer center from within, even though that may involve a restriction on expansion of computer facilities." "Restriction" is the key here. There were faculty members who were technically astute enough to see the tremendous possibilities for the technology. There were those less astute who were not convinced of the need to make exceptions to insure that the use of the computer at Iowa kept pace with the technical advancements.

On July 14 Provost Ray Heffner responded to an inquiry from state representative William Gluba concerning our provision of computer service to the arsenal. Heffner noted that the arsenal had purchased 16.2 percent of the services provided by the UCC during fiscal 1971. He included a background statement. Here are some excerpts:

The university's relationship with the Rock Island Arsenal developed because of the arsenal's interest in the theoretical work of members of the university faculty primarily in mathematics and engineering. . . . Our faculty members who are working with the arsenal staff are not experts in military tactics. However, they are interested in learning how to use computers in the management of large, complex systems involving the consideration of many parameters. . . . In addition, the members of our computer center staff learn how to deal with program problems relating to

complex systems. . . . It should also be noted that very difficult philosophical problems are raised if, as a matter of course, the university prohibits its faculty from working with the arsenal or other defense related
establishments. To do so would be making a moral judgment about the
propriety of the activities of a duly constituted and supported agency of
the United States government. . . . To impose categorical restrictions on
work of our faculty in consideration of some possible immoral applications of the work implies that someone can make valid predictions concerning the application of the work. The university accepts the creation
and dissemination of knowledge as its main missions. It has studiously
avoided making moral judgments of the work of its faculty so long as their
work is available for public scrutiny and peer review.

Centralization/Decentralization?

Professor Van Allen made a proposal that the Department of Physics and
Astronomy should be permitted to establish its own computer system on the
grounds that the service would be cheaper and more efficient in serving the
needs of the department. The issue of centralized versus distributed computing was to prove to be a contentious issue between the department and me
since I felt that I had to do what was best for the larger university community.
If such departments as physics and astronomy, which had large external resources to draw on for its computing needs, were allowed to go their separate
ways, the pool of resources for the rest of the university would be diminished,
possibly to the point that their needs would be inadequately served. In retrospect, it was, of course, a lost cause to resist the inexorable move to distributed
computing.

It was an issue that Professor Van Allen remembers well, too. He reflected
on it in an interview that I had with him on October 4, 1995:

> I was at the time a very strong supporter of the computer center, which
> centralized all the university facilities. But as life sort of developed in the
> subsequent few years, we grew increasingly dissatisfied with trying to get
> our work done in the computer center; we had in the department techni-
> cal staff and some very good computer people. We understood what we
> needed to do and thought we understood it much better and could service
> ourselves much better with a much more modest but specific computer
> within our department. It resulted in one of the only real shoot-outs that
> I remember with your administration. . . . You were flatly or strongly
> against our developing our own independent competence to handle our
> data in our department. We did see distributed computing, not as clearly

as we can now, but at that time I think we were in the forefront of recognizing that was how things were going to go. You had the proper administrative position of not wanting to see that on the grounds that it was undercutting the function of the computer center, diminishing its support and diminishing its significance on campus.

During the transition the several computer committees reviewed requests for separate computer units in part because compatibility with the system as a whole was an issue and in part because of considerations of duplication. We could only speculate then that the cost of computers might decline to the point where distributed computing would be the standard of the day except for the most exotic computing needs, which could only be handled centrally.

Computers in Instruction

Many folks within the university were still not persuaded that the computer was an important tool for instruction, especially at the undergraduate level. Happily, there were some pioneers. One of them was Professor G. R. Boynton in the Department of Political Science. On August 6, 1971, he wrote a letter to President Boyd. In it he described how he had used the computer in a summer course on public opinion at the undergraduate level. He said in closing: "There are an increasing number of courses that require active student involvement in analysis of empirical data. This is our laboratory. I cannot believe that the laboratory budgets for the physical and biological sciences were cut forty-five percent, but ours was. Somehow that has to change if the Political Science Department is to do an effective job of educating our students." The views of the Bob Boyntons were very necessary ingredients in a gradual and grudging shift in opinion about the place that the computer could and should play in instruction. A small group of us saw the implications that computers had for the university, but we felt like voices crying in a wilderness composed of faculty and administrators who were comfortable with the status quo and unprepared for the realities of the computer era.

In late 1971 NSF awarded a grant to five universities in addition to Iowa to form a consortium for "uncovering computer oriented curriculum material, classifying and cataloguing it, and disseminating it." It was called CONDUIT (Cornell, Oregon, North Carolina, Duke, Iowa, and Texas), with its headquarters located at the University of Iowa. Its first director was James W. Johnson, about whom we will hear much more later. Gerry Weeg was the driving force behind this project, and it was one more of his efforts to insert the computer into instruction.

In January 1972 the computer center staff made a report to the Faculty

Senate Budgetary Planning and Review Committee. It was a first — testimony to the growing awareness of issues related to the use of computer technology on the campus. One item stands out in the twenty-page document that the UCC staff provided to the committee in advance of the meeting: "The university is served by a computer center costing over a million dollars a year, and the university has firm budgeting for only a fourth of that. The equipment in use is old, and one day must be replaced. No provision exists for replacement."

In July 1972 I joined several members of the UCC staff in a visit to the IBM facilities in Poughkeepsie, New York, to be briefed on some of the latest computer technology developments. It became clear during the visit that IBM was taking a position that the increasing demands for support from computer technology both for instruction and research were such that a hierarchy of computers had to be developed that could be integrated and draw their strength from a core facility and, further, that these systems would ultimately include regional and national networks. I reminded IBM at the meeting that this was contrary to the position they had held (one big black box was adequate) when they reviewed our computer planning during the Bowen era.

Nevertheless, when I got back to campus, what I had learned caused me again to raise the question of possibly integrating our computer systems, especially those of UCC and Administrative Data Processing (ADP). I was even brash enough to predict that our library operations would be computerized! In the past, such discussions had inevitably touched raw nerves. ADP had a fine reputation for getting the wash out — financial accounting, payroll, etc. It also worked in a very different culture from that of UCC. But the idea of consolidation was before its time. It wouldn't be until many years later that the two systems and more would be folded into one administrative structure.

Gerry Weeg was not only a visionary but a prophet. On August 1, 1972, he sent me a memo entitled "Computing and Instruction." Here are some excerpts:

> Computer center directors have been telling university presidents that, though computing is essential to a university, it is cheap. . . . The purpose of that charade was to convince administrators that computing could remain on campus. . . . In the process computer centers have become the thralldom of research and commercial activity. . . . When economic stringencies descended upon the nation, they also fell upon computer centers. The result . . . was a strict rationing of computer funds. At Iowa, computing use for instruction and research funded by the university fell from $700,000 in 1970–1971 to $370,000 in 1971–1972. . . . We may be embark-

ing on a phase of university life in which we identify instruction as the most important part of it. . . . There are those who believe me that computing is as integral to instruction as the other great resource, the library. . . . I see that it is imperative for the university to embark on the creation of a mass access interactive computing system. . . . We need to place large quantities of terminals on this campus. They must be truly available to students, so that I can visualize clumps of ten or more in multiple locations on campus. . . . The use of this system must be free to the student.

In mid-1972 an ad hoc Committee on Computing composed of four deans (including me), two faculty members, and two administrators prepared a report entitled "Computing in Undergraduate Education at the University of Iowa: A Proposal to Make Iowa a Leader in the Use of the Emerging Educational Technology." It really had been written by Gerry Weeg, although the rest of us fully subscribed to its contents. Known as the "dream document," it envisioned in detail the use of computers distributed throughout the campus, providing support both for teaching and research. But it became more than that. It truly became the blueprint for the expansion of the computer in instruction at Iowa.

The initial implementation of the plan called for setting up some prototype training situations. Sixteen terminals were to be placed in the College of Business Administration, eight in the College of Education, and eight in the College of Liberal Arts (dedicated to the Departments of Geography, Sociology, Political Science, Psychology, and Linguistics). These academic units were chosen because of the judgment that they were ready to take advantage of the technology. Frankly and unabashedly, we felt that they would sell the system because of their readiness and enthusiasm to move ahead.

More models followed. In the case of business administration, Stanford University and the University of Chicago had already developed packages that could be used at Iowa. In the liberal arts, Dartmouth College had established a well-publicized interactive computerized instructional program. Today, it's hard to imagine how daring we thought the "dream document" plan was. We hawked it with a certain amount of bravado as well as conviction. However, it was put in motion, too slowly of course for Gerry Weeg, and it became the blueprint for the steps that led to our present system of interactive clusters.

In the fall of 1973 the UCC established the Computer-Assisted Instruction (CAI) lab, thanks to the generosity of the Iowa Measurement Research Foundation. The system included an HP 2000F time-sharing computer with thirty-two terminals. The new director of the lab, Bobby Brown, in an interview with a *Daily Iowan* reporter, said that Gerry Weeg hoped to make Iowa the "Dartmouth of the West," meaning full implementation of the dream document. The lab had the mission of working with faculty to design and evaluate ways in which computers could enhance instruction. Its establishment is another demonstration that we had the technical and philosophical leadership necessary to move us along. The lack of available equipment was the millstone, a fact that Gerry Weeg never let us forget. He noted to the *DI* reporter who did the CAI story that in 1974 the academic departments had available to them only .004 percent more money for computer services than they did during the 1969–1970 year, while the ADP had received a 33 percent increase during the same period. From an educational point of view it was a galling comparison.

Nevertheless, the budget for the UCC expanded. George Chambers, then executive vice president, was keenly aware of the issues and made every effort to be supportive. He allowed us to run deficits, with prior approval, on the assumption that end-of-year funds could be found to cover the deficits. It was a risky strategy, but, happily for all of us, it worked. It enabled the university to stay in the computer technology league, albeit never in the top rank.

On May 14, 1974, Jack Esbin, associate director of the UCC, sent me a summary report of our progress with the dream plan. Here is a paragraph from that report: "The experience of the Liberal Arts Center and the interest expressed by the Colleges of Engineering, Law, and Medicine are probably more than we could have expected this early in the 'dream.' Business Administration is a winner. It seems clear that the plan will succeed if we can only keep up with the demand being generated. An absolute minimum of one new system each year now seems critical to keep things moving."

By this time several of the surrounding public schools (for example, Decorah, Mason City, and Cedar Rapids) were watching our move to instructional computers closely and making plans to introduce their students to the technology also. Repeatedly, I expressed the opinion to my central administration colleagues that the graduates of these public-school programs would have expectations about the facilities of the colleges and universities that they would consider when choosing which one to attend. Naturally, I was not unhappy to have these allies in the campaign to integrate the computer into our educational programs.

In reviewing this history today, an obvious response might be, "What's the big deal?" It's helpful to remember that IBM was still the dominant supplier of computers in the early 1970s. At that time it was making no moves, publicly at least, to depart from the centralized, batch-processing delivery mode. Yet there were the Gerry Weegs who realized that the technology was available to make the system more accessible to users.

The Hewlett-Packard company was one of the vendors giving serious attention to these expanded possibilities. It was willing to work with us in devising a system that would be available real time to the user with a hookup to the large batch-processing IBM unit. Our first prototype HP system was installed to serve as the "field experiment" of the dream document. The second HP system was purchased by the College of Dentistry, which agreed to make fourteen of the thirty-two ports available for campus use. These extra ports were initially assigned to hospital and health administration, mathematics, dramatic art, classics, pathology, and engineering. I loved the potpourri of academic units.

The third HP unit came to us as the result of a joint agreement with Hewlett-Packard for software development. Then came the fourth HP unit, provided by the Iowa Measurement Research Foundation for the CAI lab that I have already cited. We heralded each of these acquisitions as newsworthy events, as indeed they were. In those days Iowa was a true pioneer in moving the computer to the user for real-time access.

Transitions

The UCC and the university were jolted in late October 1974 when Gerry Weeg suddenly relinquished his post as director of the UCC; he had just learned that he had a malignant brain tumor. I appointed an acting director of the UCC while we took stock. Little did I know then what a sea of trouble awaited us in finding a permanent, long-term leader for the UCC before we were ready to move forward again.

In August 1975, after an extended search, the Board of Regents approved my recommendation to appoint Howard Dockery to succeed Gerry Weeg as director of the computer center. Howard came to us from the University of Mississippi, where he had been director of the computer center and an assistant professor of mathematics. We looked forward to his leadership in helping us steer the computer ship through yeasty times.

The demands for computer time for teaching and research were increasing at an unprecedented rate. The computer center was "earning" its budget based on documented usage principally by drawing on allocations solely for that purpose that the Graduate College made to departments. However, the allocations did not cover the costs of upgrading and replacing equipment. As I noted earlier, we expected, even planned for, deficits at the end of the year, covering them from end-of-the-year university balances. Dockery, charged to maximize services at the most economical cost, worked hard at fulfilling this goal. In doing so, however, he alienated many of the computer center staff, so much so that intense distrust was generated, the center was in turmoil, and I was contacted almost daily about the intolerable state of affairs. Reluctantly and as a last resort, I removed Dockery from his position, slightly less than three years after he was hired, and reassigned him as a special assistant to me pending the final resolution of the matter. I appointed James Johnson, one of the center managers, to be acting director of the center.

Immediately after his suspension, Dockery charged that some of the computer center employees were involved in illegal activities stemming from unauthorized use of university facilities, payment for travel expenses for trips taken for private purposes, and possible conflicts of interest with companies that sold computer equipment to the university — despite the requirement that he or a staff member designated by him was required to approve all of his staff members' travel.

As a result of Dockery's allegations, President Boyd immediately asked the state auditor to conduct a special audit. State Auditor Lloyd Smith found that there was not sufficient evidence to support Dockery's charges. Nevertheless, Dockery filed a lawsuit against me and the university, charging that his job suspension and transfer was "wrongful, intentional, and malicious," that it damaged his reputation, and had prompted the University of Nebraska to withdraw a job offer as director of its computer systems. He sought $500,000 in damages. The trial on the charges would wait until the summer of 1979, after which the court ruled in favor of the defendants on all counts.

On October 27, 1977, I gave a talk at the annual fall conference of EDUCOM (Educational Computing) entitled "Distributed Academic Computing: Administrative Considerations." It was a significant statement, not because of the wisdom it contained but because it signaled a recognition that distributed computing was here with its own unique set of issues: responsibility for funding, maintenance, networking, and space. I felt some relief because, at long last, with decentralization came shared responsibility. By this time it was clear that the faculty and student body users would be more than ample to drive the budget demands. To be sure, some units were more effective in that drive than others. Our central obligation was to insure that reasonable access was available to all.

Jim Johnson's appointment as the regular director of the computing center was confirmed by the Board of Regents effective September 1, 1979. I had become acquainted with Jim as a result of my meetings with Gerry Weeg and his staff. In those meetings Jim stood out because of his well-articulated comments during our discussions. I liked his spirit, and I thought he would be able to bring the kind of fearless leadership to the center that it needed. That proved to be the case. Jim brought an enthusiasm and spirit to the center that was remarkably similar to that of Gerry Weeg.

Nearly six years later, on January 21, 1985, I got a letter that I knew would come sooner or later and had anticipated with dread. Jim Johnson, who had by then established a reputation as an innovative and effective administrator of the caliber that was highly sought on the national scene, informed me that he would be leaving on May 1 to become vice chancellor for computing at the University of Houston. I understood that it was a unique opportunity for Jim and that it was right for him to move on to new professional challenges. First Gerry Weeg and then Jim Johnson. How lucky can a university administrator and a university be!

In May 1985, the Board of Regents approved our proposal to establish the Iowa Computer-Aided Engineering Network (ICAEN) and to assess a special computer network fee from each engineering student ($100 per semester for full-time students). This action was taken because we could not provide our students with a state-of-the-art education without access to the technology and because we had to spread the costs to achieve our goal. The action was requested only after extensive consultation with the students and a great deal of soul-searching about alternative ways to finance the project. In all candor we assumed that students across the campus would be drawn into this plan sooner or later, and such has proven to be the case.

Also in May the Academic Computer Services Committee submitted its final report for the year. Among its major recommendations were to place a workstation in each faculty office within five years, to establish a pilot project for use of library information resources, to train and encourage the use of BITNET (Because It's Time Network) by the university community, to establish a campuswide electronic mail system, and to provide additional instructional computer clusters, insisting that space be provided for such clusters in all new and renovated buildings. We had faced up to the issues of centralization versus decentralization, finding and supporting qualified leaders, and generating ways, usually with bits and pieces of funding, to maintain technological currency. The "outlandish" elements of Gerry Weeg's dream — as perceived by some of the skeptics who weren't convinced of the coming centrality of the computer not only in research but also in instruction — have been met, even exceeded.

8. STUDENT UNREST:
THE WAR AND THE ROSES

"Those who wish to return home may do so without penalty" — words from an announcement by President Boyd on May 10, 1970, giving students the unprecedented option of returning home without completing their spring semester final examinations. He had made this difficult decision in the light of safety concerns stemming from persistent student disturbances. What follows is a recounting of the turbulence during the years 1965 to 1972 at Iowa. They were unique times on college and university campuses across the nation. Although the tragic Kent State episode of May 4, 1970, is frequently pinpointed nowadays as the trigger for the wave of student unrest, difficulties began several years before that, fired in part by the unpopular war in Vietnam and the draft, but only in part. Arthur Bonfield, professor of law and a longtime adviser to President Boyd, characterizes the period:

I like to call it the "period of the late unpleasantness," which was the period on this campus of the late 1960s to the early 1970s when a whole series of national things were happening and were mirrored by effects on this campus. It was the confluence of the civil rights emancipation movement throughout the country which, of course, had impact here, coupled by the Vietnam War and the social upheaval that accompanied it.

That was a very difficult, trying time because almost everything was up for challenge and not only things relating to people's views about the Vietnam War. It related to teaching, the role of faculty, the role of students, the role of authority, the role of what had been perceived values in the academy. All of those things were under challenge and required in some way a response from the university. That was a cataclysmic period in university time.

This recounting of those times will support Bonfield's assessment that they were indeed times of great change. I have entitled it "The War and the Roses" because this era had its pluses as well as minuses, with the result that universities emerged from them stronger and more vital than before.

Chronological Review of Events, 1965–1975

The decade was filled with events — daily, even hourly. The newspaper headlines and notes of those years chronicle the story. Unless otherwise noted, the headlines and excerpts are from the *Daily Iowan*, the university student-managed newspaper. They seem especially relevant since they reveal what the editors considered to be the top events of the day.

July 29, 1965 (AP): "President Doubles the Draft Quota." "President Johnson said monthly draft calls will be more than double, from 17,000 men to 35,000, to help increase U.S. forces in Vietnam from 75,000 to 125,000 troops."

July 29, 1965 (AP): "Married Men Facing Draft." "Double draft calls may mean that some married Iowans in the 24 to 25-year age bracket will be inducted into the Army."

October 21, 1965: "U of I Student Burns Draft Card during 'Sound Off.'" "Smith [a university student] said that 'Now is the time, because of my own sense of dignity, my own sense of morality, to burn my draft card.' . . . Smith faces the possibility of five years in prison and a $10,000 fine under a law signed last August 30."

October 22, 1965: "SDS Backs Steve Smith, Soldier Talks to Meeting." Part of the SDS (Students for a Democratic Society) statement issued at the meeting: "We applaud the moral courage necessary to confront the massed power of the U.S. government. The law was drafted in a spirit of hysteria and we cannot understand how the burning of a scrap of paper should lead to five years in jail." An unnamed U.S. Special Forces sergeant on campus at the time responded, "You all have a common heritage which cannot be denied. . . . The generations that went before you did not turn their backs on the law of the land."

October 26, 1965: "Fine Administration" editorial. "The University of Iowa has one of the finest atmospheres of academic freedom in the country. All thinking students — no matter what ideas they may hold to — should support an administration that not only allows, but actually encourages its students to think seriously about the world in which they live."

November 19, 1965: "Addis Says Protests Show Repugnance to U.S. Policy." Laird Addis, a faculty member in the Department of Philosophy: "The new militancy of those opposed to U.S. foreign policy has been preceded or paralleled by a new militancy in that policy itself. American intervention in other nations' affairs has taken on a crudity and a vulgarity which is opening the eyes of an increasing number of Americans."

January 29, 1966 (AP): "Selective Service to Revive Use of Tests, Class Ranks." "The Selective Service System announced . . . it is returning to the use of a testing system and class standing as guides for local draft boards in granting college student deferment" [upper half of freshman class, upper two thirds of sophomore class, upper three fourths of junior class, all senior class; graduate students carrying nine or more semester hours and making "normal progress" toward a degree usually deferred for two years for a master's degree].

January 11, 1967: From Howard Bowen's address to the faculty. "I would like to ask the support of the faculty in keeping this university as it is today, a place where we reason together as we plan our own future, not a place where we pressure and threaten one another and in doing so invite outside interference and jeopardize our traditional and indispensable autonomy."

November 2, 1967: "Antiwar Protest at Union Erupts into Violence." "Busloads of university students were hauled off to jail Wednesday [November 1] after a demonstration punctuated by occasional wild melees. The demonstration had sought to bar Marine Corps recruiters from interviewing officer candidates. [President Bowen said] 'Students involved in violations of university regulations concerning [rights to access] of fellow students will be subject to disciplinary action through regular university procedures.'"

December 1, 1967: Statement by M. L. Huit, dean of students. "Of the 108 persons arrested November 1 at the Iowa Memorial Union, twenty-two were non-students and hence not subject to discipline by the university [eleven of these had at some time been students]. Of the eighty-six students arrested, five have since canceled their registrations and are no longer enrolled. We are in the process of notifying some seventy students that they are on disciplinary probation. . . . It is unfortunate that action must be taken for offenses largely motivated by a deep and emotional concern for those involved in the Vietnam War. In their zeal to express their concern, however, these students overstepped the bounds of responsible student freedom by contravening the rights of other students and members of the academic community, and the university cannot permit this to happen."

December 6, 1967: "Protesters Lead Cops on Wild Race to the Tune of 'Dow Must Go Now.'" "By 4 P.M. [December 5] 18 persons had been arrested, more than 100 law enforcement officers had been led on wild goose chases around campus and through Iowa City, and numerous persons had been introduced to a chemical spray called Mace. The rally was against the Vietnam War in general and Dow Chemical Co. in particular. . . . Dow . . . was at the Business Placement Office interviewing prospective recruits."

December 8, 1967: Excerpt from a memo on "points of agreement" from the Bail Fund Committee, a nonpartisan student group. "(a) That on December 5, 1967, representatives of various law enforcement agencies appeared on this campus and did violently, indiscriminately, and arbitrarily beat, gas, curse, demean, and arrest members of this academic community and their families and friends; and that (b) an effort should be made to enlist financial and moral support from all possible sources so that money and influences may be used to supply bail to those arrested . . . in what seems to the committee to constitute an official purge of students, faculty, staff and their families and friends who are active or vocal in or sympathetic to the anti-war movement on this campus."

December 15, 1967: President Bowen's statement at the monthly Board of Regents meeting. "I am not happy about the student demonstrations and the wake of publicity and criticism and suspicion that follow them. The last one was effectively organized and succeeded in turning criticism toward the police and the university and away from the demonstrators. Many non-students and a few faculty were involved. Also, it becomes increasingly probable that a hard core of Maoists and of student power advocates are actively leading the movement.

"Beginning last year, when the first assaults were made on our placement office, the university has steadfastly pursued the policy that all services of the university must be equally available to all students, and that all regular operations of the institution must continue without interruption. This policy has been followed consistently — when necessary with the assistance of the police. The university has imposed penalties on identifiable students who have broken university regulations, and does not condone illegal or obstructive behavior.

"At the same time, the university has attempted to be patient, remembering that the students concerned are mostly young men and women of high ideals who feel strongly about certain social issues. Moreover, the university has been careful to avoid any infringement on freedom of speech and thought, and to observe due process in all penalties.

"The number of students involved in the disturbances is of the order of one percent of the student body. This group is augmented by a considerable number of young men and women who are not students. The overwhelming majority of the students, though they are concerned in various ways about the war and other social and political problems, are not involved in the disturbances except occasionally as bystanders and are carrying on their work in a normal way. In fact, the university as a whole is enjoying a very productive year."

January 24, 1968: Minutes from collegiate deans' meeting concerning enrollment and the draft. "Students who started the second (or higher) year in fall 1967 are exempt but those who began graduate study then are eligible for the draft. Deans Rhoades and Spriestersbach estimated that the enrollment in the Graduate College will decrease by 925 (19 percent) and the Law School by 160."

February 21, 1968: "Camel's Back Is Breaking," excerpt from *DI* editorial quoting an editorial from the *Daily Cardinal*, University of Wisconsin. "We are fighting a war that no one understands, that no one likes and that millions oppose. More tragic still, we are fighting a war that no one controls. . . . It is time the university, our administrators, and our faculty followed the lead of the students. It is time they said, as a university, as administrators, and as a faculty, that they condemn the war in Vietnam and call for its end. Now."

February 29, 1968: Excerpts from a university memo from Vice President for Academic Affairs Boyd entitled "University of Iowa Students and the Draft." "Difficult though it may be to do at a time such as this, the 'draftable' male student should try to concentrate on continuing his educational goals. . . . It obviously behooves men to be prepared for the possibility, to know what the university is doing and will do to help keep their draft boards apprised of their progress, and to know university policies relating to interrupted studies." [Topics then covered: liaison with Selective Service, proportional credit, proportional refund of fees, reporting student status, resumption of studies, financial assistance, and interrupted programs.]

April 19, 1968: Excerpts from my memo to Bowen and Boyd concerning the university and the draft. "Our position has been that we could not defend the need to defer individual half-time teaching assistants as critical to the operation of the undergraduate program at the university. Further, we have urged all to keep calm and have counseled departments to appoint draft-eligible, competitive applicants to assistantships, traineeships and fellowships. In support of this counsel is our conviction, without any solid basis in fact, that DOD will announce in May or June that it is calling for draftees according to certain age breakdowns."

May 1, 1968: Excerpts from a special bulletin from Gustave O. Arlt, president of the Council of Graduate Schools in the United States. "We have reluctantly come to the conclusion that there will be no administrative changes in the Selective Service System in time to save us from a bad situation in the fall of 1968. . . . We will continue to keep Congress informed of the scandalous confusion that the present law has produced."

October 14, 1968: Excerpt from IMPORTANT NOTICE to college and university presidents from the director of the National Science Foundation concerning a congressional provision in the appropriation to NSF for 1969. "That if an institution of higher education receiving funds hereunder determines after affording notice and opportunity for hearing to an individual attending, or employed by, such institution, that such individual has . . . willfully refused to obey a lawful regulation or order of such institution and that such refusal was of a serious nature and contributed to the disruption of the administration of such institution, then the institution shall deny any further payment to, or for the benefit of, such individual."

November 2, 1968: "SDS Ignores Warnings, Hold Anti-Code Rally." "Members of Students for a Democratic Society and other speakers blasted the 'repressiveness of the university' and 'its involvement in the corporate structure of America' at a teach-in rally [on the east steps of Old Capitol] Friday noon [November 1]. The rally, whose expressed purpose was to 'violate the Code of Student Life' lasted about two and one-half hours and was attended by a stationary group of about 125 persons."

December 7, 1968: "SDS Stages Repeat of Anti-Code Rally." "[SDS], already threatened with disciplinary action for holding an unauthorized rally on Nov. 1, held another rally Friday afternoon [December 6]. . . . The main purposes of the rally, according to the SDS were to violate the Code of Student Life and to show support for three students charged with violating the Code. . . . Howard J. Erhlich, associate professor of sociology and anthropology . . . and Robert F. Sayre, associate professor of English, also spoke at the rally [in support of the demands]."

February 7, 1969: "Tear Gas Routs Symposium." "A tear gas bomb exploded in the Union Main Lounge . . . sending 1,200 persons scattering and delaying the final session of an explosive Symposium on Student Power. . . . The symposium moved upstairs to the Ballroom without incident. . . . The symposium has been under continual fire since it began. Young Americans for Freedom (YAF) began the protest against the speakers who were brought here and brought several state legislators to observe the conference. Most of the legislators were appalled by instances of obscene language used at the first . . . session and have been criticizing the conference since returning to Des Moines."

February 13, 1969: "Bowen Urges Cool Heads/Boyd Praised." "Bowen cautioned all legislators not to overreact to the very small minority of activists who are on any campus. 'What the activists want is publicity. . . . The best way to handle them is with the least amount of attention.' . . . The Faculty Council . . . commended . . . Boyd for the dignity and presence of mind he showed at the symposium. . . . Boyd . . . was on the stage during the session in which objectionable language was used by a former student. He has been criticized by some state legislators for not attempting to end the session. Boyd replied to that criticism by saying he thought any interference on his part at that time would have resulted in violence."

February 14, 1969 (AP): "Campus Demonstrations Spread Across the Country." "More than 30 persons were arrested at the University of California at Berkeley. . . . Tear gas and bared bayonets were used by police and National Guardsmen at the University of Wisconsin at Madison to control moving bands of demonstrators who ranged in number from 500 to 3,000. . . . Police fired tear gas canisters at Duke University students . . . in a demonstration that followed the 12-hour occupation of the administration building by 30 to 40 black students. . . . In New York about 100 City College students invaded the school's administration building and occupied two floors of offices for four and a half hours. . . . About 400 students at the University of Chicago . . . voted against ending their occupation of the administration building immediately. The occupation was in its 15th day. The university suspended 22 demonstrators, bringing the total suspended to 80."

May 7, 1969 (AP): "$91.4 Million Regents Bill with 'Riot' Rider Passed." "The appropriation bill, as passed, contains a stiff 'antiriot' provision which, in effect, would bar from the state's three universities any student or faculty member convicted of promoting or taking part in a riot resulting in property damage or personal injury."

May 7, 1969: "Students Extend Boycott for 2 Days — Class Attendance Estimated at 50% — Sutton Declares University Closed." "[Dean Philip Hubbard said he] 'was not sure what benefits the group expected to gain from the continued boycott. If it is an attempt to gain publicity for the cause of lowering tuition, the publicity should be directed at the group they are trying to influence — the Iowa legislature.'"

May 10, 1969: "The 'Siege' of Old Capitol — All Quiet on Eastern Front." "The university employed the oldest known method of keeping people out of somewhere they shouldn't be in on Friday [May 9] — they locked the doors."

May 10, 1969: "Old Cap 'March' Becomes 'Sit-in' on Tuition Boost." "About 14 students marched on Old Capitol Friday morning [May 9] saying that they intended to take over the building. . . . [They] demanded that Huit [dean of students] obtain for them a copy of the university's proposed budget so that they could call a referendum on priorities [in the light of proposed tuition increases]."

August 3, 1969: "Campus Calm, but Some Students Simmer," *Cedar Rapids Gazette,* from an interview with a graduate student who described himself as a "Marxist-socialist by conviction, with reservations," from a series of interviews with acknowledged "left wing" students in an attempt to explain why the Iowa campus had been relatively calm. "[President-elect Boyd] has already passed one big test. That time he was at a student power conference and a student asked a long rambling question using every four letter word in the book; that was a set-up, pure and simple. I mean it was planned. I know that for a fact. The so-called 'Yippie' group on campus set that student up to bait Boyd in hopes that Boyd would try and shut him up, in which case the 'Yippie' politicos were prepared to raise the issue of 'Free speech and assembly.' . . . If they could get Boyd to make a fool of himself, to lose his cool, they could say free speech was denied here. . . . But Boyd foxed them . . . by staying in there and keeping calm."

August 10, 1969: "Iowa Student Protest Movement Split," *Cedar Rapids Gazette.* "In summary, the three student protesters at the University of Iowa interviewed expressed the views that violence is a necessary weapon for those who believe in closing down the university altogether; violence is to be deplored, but is probably inevitable in connection with student demonstration at Iowa; and violence is possible at Iowa if responsible student protest leaders lose control of the various left-wing groups on campus."

September 27, 1969 (AP): "Nixon Calls for End to Viet War in '70 but Wants No Deadline for Pullout."

September 30, 1969: "Committee Sets Moratorium Plans — Antiwar Boycott Teach-in Oct. 15." The article announces "a vigil by the American Friends [during which] a list of war dead will be read"; "[a] 'teach-in' . . . from 11 A.M. to 1 P.M. on the Pentacrest"; "a candlelight march from City Park to Old Capitol"; "boycott of classes for the entire day"; "the issuing of daily pamphlets of Associated Press war roundup reports."

October 7, 1969: "October 15, 1969: Day of Inquiry," university memo, Office of the President. "I have been requested to suspend all classes on October 15. I decline to do so for two reasons: (1) As a matter of practice, adherence to class schedules and the question of attendance have been primarily collegiate matters at this university. . . . (2) Even if I felt that decisions of class schedules and attendance should be withdrawn from the colleges, I would not be inclined to suspend classes because of the internal civil liberties issues involved. . . . The agonizing question of Vietnam itself [and associated complex issues] . . . cannot be realistically discussed without considering such factors as institutional autonomy and the politicization of the university."

October 16, 1969: "University Pauses for Moratorium — 6,000 Take Part in Candlelit Rally — Moratorium Is Opposed by 3 Groups." "An eighth of the population of Iowa City marched from College Hill Park to the Pentacrest, then stood shivering in the 40-degree chill beneath a haze created by hundreds of lighted candles . . . as part of a nationwide day of demonstrations for peace in Vietnam. . . . The university's United Republicans passed a resolution commending President Nixon for his 'courageous refusal to be swayed by the Oct. 15 Moratorium,' President Boyd for his decision to hold classes Wednesday, and 'deep concern that some university instructors canceled classes to observe the Moratorium.'"

December 11, 1969: "Student Protest Results in Scuffle." "About 15 students entered the Career Placement Counseling and Placement Office . . . and attempted to remove a Department of Labor recruiter . . . for what they called Labor Department's attempt to break the General Electric strike. . . . The students claimed that the university was operated on student money and that therefore Chaiken [the recruiter] should not be allowed to interview on the university's property. . . . The students said they represented the university, to which Huit [M. L. Huit, dean of students] replied 'The hell you represent the university.' This was responded to by Jerry Seis, corresponding student from Iowa City, who said 'Get the f—— out of here and bust her [Helen Barnes, Placement Office director] for stabbing me [with a pencil].'" The students finally left the office.

January 4, 1970: Spriestersbach confidential note to the file concerning a meeting of the Johnson County Law Enforcement Advisory Council. "Pat McCarney [chief of the Iowa City Police Department] indicated that he and the sheriff would cordon off the university and arrest anyone who strayed from the premises and got into trouble. He complained about harassment of the city police and indicated that they simply were not going to be given enforcement tasks by the university in which they would be criticized."

January 16, 1970: "Boyd Dissolves Judicial System — Garfield Chosen to Hear Cases." "University judicial committees were dissolved and replaced by a 76-year-old former Iowa Supreme Court Chief Justice, Theodore G. Garfield. . . . Boyd declared the university could not function effectively without an operative judicial system. His move came after Student Senate revoked student members' credentials on university committees."

January 19, 1970: University memo, Office of the President. "The events of January 13th involving the university judicial system have raised serious and substantial questions regarding the responsible governance of the university. These events were: (1) A group of students, apparently led by several of the students who were on trial, disrupted and took over the hearing being conducted by the Committee on Student Conduct to consider their case, thereby forcing the chairman to adjourn the hearing. (2) In response to a mandate from the Student Senate, two of the four student members of the committee attending the hearing walked out and refused to serve, thereby preventing a quorum of at least three students as required by the existing procedures. (3) The Committee on Student Conduct exceeded its authority by rendering a decision invalidating a lawful university regulation. . . . As a result of the events of the 13th, I have concluded that I must, as an emergency measure, suspend temporarily the present university judicial structure for handling student non-academic misconduct . . . and appoint, on an interim basis, an independent hearing officer to adjudicate cases of student misconduct."

March 26, 1970: University of Iowa News Service. "President Boyd announced . . . the imposition of sanctions against five students and Students for a Democratic Society (SDS), a student organization, for violating sections of the Code of Student Life during an incident December 10 at the Office of Career Counseling and Placement. . . . The disciplinary sanctions imposed . . . include suspension of two students until the end of the 1970 fall semester. . . . In all five cases the students were placed on disciplinary probation effective immediately. . . . During the probation period, [SDS] recognition as a student organization will be withdrawn."

April 16, 1970: "500 March in Moratorium." "The crowd walked from College Hill Park . . . to the Post Office and back to the park chanting peace slogans and singing. . . . Alan Spitzer, chairman of the Department of History . . . urged that protest of the Vietnam War continue for several reasons — to block the expansion of the war to Cambodia . . . and to show that people do not accept Nixon's Vietnamization plan."

April 21, 1970: "Protesters May Face Penalties." "The demonstration [at the university recreation building] forced postponement of an annual regional Pershing Rifle precision drill meet . . . when a crowd of approximately 150 demonstrators staged a shout-in and later surrounded the drill team from the University of Wisconsin."

May 5, 1970 (AP): "National Guardsmen Fire on Kent State Protesters." "Four students in a crowd pelting National Guardsmen with bricks and rocks were shot to death at Kent State University Monday [May 4] when the troops opened fire during an antiwar demonstration. Two of the dead were men, two were women. . . . The shooting came after a force of 100 guardsmen, their supply of tear gas exhausted, were surrounded by about 400 demonstrators."

May 6, 1970: "Windows Broken Tuesday [May 5] — Students Roam City After Rally." "Fifty-one persons — mostly university students — were arrested early Tuesday when a rock and firecracker throwing incident at the men's dormitories [Reinow I and the Quadrangle] at about 11:45 P.M. Monday [May 3] mushroomed into a student-police confrontation. . . . After the crowd of students swelled to 300 to 400 it moved across the Iowa River into the main university campus and then moved south toward the Iowa City National Guard Armory. . . . Over 50 windows were broken. . . . Once in the downtown area, about 55 to 75 students started a sit-in in the College–Dubuque Street intersection. Meanwhile a crowd estimated at 400 converged at the Clinton

Street—Iowa Avenue intersection and broke several windows at Iowa Book and Supply. . . . At about 2 A.M. . . . the crowd moved onto the Pentacrest. Once there, attempts were made to break into Old Capitol, but they failed. . . . As the crowd moved toward the Civic Center windows were either cracked or broken at Whetstone's Drug Store, the Red Ram, Bremers, the Dey Building, Iowa State Bank and Trust Co., Fuiks Jewelers, Herteen and Stocker Jewelers, Hagen's Appliance, First National Bank, and the Post Office. Meanwhile, the students at College and Dubuque continued to block traffic. . . . Finally, the order went out that everyone was to clear the areas or be subject to arrest. . . . About 3:45 A.M. some 22 highway patrolmen and sheriff's deputies . . . started marching around the corner of Capitol Street, east on Washington Street toward the crowd which at the time numbered from 150 to 200. . . . The order was again made that the area must be cleared and all those not leaving will be arrested. By 4 A.M. the crowd had completely dispersed. . . . Nearly 3,000 persons earlier Tuesday evening had attended a 'non-violence rally' called after violent demonstrations occurred in downtown Iowa City early Tuesday morning."

May 7, 1970: Statement by President Willard L. Boyd. "As a result of the recent violence and threats of violence on the campus, I have determined it to be necessary, for reasons relating to the physical safety and well-being of all members of the university community and the protection of university property, to exercise the emergency authority vested in me to suspend, effective immediately and pending final action on the charges, any student at the university who is charged with any violent or disruptive violation of university regulations."

May 8, 1970: "Trouble Mars Protest; 250–350 Arrested." "Early in the evening [May 7] about 50 persons broke into Old Capitol in an attempt to occupy the building but left voluntarily after three Iowa City patrolmen — two armed with shotguns — and [the city manager] asked them to go. Police arrested 250 to 350 demonstrators sitting on the steps of Old Capitol at 2 A.M. today. . . . Damage to Old Capitol was confined to several broken windows, a smashed painting and a broken ceramic floor ashtray. The break-in came after several persons at a rally on the Pentacrest attempted to turn what had been several hours of peaceful protest into violence. Someone broke a basement window of Old Capitol and then opened a basement door. About 50 students entered the building and started yelling and clapping. One person set off what was later revealed to be a smoke bomb. Several students yelled fire and one television station flashed a bulletin saying the building had been set on fire."

May 8, 1970: "Boyd Ordered Area Cleared — More Than 200 Arrested,"

Iowa City Press-Citizen. "[Among those arrested were three clergymen.] They were Rev. Roy Wingate, Rev. Ronald Osborne and George Forrell, who is head of the university's School of Religion."

May 8, 1970: Statement by President Willard L. Boyd, Office of Public Information. "When members of the university community act in such a way as to require the calling of outside help to preserve order, they take control of the university away from that community and put it in the hands of the civil authorities. A minority on campus have forced this situation on us. Those arrested last night are now subject to civil authorities, and the disposition of the charges is beyond our control. Despite this, I have urged the presiding judge, in assessing the sanctions, to make a distinction between those who protested in a non-violent way and those who protested violently. For the latter I hold no brief. For the former I urge that great weight be given to their rejection of violence."

May 9, 1970: "Early Morning Bulletin." "The Old Armory Temporary caught fire at approximately 3 A.M. this morning. At . . . 4 A.M. the building was almost completely engulfed in flames. . . . The building houses the university rhetoric program and writing lab."

May 10, 1970: University memo, Office of the President. "Classes at the University of Iowa will be held as usual on Monday [May 11] and through the close of the final examination period, May 26. In light of recent events and the tense emotional situation on campus, however, a number of students, fearing for their safety, have expressed the wish to return home. Their concern on this score has been heightened by the circulation of an incredible number of rumors throughout the university community, and it does not seem likely that their fears will diminish quickly. Those who wish to return home may do so without penalty. But before they leave, the university will need a clear indication of their choice of (1) completing their work at a later date; (2) accepting a 'pass' or 'withdraw' grade; or (3) accepting a grade based on the work completed through May 3."

May 11, 1970: "Highway Patrolmen Here for Indefinite Stay." "According to Lyle Dickinson [state highway patrol captain] approximately 180 highway patrolmen are headquartered at the Ramada Inn [now Express Way Motel]. . . . Dickinson said that about 200 to 300 national guardsmen were still stationed at the Johnson County 4-H Fairgrounds but that no plans for moving them into Iowa City were being considered. . . . According to Campus Security director William Binney, lights are being left on in the lower levels of most university buildings during the night to provide better security. Binney said Campus Security was still receiving a large number of bomb, damage and fire threats, although no violence has occurred since the fire in the East Hall Annex Saturday night [May 9]. . . . Binney said many of the university buildings were occupied Saturday night by faculty members in an attempt to prevent further damage. . . . Many faculty members have moved valuables from their offices to prevent their loss in the event of violence."

May 12, 1970: "2,500 Vote for UI Strike." "Some 2,500 persons, packed into the Main Lounge [of the Iowa Union], voted overwhelmingly Monday [May 10] to continue a general strike on the university campus in a 'non-obstructive, nonviolent way.' . . . Robert Corrigan, . . . professor of American Civilization, received a standing ovation when he told the crowd he could guarantee that 'the Faculty Senate will vote to abolish ROTC' on the university campus tomorrow [May 12]." [Subsequently, there was a tie vote by the Senate, and, ultimately, the regents deferred any action on the matter.]

May 12, 1970: "300 UI Students Exit Campus Early." [At least 11,796 of the university's 18,937 students ultimately chose to leave.]

May 12, 1970: "Explosion Still Mystery." "Campus Security officers investigated reports of a loud explosion sound and flash of light near a road grader . . . parked in a median strip near the intersection of Grand Avenue and South Grand Avenue. . . . The blast moved the grader several feet."

May 14, 1970 (AP): "Campus Protests Continue." "The student strikes information center at Brandeis University . . . reported 267 schools were on strikes of indefinite length. . . . The White House announced that Julie and David Eisenhower have decided not to attend their graduation exercises at Smith and Amherst colleges, which are among the campuses disturbed by antiwar protests."

May 16, 1970: Spriestersbach note to the file. "There are . . . identifiable groups within the business community: (1) A group (probably relatively small) which feels sympathetic to the students because they believe that the students' concerns over national issues are sincere and that the students have the right to express their concerns . . . short of violence. (2) A relatively large group that feels that law and order must be maintained at all costs. These people feel that the university has taken too soft a stand. (Kids who get out of line should be kicked out of school. The university should have the guts to do so.) Among this group are business people who stayed in their stores at night with guns and accumulated bricks and other missiles on the roof tops of their businesses to throw at students who might mass in front of their stores. Joining this group are workers who would love to have a chance to beat the hell out of any hippie types, and those who would really have liked to have had disturbances get out of hand, to show the students that they [the students] could be controlled. . . . The same group is irate because they are losing business as a result of the options provided to students to leave school early. Among this group there is a lot of talk about a 'communistic conspiracy.'"

June 24, 1970: "Regents Hear Views on Campus Disorder." "Each of nearly 40 speakers were allotted five minutes for presentations. . . . 'Repressive tactics are certainly not the answer,' Stow Persons, UI history professor and chair of the Faculty Senate; . . . 'Students need to see their efforts bring about change,' Jerry Schnoor, Iowa State student body president [and now UI professor of civil and environmental engineering]; . . . Student Body President Robert Beller submitted a statement calling for a more active student role in all decisions and free access to the regents and a permanent place on their agenda; Pella physician Peter Van Zante said 'the police should be given the authority to use all force necessary, even if they have to carry machine guns to quell riots'; Ben Summerwill, speaking for the Iowa City Chamber of Commerce, advocated keeping 'criminals, dope addicts and the like off the campus.' . . . Iowa State instructor Gary Widmer called for direct presidential responsibility for misconduct and investigative and hearing officers to handle charges. [He] called for relaxed rules of evidence, closed hearings and presidential authority of suspension without hearings when the president deemed such necessary for security reasons. . . . Stanley Redeker, board president, said some sort of policy will be formulated by the board in July."

July 10, 1970: "Campus Disorders and Student Unrest," Board of Regents minutes. "This Board, charged by law with the responsibility for the governance of the public universities of Iowa, reaffirms the following beliefs and intentions which will continue to serve as bases for the discharge of the board's responsibilities:

1. The citizens of this state have established and supported the state universities in order to make higher education available at reasonable cost. It is the responsibility of this board to insure that this purpose is not subverted.

2. Neither violence nor the threat of violence has any place in a university.

3. Freedom of inquiry and freedom of expression are indispensable elements of academic life.

4. The freedom to express dissent by lawful means, including peaceable assembly and petitions to authorities, is no less important on a university campus than elsewhere in our society.

5. The exerciser of this freedom to dissent must not interfere with the rights of others.

6. Adaptation and change are necessary processes by which an institution renews and preserves itself."

August 3, 1970: University memo from Willard L. Boyd, Office of the President, to Congressman Ichord (chairman, U.S. House of Representatives Committee on Internal Security). "I am responding to your letter requesting a list of guest speakers at the University of Iowa. . . . The number of . . . speakers is appropriately great and spread throughout the university with no attempt to centralize these programs. . . . I enclose copies of the two most recent reports of the [University Committee on Cultural Affairs]. . . . Universities must not be prisons of dogma but rather ports for conflicting points of view. . . . We must be willing to reason, to tolerate, and to respect. We must recognize that there can be honesty in our differences, that respect can emerge from diversity, and that progress takes many forms."

October 3, 1970: "Old Armory Fire Caused by Wiring." "State Fire Marshall Wilbur Johnston reported that the fire which destroyed Old Armory Temporary Building . . . probably resulted not from arson, but from poor electrical wiring."

October 7, 1970 (AP): "It's Get Tough Time in Colleges, Legislatures." The American Council on Education . . . reported . . . that the vast majority of 384 institutions responding to a survey said they had made physical and policy preparations to cope with turmoil." [Institutions included Southern Illinois University, University of Washington, University of Wisconsin, California system, Stanford University, Oklahoma State, Northwestern, University of Cincinnati, and Brandeis University.]

December 12, 1970: "Students Protest DIA Visit in Placement Office Sit-in." "About 100 students staged a two-hour sit-in outside the University of Iowa Placement Office . . . to protest the presence of a recruiter from the Defense Intelligence Agency (DIA). The demonstrators left the Union shortly after Robert Engel [assistant to the president] . . . told the group that the DIA recruiter had canceled the interviews."

December 17, 1970: "UI Charges Filed against Protesters — SDS Cited for Sponsoring Sit-in." "Seven students and three non-students have been cited . . . for violation of university and Board of Regents rules during a sit-in at the Placement Office on December 9 and a related incident at the office of the dean of the College of Liberal Arts the same day."

February 11, 1971: "Student Protest of Expansion of Indo-China War," Board of Regents minutes. Robert (BO) Beller, Student Senate president was given permission to read a statement. "At a mass meeting the evening of February 10, 500 people decided to implement the [demand that the U.S. get out of Indo-China now]. We will act to stop university involvement in the war effort and university contribution to the domestic oppression related to the war-unemployment. Therefore we demand that (1) The University of Iowa end complicity with the war — abolish ROTC, war research and war recruiters. (2) The university end all layoffs of campus workers."

February 12, 1971: "Protesters Raid ROTC; One Arrest." "A group of about 50 persons, some of them wearing war paint, left the Union shortly after 6:30 P.M. intending to confront an ROTC drill team in the Recreation Building to protest U.S. military involvement in Laos. Finding the door of the Recreation Building locked, the frustrated protesters moved to the Field House and ransacked the offices of the ROTC headquarters. . . . They left shattered windows and scattered furniture in their wake as they moved to the inner court of the Quadrangle Dormitory. . . . A war-painted figure produced an American flag which was burned as the whine of a fire alarm started in the dormitory. . . . The demonstrators ended their rendition of 'My Country 'Tis of Thee' and fled in all directions. . . . The alarms were quieted and a mass of about 60 chanting people moved across the Burlington St. bridge, followed by a few snowball-hurling dormitory residents. Stopping at Campus Security only long enough to throw a few snowballs, the chanting mass then marched with arms linked to the Iowa City Post Office. In drum major fashion, the shouting leader of the group led them around corners, stopping traffic at several intersections. A small fraction of the protesters moved into the Post Office in an attempt to storm the Johnson County Draft Office on the second floor. Their path was blocked by a high wire fence on the steps. Before a battering ram could be found, the Iowa City Police arrived to close the building. The dwindling group of marchers, followed by an expanding group of spectators, turned toward the Navy Recruiting Office at 221 S. Linn. A firecracker exploded, breaking a small hole in the glass door of the recruiting office. The hole widened as chunks of ice were thrown against the glass. The milling group, now numbering less than 40, trudged its way back to the Pentacrest and the steps of Old Capitol. A short debate over the accomplishments of the evening ended as the straggling group adjourned to the Union for coffee."

March 10, 1971: "Garfield Recommends Suspension of SDS." "Hearing officer Theodore Garfield has recommended immediate one-year suspensions of the Students for a Democratic Society . . . and one student, as well as probationary status for seven other students. . . . The sit-in, which gave rise to the charges . . . occurred December 9 at the Union Career Counseling and Placement Office following a rally sponsored by SDS."

April 4, 1971: "Boyd Hits SDS, Ten UI Students for DIA Protest." "Boyd followed the recommendations of Theodore Garfield. . . . The defendant's brief argued that they had been forced to violate regent and administration rules 'because attempts to establish lines of communication between students and controversial recruiters had been blocked or ignored.' In response to their brief Boyd said, 'The facts do not bear out this contention. The essence of the argument is that the ends justify the means. Protest must be accomplished without impinging on the rights of others.' . . . Bruce Johnson [the student suspended] said of Boyd's action against SDS, 'He can kick us off campus, but we're not going to go away.'"

April 28, 1971: Statement by President Willard L. Boyd. "In view of the fact that no other suitable facility is available where interested students can hold a rally on Saturday, May 1, the university is prepared to grant permission for such a rally to be held on the Macbride field campus." [Twelve miles from the main campus, isolated and well removed from university classrooms and Iowa City streets.]

May 1, 1971: "Iowa City Peacefest Starts This Morning." "The Iowa City peacefest . . . gets off the ground at Macbride field campus. A parade of guerrilla gardeners, which begins at 12:30 P.M. . . . and a rally scheduled for 10 P.M. on the Pentacrest are being billed as the places to go if you don't or can't reach Macbride field campus. . . . Events scheduled for Sunday will take place in the Union. . . . Workshops . . . include Economic May Boycott of the War by the International League for Peace and Freedom; Christians Affirming Life; Vietnam Veterans Against War; Draft Resistance and Repeal; Sexism; Day Care Organizing; People's Peace Treaty Organizing; ROTC — The University's Role in the War; and Building a Student-Worker Alliance."

May 6, 1971: "Anti-War Violence Strikes City — Scattered Arrests Follow Three Hours of Trashing." "A handful of people were arrested Wednesday night [May 5] after a crowd of anti-war demonstrators estimated at an average of between 400 and 500 people ranged through Iowa City for four hours breaking windows and blocking traffic. About 100 law enforcement officers, including Johnson County Sheriff's Deputies, the Iowa Highway Patrol and the Iowa City and Coralville Police Departments, dressed in riot gear, charged down Clinton Street and into the Pentacrest to break up the crowd shortly before midnight."

May 6, 1971: Statement by President Willard L. Boyd. "Last night's unlawful activities cannot be related in any way to the cause of peace. . . . Those found guilty of willful destruction will be dealt with to the full extent of the civil laws and will be subject to sanctions under the regents' rules of conduct. The volunteer student monitors cannot be praised too highly for their heroic efforts to protect the safety of others and to limit the damage to property. . . . We are all in their debt."

May 7, 1971: "Disturbances Continue." "At least seven persons . . . were arrested Thursday night [May 6] during an anti-war demonstration on the Pentacrest and subsequent confrontations between police and about 800 demonstrators in downtown Iowa City. . . . The arrests followed an attempted march to the county courthouse earlier in the evening which was broken up by sheriff's deputies."

May 8, 1971: "Explosion Shakes Iowa City Civic Center." "An explosion caused an estimated $3,500 to $5,000 worth of damage to the Iowa City Civic Center early Friday morning [May 7]. . . . No one was injured. All windows on the south side of the courtroom and council chamber were blown out and a hole three feet by five feet was blasted in the foundation. . . . 'These people knew what they were doing,' one investigator commented."

May 11, 1971: "Massive Bust, Tear Gassing, Rip Protesters." "Law enforcement officers charged a gathering of anti-war demonstrators downtown Monday night [May 10] and made a large number of arrests. Using tear gas for the first time in the week of demonstrations and flailing night sticks, Iowa City police, Highway Patrolmen, Johnson County Sheriff's Deputies and Campus Security charged a gathering of anti-war demonstrators downtown."

May 11, 1971: "40 Stage Sit-in in Boyd's Office after Rally on Monday Afternoon." "The sit-in broke up after it was learned that Boyd was out of town. The purpose of the sit-in . . . was to demand an end to layoffs of university employees, and an end to university support of the ROTC program on campus."

May 12, 1971: "Police Charge Crowd Gathered Near Dorm — Dorm Protesters Gassed by Police." "Late Monday night [May 10] police had chased a crowd of demonstrators from Campus Security headquarters. . . . Some crowd members were chased to an area around the men's dormitories when the crowd began rolling large pipes from a construction site on Grand Avenue down the hill to police. . . . A crowd outside Hillcrest dormitory had begun throwing rocks and bottles at police about 1:30 A.M. Tuesday when the police charged toward the crowd and fired several tear gas canisters into the crowd and at the dormitories."

May 13, 1971: "Sharp Fight Marks Tuesday Demonstration." "Seven persons were arrested and at least 16 highway patrolmen and three students injured in a confrontation near Quadrangle and Hillcrest dormitories here late Tuesday night and early Wednesday morning. Six of the patrolmen and three university students were treated at University Hospital and released."

May 14, 1971: "A Special Announcement to the University Community," university memo, Office of the President. "The university has suspended outdoor rallies at night for the time being. This decision comes in light of recent serious crowd disturbances in the city and on the campus, and also because of the need for undistracted preparations for final examinations beginning next Wednesday [May 19]. In order to assure opportunity for the exercise of free speech rights, meeting rooms will continue to remain available for groups which seek arrangements in advance."

August 12, 1971: "Action Asked by City Attorney," *Iowa City Press-Citizen.* "Approximately 200 criminal charges filed in City Police Court as a result of student disorders May 7 and 8, 1970, soon will be dismissed, Judge Joseph Thornton said today."

September 17, 1971: "Stuit Blocks Credit to Action Studies Class." "[Dean Stuit, College of Liberal Arts] said he refused to allow credit for 'History of Non-Violence' . . . which . . . contrasts violent and non-violent approaches to contemporary problems.' . . . At the same time . . . Stuit attacked the Action Studies program, charging that 'Action Studies has used subterfuge in gaining permission to grant credit through departments.'"

May 2, 1972: "Anti-war Group Discusses Lack of Student Involvement." "The 'Committee to End Computerized Death,' meeting . . . to discuss the lack of student involvement in their cause decided to cancel picketing of the University of Iowa Computer Center. . . . No more than two persons picketed the center at any one time Monday [May 1]. The group is picketing the center as a protest to the UI's connection with the Rock Island Arsenal."

May 5, 1972: "War Rally Sparks Trashing." "What began as an 'anti-war' rally Thursday [May 4] disintegrated into widespread vandalism in downtown Iowa City and resulted in an order from Governor Robert Ray putting the state Highway Patrol in charge of all law enforcement. . . . The crowd fluctuated from about 100 to nearly 800 during the rampage." [Forty downtown establishments suffered damage.]

May 10, 1972: "3,000 Protest in Streets." "A slogan-chanting crowd of anti-war demonstrators blocked intersections and marched peacefully through Iowa City for nearly four hours Tuesday night [May 9]. . . . The mostly-student crowd, which grew to nearly 3,000 persons, was sharply different from a much smaller group which trashed downtown Iowa City last Thursday [May 4]."

May 12, 1972: "Protesters Block I-80." "Antiwar protesters . . . Thursday night [May 11] blocked a portion of Interstate 80 for a short time before being routed by police and tear gas in the third evening of demonstrations in a week. The protesters reached the Interstate after a confrontation with Iowa highway patrolmen at Dubuque Street near City Park and after sometimes running, sometimes walking through streets, yards and pastures in the north part of the city. Police reported about 1 A.M. Friday that 19 persons had been arrested."

June 7, 1972: "UI Suspends Piller." "[Mr.] Boyd announced Tuesday [June 6] that Simon Piller, A2 [liberal arts sophomore] . . . has been suspended for one year as a result of his use of campus facilities to aid SDS while the chapter was under a previous suspension. At the same time, Boyd said that SDS will be suspended from the university for three years."

The student unrest that had built up to a white heat during the springs of 1970, 1971, and 1972 ended at Iowa, almost without a whimper, after the 1971–1972 spring semester. Our best guess was that the mass protests here were over, so much so that those of us who had been centrally involved during those days and nights had a party to celebrate. We were confident that, one way or the other, the U.S. would be getting out of the Vietnam War and the draft would become a thing of the past. There is no doubt in my mind that, troublesome though the student unrest had been, it had had an effect on the nation's attitude toward war, especially the war in Vietnam. In retrospect, it marked the beginning of a continuing struggle among peoples worldwide to determine without outside interference what the nature of their futures should be.

January 27, 1973 (AP): "Draft Ends, but System Intact," *Iowa City Press-Citizen.* "For the first time since 1948, men aged 18 through 35 will not face induction" without an act of Congress. The fact that the *Daily Iowan* chose not to print the story on its front page suggests that the issue of the draft per se was no longer paramount in the minds of the students.

April 29, 1975 (AP): "U.S. Ordered out of Vietnam."

April 30, 1975: "War Ends in Vietnam."

The Administrative Liaison Group and the Administrative Liaison Officer

The student unrest required institutional responses, often under circumstances that did not allow extended consultation and deliberation. Personal and property security were frequently threatened and had to be secured without delay. At first the central administration attempted to deal with these problems on an ad hoc basis. Frequently, however, the most recent message tended to get attention before the previous one had been dealt with. Adding to the problem was the lack of an adequate network of communication up or down the university administrative system for taking decisive actions. Centrally, different people dealt with the problems as they came up, but we muddled through during the spring of 1969. As tensions built up during the early months of 1970, and in the absence of any sense of how long the circumstances would continue, it became clear to President Boyd that forming some type of quasi organization would be necessary.

Robert (Bob) Hardin, then vice president for health affairs, and I in the central administrative group had military experience in organizing groups for ad hoc situations. Gradually, we were given more and broader assignments to deal with the flood of messages and concerns associated with the unrest. By the end of the spring of 1970, Bob and I had moved in as a team to orchestrate the central administration's decisions. In July I accepted the assignment to draft a protocol under which the group would function.

The title of Administrative Liaison Group was chosen because it masked the true functions of the group, assuming, as we did, that it would not appear in any official minutes or regents dockets. And it never did. Nevertheless, the protocol was distributed to the selected group of persons, primarily staff, who would make up the organization. Assignments were meted out, communication nets were established, and the group was placed in a readiness mode that allowed us to assemble literally at a moment's notice.

During the times of disturbances we had twenty-four-hour coverage. There was an administrative liaison officer (duty officer) and a "headquarters command," the Administrative Liaison Group (ALG) — ten to fifteen or more persons depending on the circumstances. I served as chair of the group; Charlie Mason kept notes. Sometimes, we sat in continuous session. On calmer days we met regularly every Monday morning to get reports from our assigned observers among the group. However, beyond the documents that outlined the organization and responsibilities of the group, I do not recall that a single official university document was ever written under an ALG imprint.

During the times of high tension (the springs of 1969, 1970, 1971, and 1972) we found special places for the ALG to function on a twenty-four-hour basis. In the spring of 1969 we chose Oakdale Hall; in 1970, 1971, and 1972 we chose a conference room and associated spaces in Westlawn, complete with telephones, a situation map, and even bunking accommodations for those of us who remained around the clock.

The organization was in many ways the antithesis of the deliberative, democratic university organization. But it worked. Many of the faculty were aware of the "shadow" group, and few objected to it. On the contrary, many expressed appreciation for our efforts in serving as the buffer between the several police forces and the academy, and, on many occasions, walking very fine lines for which there was little, if any, precedent.

Some of the folks who were part of the ALG in those days are still actively involved in the administration of the university today. Dick Gibson, for one, was my right-hand person in the "bunker" because he had good sense and a level head, and because he knew the physical layout of the campus better than anyone else. In his commentary below, Dick mentions drawing on those experiences during the recent spring floods of 1993. Phil Jones (then assistant vice president for administration) also was part of the group in its later days. He is now the "official keeper" of its memories and, as he says in his commentary, draws on that experience in dealing with unusual issues even today.

There were times of great stress, of course, but there were also funny moments as well. Having lived through them, the members of the ALG found that they had established trusts and bonds with persons they would never have known otherwise. As I think about the group now I am somewhat surprised that we never organized ourselves into a special "alumni" organization with meetings and appropriate bending of elbows.

Commentaries

George Chambers, professor of education and formerly executive vice president: "The student unrest did have a bearing on Howard Bowen's decision to resign as president. I shared a plane ride to California with Howard Bowen after he had gone out to Claremont. He had been back in Iowa attending a Grinnell board of directors and trustees meeting. Howard told me he made that decision when one of our wild SDS students had seen fit to place his body in front of Mr. Bowen's car in Mr. Bowen's driveway at 102 Church Street, and the police had to be summoned to move him before Mr. Bowen could be driven to the regents meeting. He made the decision at that point that the eras had passed him and the generation had, and that he no longer could relate to what was going on. He said he concluded that it was best for him to move on. He said he told Lois [his wife], when he walked in the house, that they would be leaving Iowa soon."

Mary Parden, formerly administrative assistant to presidents: "President Bowen just couldn't understand, though he had two sons of his own. I don't know that they were rebellious, but he just couldn't understand these kids who had it so good, so to speak, doing this.

"The first movement had to do, I think, with hours. It had nothing to do with the Vietnam War or anything else. One of the radical groups made an appointment to see Mr. Bowen, I'll say at three in the afternoon. I think it was as simple as student hours, you know, shutting the door. Well, the student came, accompanied by about twenty-five friends. When it got to be five o'clock, I said, 'Now we're all going home!' and we went. That was the first and we had a couple more sit-ins at Jessup later. Then we were more experienced and they were pretty short-lived.

"I stayed in the office the day of the sit-in. I only let — and it worked — the one who had made the appointment in. I just plain stood at the door. I was old enough — I think I had a mother image. You know, they all had mothers. I didn't know who the kid was at all. He said, 'You're kind of between a rock and a hard place.' So the rest of them just sat down, some of them on the floor because there weren't chairs enough, but they did absolutely nothing. Well, there was a guy who kept going in and out of the window. There was a ledge around Old Capitol and so you could walk on it. I don't know why he was going in and out of the window. He came out a couple of times, it was right by me, and I looked at him coldly and said, 'You do that once more and I'm going to have you arrested for breaking and entering.' So, he didn't do it anymore.

"They just finally left. Oh no, we didn't do anything. I just sat there at my desk. There wasn't much dialogue; there was a little, and I've forgotten what they were talking about, and they didn't know what they were talking about. Oh, the labor unions. Somebody was talking about labor and he didn't have any more idea of what he was talking about than the man in the moon. I just let him talk. I felt, well heavens, I'm not teaching economics. When the fellow with the appointment came out, they all followed him out. They didn't hurt anything. They didn't do anything.

"My thought about this whole rioting, as I call it, was they were going to have a day in May. They even had a name for it because the *Iowan* was mixed up in it, and that was before they got radical. They really thought that it was kind of a show of solidarity against the Vietnam War. I think the thing just escalated and got out of hand. One of the problems was the weather was so nice. If it hadn't been so nice, I'm sure everywhere in the country, certainly here, they would never have gotten off the ground.

"There was a regents meeting and Mr. Boyd wasn't there the first day they moved into the campus. Somebody called me and said, 'Those kids have got a pig out there on the front yard, and it's being abused.' So I called security or the police and said, 'You'd better come and get the pig.' Which they did. So that ended the animals. I think the first night they were just playing out there on the front yard. Now somewhere in here, I don't remember the timing on this, during the lunch hour somebody broke into our office and threw my typewriter out the window. We didn't lock the files at noon — they could have just dumped the whole lot. By Saturday the thing really got cooking. We took the files and stuff out while I was there. We took all the pictures down and we took our file cases out and then we physically moved ourselves.

"Sandy wasn't as disturbed by it as Howard had been. Of course by this time it had gotten national, and this was not just an isolated incident as it had been. I think his main reaction was, one, he thought it was silly, as all of us over seventeen did. The second thing was he was afraid something would happen, that some student would get hurt, or there would be severe physical damage. We never got close to having anybody sit in the president's office. That day I was there with Captain Dickinson when they were milling around, and some little hysterical girl came in and said, 'What's the *Des Moines Register* going to think when the Highway Patrol is giving the orders?' And I said, 'They're going to think for once the university is using some sense!' Think of how excellent the Highway Patrol was. They were just superb.

"Everybody was afraid. By everybody I mean nationally, that it was all going to start again in the fall because of elections. We laughed and said all the kids went home and their folks told them to study and shut up.

"We had another sit-in in Jessup Hall over daycare. They sat down in the hall first, and, by that time, there were some regulations about students not impairing our getting to work. I had gone across town to lunch. I came back, and Arthur Bonfield, who was out in front, said to me, 'Are you afraid to go in there and unlock the door?' And I said, 'Arthur, you've got to be kidding!' So, I just walked up the steps, pushing young bodies aside as I went, only I didn't need to push them — they stood. We got to the door and some boob was standing in front of it. I looked at him and said, 'You're in my way!' At which point he moved and I opened the door with my key and went in. Well, some of them came in, and I remember a girl stood on one of the chairs, and I said to her, 'You get down from that chair!' and she got down. You just sort of had the feeling you had a bunch of preschool kids that you didn't know what to do with. Some of them sat around. It got to be five o'clock, and I said, 'We're going to close now,' and then they just all herded out."

Richard Gibson, associate vice president and director for finance and university services, and director of Facilities Services Group: "I always thought that one of the most unique aspects of those times of unrest was how the university, contrary to all its instincts, could reorganize itself very quickly and move to the management mode that was up to the task of dealing with the situation.

"I was in the bunker all of the time. I depended on others' eyes and ears for what was going on for the whole three years. Our communication system depended a great deal on the telephone. And we used radios — a very obsolete technology compared to what we have nowadays. It was a patched-together thing that depended very much on the people that we had out watching: faculty representatives, staff representatives, ALG people, watching what was going on and getting it fed back to a central location. It worked quite well. In fact, I think we were the envy of all the public safety agencies, even the Highway Patrol. We knew what was going on far ahead of when they did.

"We had one of their officers sitting in our bunker, and we also had people sitting in their bunker at one point too, so we had a good system going, and we also had good communication with the Iowa City police, sheriff's office as well as the Highway Patrol. We kept a situation map and a journal or a log.

"We put together a group of volunteers and we had one in every building. They were our line of communication into the buildings in terms of passing them information they needed to know, making sure the places were locked up or unlocked as necessary, and serving as our eyes and ears in the building. They walked the buildings a few nights, as I remember, because we were under considerable fear of arson and bombs.

"Another thing that we did that is not very publicly known: I don't think it ever appeared in the papers, but we replaced all of the glass on the ground floor of Jessup Hall with Plexiglas. Probably some of it is still over there, as a matter of fact. How did we ever get that done without people noticing that that was what we were doing? Those windows are right on grade.

"We had faculty watching us constantly in the bunker, and participating in the skull sessions and decision-making sessions where we were plotting strategy and pulling together intelligence. It looked like a sort of bunker man-agement, and it was. It still was very well observed by very responsible, con-cerned people. . . . If it hadn't been for the oversight, we probably couldn't have run the university that way.

"The faculty were always in a difficult role in the whole thing. We were asking them to help us, asking them to give us information. At the same time they were out there to make sure we weren't misbehaving or that others weren't misbehaving toward students, and towards faculty and staff if they happened to be involved. They had a very complex role to play and did a marvelous job as I recall."

Philip Hubbard, then vice president for student services: "The ALG met as needed, and it was needed quite frequently because all of us tried to keep our ears to the ground and get wind of student activities, protests, whatever they were planning, so that we wouldn't be caught off-guard. The director of stu-dent activities, Kevin Taylor, was a member of the group, so he was in the Union all the time. He generally knew everything the students were doing. He went to all the student government meetings, and, if they needed something, they went to his office to get it. That was the way we learned of potential things. But I also went to the student meetings. If they organized a protest meeting, I went.

"The students were in contact with students from other campuses. They were telephoning their compatriots at Wisconsin, Columbia, Berkeley, all of these schools where there were protest activities, and so they knew what was going on. Many people interpreted this as being a conspiracy but it was no better organized than that. They just talked to one another and got ideas. I was a member of the CIC group [Big Ten Committee on Institutional Cooperation] on student affairs and I would go to their regular meetings and we would talk about what was going on at our various campuses, because most if not all of the Big Ten campuses were in an uproar. So we had our way of communicating, the students had their way of communicating. It was a pretty exciting time.

"One group was arrested in front of Old Capitol because they refused to disperse when we told them to. Among that group was one of my sons. I was inside of Old Capitol looking out and I could see him there. When they came, he looked very, very unhappy but he stood his ground and he was arrested with the rest. The interesting thing was, very close to him was Professor George Forrell, who was the director of the School of Religion. He was arrested also. Well, this was a matter of principle. He just felt that the students, however misguided they may have been, were protesting what they felt to be an unjust situation in which people who were not able to defend themselves adequately were being threatened by a very powerful force which, as the students saw it, had no legitimate basis for being in Vietnam. They were there as aggressors, or at least as oppressors, and so they were protesting that. Professor Forrell and Mike, my son, and I, and many of the university officials didn't really agree with their tactics, but we thought that people who felt that strongly about something had a right to protests and we would do everything we possibly could to assist them.

"Of those things that was most difficult to deal with was their desire for publicity. Anything they were going to do they'd announce it to the media and the media would send their reporters here and the TV cameras would be there and, of course, it was just like all other cases where the TV cameras show up — people would perform. They would put on a big show of force and it would be written up in the newspapers and people all over the state would get alarmed and there'd be letters to the president and people would invite me to speak and demand, 'What in the world are you doing to those students at the university?' The Cedar Rapids Association of Accountants, who had invited me to speak at one of their luncheons, asked me, 'Why are you turning the students against business?' We told them, 'The students have their own minds, we're not turning them against anything.'"

Howard Sokol, formerly special assistant to the vice president for academic affairs: "Judge Garfield was a very grumpy-looking guy, and one of the lawyers involved was a student lawyer who is now quite a well-known defense lawyer. After this was over, he went in to see Dave Vernon, and he said, 'You know Dean, people say that he's an old goat. Old he may be, but smart he sure is!'

"We had all the trappings, a court reporter, and they took down every word. One of our witnesses was Lieutenant Saylor, who was an old sodbuster. He'd been in the service. He was one of our detectives. They were grilling him about his background, as though he had been some sort of a real pig. So they said, 'Lieutenant, what did you do in the service?' 'Well,' he said, 'I was a VD Control Officer.' They said, 'What does he do?' 'He goes around and talks to people who have the clap to see where they got it.' Well, of course, stuff like that kind of destroyed the hearing to some extent.

"There was humor connected with the trials from time to time. One had to do with some of the dorm residents who were accused of rolling culverts down into the Riverside–Burlington Street intersection. A law student was defending the dorm students. He got up and said, 'I'm so and so.' The judge looked over his glasses and said, 'Oh, your name's so and so? Oh yes! Was your father lawyer so and so from Burlington?' He said yes. He said, 'I remember that famous Bond case that he represented the city on an appeal.' He went on, and here this kid is who is good at 'gung ho,' he's getting put right back in the upper classes.

"On Easter I was home for the weekend from the legislature, and I got a call that the student protesters were clearing out the Language House, which was on Clinton Street, now torn down. It was Sunday afternoon, and we had a little trouble assembling a crew of police or security to go over there, but we did. And we escorted them out of the front door.

"Spriestersbach was in the headquarters that day. His grandson was playing out there on the Pentacrest. His father was part of the group. When we asked Sprie if we should clear the building, someone said, 'You know, your grandson is out there playing.' The answer came back that, 'His dad's going to have to take his licks just like everybody else.'"

Lyle Dickinson, captain and area commander retired, Iowa State Patrol: "The chain of command was one of the major problems in this whole time period: who was going to be in charge? The law says that we [the patrol] cannot come in and do anything unless we are invited in by the local mayor. He has to call the governor. I had certain limits of authority where I could come in town and assist the police on an emergency type situation, but one of the biggest problems was the lawyers for the city and the state and the university arguing over whose problem it was. The city said, 'It's not ours, it's the university's. The university is state property.' They were very, very frustrating times for all of the law enforcement people . . . waiting for the word from the hierarchy to come down. . . . A section in the law says that state patrolmen shall have all the powers of the peace officers within the boundaries of the state. Now a sheriff's authority is limited to the county, and the city is limited to the city. By statute, a patrolman does not set up a regular patrol beat within a city. It doesn't exclude the fact that as I ride through Iowa City on 218 or Highway 6 that I can't stop somebody for a violation. But I don't set up radar or anything like that within the city limits.

"[The troopers] had a hard time understanding why, when you burn down a building, do you stand around and wait for another one to burn? They felt that action should have been taken. . . . You want to remember these were young men, the vast majority of them ex-military, young people who had gone into the service out of high school or college and then come in to the area of law enforcement. The vast majority of their lives was very, very structured, disciplined. In the late sixties and early seventies, things had changed rather drastically from what we had been used to. There's an awful lot of us that had never heard, 'You son of a bitch,' spoken directly to our face before. It was not done. But we were now in an era when this was commonplace for a lot of these young people to address anybody in the foulest of language. Of course, generally, on a one-to-one basis, they probably wouldn't have done it. But when you're standing in a great big crowd of hundreds, it's pretty easy to call somebody a foul name and get away with it. The men were basically frustrated.

"We had officers walking the campus later on and visiting, and going into the residence halls. This was my idea. Let them see us on a different plane. Let them see us without our batons and our helmets. Go in, sit down in the residence hall, and eat lunch with them. Sit on the fence over there on the Pentacrest and talk to them. Let them see we're human, we'll talk to you! I just had a difference of opinion. I didn't think that guns were going to do anything at all. We could have accomplished just as much with a riot baton as we could with a shotgun, and I was opposed to that particular thing. I think that once we got into more closely watching the residence halls and everything, I think it went on fine.

"I don't think there's any question [about the presence of outside agitators]. I say this because I personally talked to an undercover B.C.I. [Bureau of Criminal Investigation] agent who had been in Madison, Wisconsin, who knew that they came down here. I honestly believe that the Students for a Democratic Society moved some professional agitators in here. They came to the meetings, but they did not officially participate other than in the background to get them all riled up and say, 'Come on! Let's go do this! Come on!' There's no question in my mind that they were here. "I still have some very strong feelings about the night we went up the hill [toward Hillcrest] and they were catapulting rocks and wine bottles down on us as we moved across the Burlington Street Bridge. They rolled great big cement conduits down the hill, and they'd go clear on down into the river. I can't remember exactly how many officers I went to visit in the hospital that night, but quite a few of them got hurt.

"I think about those times, and, every once in awhile, I think about decisions I made. Could I have made a different one? Should I have known more than I did? We never actually had the type of training. . . . It was all an experience that we were not totally prepared for any more than the university was to handle it.

"I think of so many of the [university] people that I enjoyed so much. I think of a lot of them. I probably never had the opportunity to work with any finer group of people either. After that, I had some officers sitting in on constitutional law classes up at the Law College, some law students riding with patrolmen; we developed a very fine relationship. I was always happy that the decisions that we were able to make didn't result in any real embarrassment. There were some unfortunate instances throughout the country, and I thought that we were fortunate."

Phillip Jones, vice president for student services and dean of students: "I remember we had a situation just before Kent State. There were reports of people driving around in pickup trucks with rifles in the back. The rumors got started and I was called to check that out. I remember finding a sign on the door of the Afro-American Cultural Center that said something to the effect of 'Go home.' It turned out there was so much tension on campus around the Kent State thing that some of the black students put the sign up, trying to get people to stay away from the center. About this time the Old Armory temporary building burned.

"My role evolved into being part of the planning group, still having the responsibility for making periodic reports to the bunker. I was one of the folks who was designated to call in and give the status of activities and input for decisions that were being made in the bunker, as it was called in those days. It was very interesting because it was clear that this was confidential to the people who were involved in it. It was like having to gain security clearance. You went from very informal to more formal kinds of relations and, once inside, you realized that this was an organized effort on the part of people giving very serious consideration to things in a calm way for making some really tough decisions. Once decisions were made, they tended to have tremendous rippling effects, and a lot of times people couldn't understand, thinking this was an off-the-cuff kind of decision, when it had been thought out with the consequences already thought through. As you, Sprie, would say from time to time, we needed to be overprepared. Every time we would have the anticipation of a crisis was the time to plan, not when there was a crisis. And we use that approach to this very day.

"It was a basic principle that no one person made a decision, and that there should always be administrative control of law enforcement until law enforcement had to do its job as law enforcement. At that time the university administration withdrew. But there would be observers, primarily from the faculty, to observe the process and to make determinations about whether the decisions that were being made were appropriate for a university.

"When a decision had to be made for police actions to be taken, it would only occur after a period of jawboning, trying to talk our way through, trying to compromise for reasonable kinds of activity, and that dissent was not only tolerated but necessary. It was understood that people had the right to dissent but they did not have the right to disrupt the functions of the university. 'Reasonable time, place and manner' was kind of the watchword. Two things, it seems to me, are basic: a forum for the free exchange of ideas and people having the right to dissent in reasonable time, place and manner.

"There was a two-position kind of thing. There was the issue in society and then there was the university. And while they might be against the CIA, we would say, 'We don't have any problem with you being against the CIA but you must do it in a reasonable time, place and manner.' And they were saying, 'You should allow us more latitude to disrupt them,' and we'd say, 'No, there are other students who have rights also. You may dissent but they also have a right to their expression, and therefore we're going discipline you for abridging other students rights.' That became part of the debate and the discussion and actually was much more educationally relevant because it was playing out democratic principles in more dimensions.

"I don't think, during the time that I was working in this area, that anything that we dealt with had been significantly influenced from the outside. I think that what happened at Wisconsin, what happened at Berkeley, what happened at Michigan began to be the base for the students' activities. . . . But I don't think that there was any outside agitation. It was basically the thoughts and actions of students who were here, many of them graduate students."

Dorsey (Dan) Ellis, former vice president for finance and university services, now dean of the Law School, Washington University, St. Louis: "I remember the demonstrations on the Pentacrest. At that time I was young enough that I could pass for a student, especially since I had a full beard then. I put on my field jacket and my utility cap that were left over from the Marine Corps and went wandering around the Pentacrest. None of the students paid any attention to me; they thought I was one of them. That gave me a kind of worm's-eye view of what was going on. An awful lot of it was clearly posturing. I recall a demonstration that was focused on the steps of Old Capitol. The crowd wasn't very large, and that was clearly upsetting the organizers. Then somebody pointed out that movie theaters hadn't let out yet and, as soon as they did, those who had gone to the movies for the evening would no doubt join us here because this was where the action was. It's that kind of thing that appeared on television as being a large crowd of student demonstrators. I remember one line in particular — an organizer standing up on the Old Capitol steps exhorting the group to do something, and her catch line was 'Come on Iowa. The University of Iowa hasn't made it to the *New York Times* yet.' I also remember the sickening, sweet odor of marijuana in the crowd."

Robert Engel, professor of education, formerly special assistant to the president: "I remember standing over at the intersection of Iowa Avenue and Clinton on the Old Capitol side of the street; there had been a lot of trashing. They had trashed Iowa Book and Supply and the street had been closed. Three or four students, one of whom I recognized as a kind of leader of unrest, came running across the intersection saying, 'Let's get Jessup Hall,' and I remember standing out in front of them and said, 'This is your home; think about it for a moment.' Well, they weren't interested in thinking about it for a moment, at least as far as I could tell.

"I remember getting a call when I was assistant to the president from our student body president at the time, saying that the sheriff and some deputies were down at the Iowa Memorial Union. He wanted me to come over and get them out. I said I was sorry, but if the sheriff has a reason to be there, then he has as much right as I do, or more, to be there. The student said, 'I took a class from you, and you said something about the university being a sanctuary.' And I said, 'It is, but not to that extent.'"

Mary Jo Small, associate vice president emeritus for finance and university services: "On that week in May in 1970 there was the big political push to get Congress to vote a date certain to withdraw. There was a petition circulating, for Amendment 609, as I recollect. We wanted to have somebody tell the students that this was a good thing to do. They kind of pushed me out there. What I basically said was, 'Write your congressman.' The crowd thought that was wonderful. So I thought any crowd that thinks 'write your congressman' is a revolutionary act is not very revolutionary. I always thought it was basically a fairly benign crowd."

Margery Hoppin, then director of sponsored programs: "It was a sad time. Working in the basement of Old Capitol we were a target; Old Capitol was a target. Students would meet out in front and then they would try to push in to the building. I recall standing in the hallway there, putting my shoulder to the door with some of the staff, trying to keep them from breaking in. One student or group did break into my office through the window and took an air conditioner and set fire to a bulletin board. It was a scary time. We were cautioned to have duplicate files and were told what to do if a large mob came in. Finally, it became so bad that the president decided to move all administration out of Old Capitol. He was afraid this lovely old building would be destroyed, so they moved the president's office and our office into Jessup Hall, so Old Capitol was no longer a symbol."

James Jakobsen, associate dean of the Graduate College: "The Graduate College stayed open during the protests and tried to function normally. At that time the offices were in the Old Capitol, which was, to some extent, a focal point for demonstrations and meetings and discussions, on the steps or on the lawn. That made the conduct of Graduate College business somewhat difficult. It got so bad that, in fact, the authorities didn't allow people, either students or staff, to go into the Old Capitol. That made it a difficult operation for us, especially the handling of theses. We had a short period of time when a student would deliver a thesis, be met at the door by a state policeman, hand the thesis in to a state policeman, who would bring it to the office. The student wasn't around at all. When we were through checking it out we'd have to do the opposite: have the student come to the door, the state policeman would come, pick up the thesis. There was concern for the safety of the building. I can remember coming to work when the windows of my office would be broken, rocks and bottles thrown through them. While that was disruptive, I don't think it had a great effect. Graduate education didn't veer off, or expand enormously because of it, or condense enormously because of it."

Frank Horton, then professor of geography and director of the Institute for Urban and Regional Research located on the second floor of the president's home: "We had two grants from the Department of Defense, one on geographic information systems and one on environmental change detection systems. So, here comes this mob of kids walking up to the institute at the president's house. They had a spokesperson who demanded something about the defense contract. So, I said, 'I'll tell you what. Since you're all here, I think the way to really handle this is for me to read these reports to you.' And so I brought them out, and started to read them. And you know how boring those things will sound. I just kept reading and people started drifting away, drifting away. Finally, I looked up and no one was there! I went back in and that was the end of this great protest for our defense contracts.

"And then I remember being asked to stay in the house over night, because there was concern about fire bombing and so on. Mike McNulty [then a faculty member in geography] was involved in one of the contracts; I asked Mike to stay up there with me. We brought one of the logistical games up, and, I don't know if it was legal or not, but we brought a couple of bottles of wine up. We played logistics games, had a bottle of wine, went to sleep, and stayed the night.

"I don't think the unrest had much of an impact on the activities of the Graduate College. I think it probably affected the undergraduates a lot more, and that's understandable.

"During that whole time, both as a faculty member and as an administrator, I never remember great confrontations between students you worked with and knew and taught and the faculty. It was always a mass. But in terms of the people you interacted with on a regular basis, I think everybody was civil. Most of the conversations were still academic conversations, they weren't political confrontation. I always thought that was a real plus for the university, that you didn't get acrimony among people who knew each other. I always remember that as it was kind of a civil time during a time of civil disobedience."

Sam Becker, professor emeritus, communication studies, and formerly acting vice president for academic affairs: "I think those years had some good effects and some bad effects. They forced us to listen more to students and respond to them. They forced us to be more flexible and, when a student has a good idea, to consider it. At the beginning of that period, programs and departments had become less flexible, less willing to try something new. A saving grace has been that we loosened things up for students. Now when we revise our graduate curriculum, we wouldn't think about doing it without some student input, and that has been positive. One of the things I worry about, and that has never been regained, is the notion of being able to disagree strongly but respectfully and still be civil to each other."

Gordon Strayer, director of the Office of Public Information: "There was no way to put a good face on the unrest as far as the public was concerned. The public by and large was the generation beyond the student generation and found these young people pretty hard to take, especially those who had missed military service themselves in the previous couple of wars — and the men who were doing their best to be deferred from military service because they were in college — turning around and raising all this hell. It had not been the fashion to question, to doubt, what the government told you and to question governmental actions. Now everybody does this; this is one of the things that came out of that time. We lost our innocence, if we ever had any.

"My office did what we called a special report. Schools all over the country were making reports to their alumni and various constituencies — if they were state schools, to the boards of trustees, parents, and students. Most of these were just sort of public relations apologias. They said almost in effect,

'Look, whatever you read in the paper or saw on television about the strife on our campus, well that didn't happen. But, if it did happen, it was caused by out-of-state students or people from out of town; it wasn't our students who were doing this.' We didn't play it that way. We did a report that showed pictures and used some newspaper clippings and freely acknowledged that it did happen, but we also had some things in there that showed, or tried to show, what a hard time it was for a university. I had a wonderful little letter from a doctor who was from, I think, Anamosa. He was way up in years, and he was down here for continuing medical education. I think he got bored and left his nurse to take notes and wandered up onto the campus and talked to people, to students, almost the whole of one afternoon, and then he went home and he wrote a letter to the editor of the local paper, which we picked up in the clippings and used. He cited the thinking that these kids were doing and wound up saying, 'I guess if I were fifty years younger, I'd be with them, too.'

"It was a terrible time for the history of this university, for people to have to go through this. We had excerpts from mail that came in to Sandy Boyd's office, and one parent or set of parents would say, 'You should throw those animals off campus.' Another one would say, 'I'm trying to understand what my children are going through on this.' We put this together in my office and took it to Sandy. He'd always been not one to push out the bad news in front of the world, and he looked at this a long time. Finally, he looked up and said, 'This is what you folks think we should do?' And I said, 'We think we should because people know that this is happening; maybe this helps them understand why it was happening.' He said, 'I think you should go with it.' One of our deans, when he saw me after this said, 'Gordon, there's no excuse for you showing those pictures of policemen on the campus. (We had one shot of the Iowa Avenue–Clinton Street intersection and there were just thousands of students out there.) There's no excuse for doing this.' And I said, 'Well Dean, this happened.' He said, 'No, you didn't have to show the world about it.' This was head-in-the-sand kind of thing. We felt we were doing the right thing. The then head of the Alumni Association, however, denounced me and printed it in the next issue of the *Alumni Review* for doing this and did his best to distance the Alumni Association from having any part of it. Alumni and some of the people who contributed to the foundation of course were saying, 'You won't get any money out of me until you can do something about those students.' For people to be governed, they've got to want to be governed. You can't govern a mob. We had mob scenes. It was a bad time for the whole country.

"The legislature was very unhappy about all of this. The legislature was in session that spring, and their appropriations in effect were just a few dollars within being exactly the same as we'd had the previous two years. They gave us nothing as I recall for buildings. So we had a two-year hiatus, when there was really no growth. Somehow they managed to eke out some salary raises, not very many though. They were punishing us. The legislators, by and large, were older men, and many of them were veterans of WWI or WWII and just could not see this, could not understand it. It was hard for people, even people with good sense, to see this kind of thing, this 'Hell, no, I won't go' business and this rebellion against the government. This was part of Sprie's and Boyd's magic, if you will, for keeping the lid on things. We had these meetings of the administrative group, sometimes several a day, moved out to Oakdale. For at least one year we had our headquarters out there, clear off the campus. And the governor came to town and the president of the Board of Regents, and they were satisfied with what we were doing, and, while they could have sent the National Guard in here, the governor kept his cool, and the president of the regents helped on this. It could have been a lot worse than it was. We were convinced that a major show of force by the government simply would escalate it, because that's how people reacted; they didn't back down when the troops came in, they started throwing things. It was a bad time."

Willard L. Boyd, president emeritus of the University of Iowa: "I look at the whole thing as a continuum of change in the society. I believe firmly in the civil rights movement. The thing I think most about is the accessibility of the institution. The civil rights movement obviously created a lot of positive participation on the part of white liberals. Yet, at the same time, for Afro-Americans it was understandable that they wanted to be able to stand on their own feet without white liberals. The war was there and the war brought a lot of people together. However, they were primarily white males because, though the SDS would talk about every social issue under the sun, there were very few blacks who would ever come out to SDS demonstrations. First of all, they were afraid that they would be the first to be arrested just by virtue of the latent prejudice in the society.

"Sometimes I think that the greatest problem was that demonstrations choked off discussion about the other side of the war issue. But there was the opening up to all of the other groups such as the Mexican Americans, Native Americans. Then the very important opening up to women, because the university was in fact closed to women as far as faculty was concerned. And then I remember coming along by the Old Capitol and there were a bunch of students with disabilities trying to get up and down its steps, and they were having a great time. I think that the important thing was the opening of the institution to all people based on merit.

"I don't really think our curriculum changed very much as the result of those times, but we had some opportunities, which I had always believed in. We had the Bachelor of Liberal Studies, which was designed to meet the needs of individual students. But basically the curriculum did not change here.

"I think there was a broader context. There was a national president of the SDS who said, 'Goals achieved are no longer goals and people need goals to live by.' This was basically the antiwar motivation; the SDS was a movement of young white males who were relatively affluent. Their parents had come out of the Depression, were busy trying to make a living so the kids could have things. And these kids were in a position so they could come to the university, and they were waiting to change the society. The war came along and there were other concerns, such as inequities in the society, that even now we must continue to address. At the same time many people were in [draft] deferment in the university, and remember that blacks were fighting the war. The blacks had the burden of the war because they were the ones who had been held in subjugation so they just didn't identify with the antiwar in great numbers.

"But the response was not so much in response to the SDS as it was to the war. And then the war swamped the SDS. I recently read a book by a woman of the SDS who talks about the fact that on most of the campuses the talking was always done by males and that the women members were not allowed to talk. So you see a lot of changing going on. I see it as the opening up of the society. While I think it was an important thing to get us out of the war, I look at this as a long term civil rights issue which has opened up the universities and opened up the society, I say, based on merit."

Arthur Bonfield, professor of law and advisor to Presidents Bowen, Boyd, and Freedman: "Sandy [Boyd] stood up for the principle that if you broke lawful and proper rules, you ought to be willing to take the punishment. Whether you were willing or not, you'd get the punishment, and, similarly, he was going to maintain this campus as an open forum for the expression of ideas, however popular or unpopular, whether at one end of the political spectrum or another. Unlike some universities, where they caved in to one side or the other, this university never did because of the leadership of Sandy Boyd, who really made an effort to live on principle and keep this as an open forum, at the same time enforcing the rules.

"Judge Garfield, a former justice of the Iowa Supreme Court, was brought in to preside over sanction hearings in very difficult circumstances but did so in a way that this university again stood up for principle.

"There were lots of different pressures that Sandy Boyd had to stand up to. People didn't want certain people speaking on campus. . . . People didn't want people from the left speaking on campus. Sandy stood up to that. This was an open forum. So long as they obeyed the law, and they demonstrated lawfully, that was fine; they ought to be able to speak. But, of course, the people from the left, once they thought they had power, thought that they weren't going to let the people from the right speak. Oh no! Sandy believed the principle — what's good for the goose is good for the gander — and the principle was an open campus forum with ideas of all persuasions.

"Sandy not only had the intellectual courage; he had personal courage, personal physical courage of a kind you don't often see. . . . When he was a professor, when he was vice president, when he was president, he was simply Sandy to everybody on campus. He had a wider acquaintanceship of people on this campus than I believe anyone on the campus had, and he was universally loved by people because he was one of the people in the sense that there was no social distance between him and others; he was just everybody's buddy, and he would talk to anyone without regard to their politics or even, frankly, their good manners. That served him very well during periods when there were several thousand students on the Pentacrest, and there were a fringe number who threatened violence and were willing to engage in illegal, unlawful violence or other improper conduct. In those circumstance, multiple times I saw Sandy walk into a crowd of a thousand seemingly hostile people, get in there, talk to them, and ultimately make a speech and most often calm them down. He was willing to put himself on the line, and he was successful in doing that because everyone respected Sandy, even those calling him a tool of this, that, or the other thing.

"Another occasion when Sandy's principles showed was during the time that students were allowed to leave the university before the semester was over [May 1970]. Sandy was incredibly conscientious in not wanting to do that, but finally did it only after being persuaded that that was really essential to avoid harm, potentially even violence, harm to students, to faculty, the university. However, we need to remember that he never closed the university. What he was dealing with were students who were terrified.

"There were allegations that the trouble was created by outsiders rather than insiders. I think both are true. That is, on the one hand there was a social revolution going on in the country. Just by watching TV you could see it. Again, I want to stress it was not just the Vietnam War. There were many people with many different views as to why this was happening, and I might also add, this kind of unrest was going on in Europe. They weren't fighting the Vietnam War; we were fighting the Vietnam War. And secondly, what did the Vietnam War have to do with whether or not there ought to be student evaluations of faculty? What did it have to do with certain efforts to diversify the faculty and certain efforts to try to eradicate the racism that was present and open things up for women? There was also a sexual revolution going on in this country at the time; there were all kinds of things going on and, I guess, to the question 'inside-outside,' it is perfectly clear that we had our own indigenous levels here. But it is also clear that there were some from the outside — I mean outside the university and outside the university community — that suddenly seemed to appear and pop in here, and that increased trouble was a result of it. So I don't have any doubt that while the bulk of the protests and the bulk of the problems were homegrown and went beyond the Vietnam War to a larger social revolution, larger issues, civil rights, issues of reform in education, challenges to authority, challenges to the existing order, that most of it was local, but there clearly was some element who introduced themselves from outside solely for the purpose of fomenting difficulty.

"There are a number of legacies from that period, some good, and some bad. Clearly, one of the legacies that came from it is a greater university responsibility for teaching of students. A second was a university commitment to try to make this a more open place to more different groups. I'm thinking now specifically about blacks and minorities; I'm also thinking about more equal roles for women. I hope that the clock has not turned back on this, that the university got out of the business of *parens patrei*; that is, got out of the business of *in loco parentis*. The university used to treat the students as its children."

David Vernon, professor of law and former acting vice president for academic affairs: "Those times were not a plus for the university or the country, in my opinion. I never understood why the people who were opposed to the war were attacking the university, which was not engaged in a war. I could understand the civil rights movement attacking those who were discriminating, but to use that as an analogy is wrong because the university was not involved in that damn war. I didn't like the war any more than the people who were being disruptive. I minded the disruptions. I just read a piece the other day, and a reference was made to that group of people as being sort of neo-Nazis. I have not called them that yet, although I have called them hooligans.

"I think it had an impact. I think it moved the universities away from doing research that might have helped the armed forces. I thought that was a little bit absurd. Other than that, I couldn't see any particular merit in most of the positions taken. It was not that the war was bad. I view it very cynically and believe that the protest movement had lots to do with the draft. And that's how we ended the war. Middle Americans didn't want their kids drafted, and therefore the war was ended. That may be a cynical observation by me, but I believe it. Although I think it did a lot of damage and there's one holdover, although not a great one, that has to do with the role of students, but faculty members are now finding it easier to forget. They capitulated too easily to the excesses of the militants. There was no reason to do that. But the good thing is that we finally listened to the students.

"What it did accomplish was that it brought together within the university a group of people from the core of the place to the fringes who worked to try to hold the place together. And there developed a quite amazing camaraderie that was very important to us as a morale matter, and it supported the university for many years thereafter. I thought that was one of the good things. It's really hard to put your finger on it, but I really believe that we learned to trust each other and to work together. It lasted a long time.

"Governor Ray's willingness to let us determine our own fate was, I thought, one of the key factors. The Board of Regents' willingness to send an observer [President Stanley Redeker], who was just that, who was there not to do anything but to explain what we did, was a stunningly important thing to have happened. The faculty, I thought, to a very great extent acted well during that time. Sure, we had some oddballs, but I thought the faculty was helpful in trying to keep the institution functioning to get this thing done and get through a difficult time. It was my idea initially to give people the option of taking exams or not as they wished, and, if I had it to do again, I think I would not recommend that. That was for me almost the low point, even though it was my idea. It got us out from under, but it sacrificed an awful lot in terms of academics. It probably was a mistake. Now it's hard to tell what would have happened if we had had exams. But the trouble did end on the spot. That was a plus, because we were all tired and we would not have been able to go forward much longer.

"I have just finished an article/essay [November 1995] on a fifty-year review of the 'free' speech on campus and concluded that the worst times for free speech were the late 1960s and early 1970s. I have concluded that that era made faculty and administrators realize that there was something called 'students' on the scene and that students are vital to the institution. Nobody really believed it until they showed us how important they were. The care and feeding of students became a major operation for us. But the fact is that the majority on campus was able to stifle dissent by shouting down those who disagreed. I thought the impact was negative. There was substantial intolerance on campus at that time toward speakers who were controversial, and it continues to some extent even today. I think that is a holdover from the days of the Vietnam protest."

During the years of student unrest it was difficult for us to imagine that anything good would come out of the experience; indeed, sometimes we wondered whether the unrest would ever end. I think, however, that the university ended up stronger when the unrest was finally over. It knew itself better and understood its core values better; it acknowledged, sometimes grudgingly to be sure, a new and appropriate respect of its students. Perhaps most important, the university did more than survive the ordeal; it lived up to its founding premises of open inquiry and dedication to learning, in spite of fear and dissent. An institution singularly devoted to expanding knowledge, the university learned it was unsinkable because it was irreplaceable.

9. THE LASER CENTER: WILL-O'-THE-WISP

The Laser Center, now called the Iowa Advanced Technology Laboratories, is situated on the east side of the Iowa River, north of the Iowa Memorial Union and directly across from the Art Building. It was designed by Frank Gehry, an architect with a national/international reputation, known for daring, even avant-garde designs. One can imagine the building to be a jumble of various sized and shaped farm buildings, including silos, bunched together. Most of its exterior has a silver sheen, very unlike the masonry and brick exteriors of other university buildings. Controversy has swirled about both its design and the uses originally proposed for it.

A brochure detailing the laser initiative was produced in 1987. The headings of the brochure reveal its scope: "Taking the lead"; "The opportunity is now for Iowa"; "Why and where does Iowa fit?"; "The University of Iowa — a plan of action"; "The need for statewide commitment"; and "New wave into the twenty-first century." There were, of course, several years of antecedents before the brochure. The residual history to date has largely ignored those antecedents. It has also glossed over the reality that the university administration that followed the Freedman era lacked, in my opinion, the vision, determination, and guts to complete the laser initiative. What follows is a recounting of a story that could have ended with a unique, vibrant intellectual center at the University of Iowa instead of a will-o'-the-wisp.

Beginning in the late 1970s, the economy of the state was in a doldrums, and the state legislature was casting about insistently for ways to jump-start it. Not surprisingly, they looked to the state universities, not only for ideas but also for potential products that would breathe life into the state's economy. We felt the pressure in central administration; in fact, it was intense. We were called to repeated meetings in Des Moines and pressed for ideas on ways we could help. A not-too-implicit agenda was, Why don't you people dust off those ideas and inventions that you have sitting on your shelves and make them available to the private sector for development? If we had had any at that stage, we would, of course, have been delighted to comply. While there are thousands of ideas in the collective mind of our faculty, they are there as parts of conceptual frameworks of a faculty driven primarily to examine constructs and better understandings of natural phenomena rather than the development of better mousetraps.

Nevertheless, those of us in central administration began to think systematically of ways that the university could do its part. Because the calls were coming so regularly and insistently from the legislature, the "SWAT Team," described in chapter 4, was on standby, frequently on weekends, to respond to forty-eight- and seventy-two-hour turnaround times to supply the various legislative committees with information and responses to a host of questions.

This, then, was the zeitgeist when Bill Stwalley, then professor of chemistry and physics, and now professor and head of the Department of Physics at the University of Connecticut, came to my office to give me a report on what he had learned during his one-year leave (1975–1976) to serve as a visiting program officer at NSF (a customary practice by NSF at the time) and several subsequent years consulting for them. Since he had been interested in lasers prior to going to NSF, he was particularly attuned to observing developments in that area from the NSF vantage point. He came home convinced that there would be explosive growth in research and development involving lasers. He inquired of me whether the university would be interested in supporting some developments in the area. I was intrigued, but my understanding of the science was primitive at best, so I arranged a meeting for Bill to make a presentation before a number of my colleagues whose judgments I trusted. The conclusion was that lasers were going to be one of the waves of the future and that, with Bill's leadership and convictions, we had a chance of being on the ground floor in its development.

In May 1978 we announced through *RGN* (*Research and Graduate News*) that the Iowa Laser Center, consisting of several offices and a large laboratory, had been established in the Chemistry Department and that it was available to the entire university community. Collaborative projects were already under way, involving faculty from Coe College, the University of Colorado, Wartburg College, and National Taiwan University. We noted that a $2.75 million proposal had been submitted to NSF to aid us in becoming a regional laser instrumentation facility.

By 1985 the Iowa High Technology Council had awarded the center three grants totaling approximately $160,000, which the university had matched with another $91,450, to continue the acquisition of state-of-the-art laser equipment for the center. By that time the center had become a stopping place for state officials who regularly toured the university's facilities.

President Freedman explains what happened next in a talk given at a dinner meeting on January 8, 1986, before the Keokuk Chamber of Commerce. Here are some excerpts:

When we were first asked by state officials to design proposals for the funds generated by the lottery, we asked ourselves "What areas on the cutting edge of research, where the university already has strength, will also contribute to the economic development of the state?" We chose laser science as our highest priority because it is one of those very few fields which is going to ascend into international prominence in the next decade.

Already lasers are scanning our groceries, playing our compact discs, carving elaborate and delicate wood designs for Iowa furniture, removing birthmarks, analyzing blood, surveying roads, and probing genetic material to choose almost at random from a long, long list.

So far no region has established dominance in laser technology in the way that California and Massachusetts have done in computers and electronics. And no university has yet established an interdisciplinary laser program that combines the teaching and research in the way that we propose.

The University of Iowa is in an ideal position to move forward with laser research. We have eight faculty investigators actively focusing on laser science now — in physics, chemistry, biomedical engineering, electrical engineering, and mechanical engineering — and at least seventy-five other scientists, and medical researchers with laser-related interests. We have $1.5 million from the state in lottery proceeds, matched by private gifts, to endow chairs for three eminent professors in laser science. . . .

The state of Iowa now has the opportunity to invest in front-row seats for a research initiative that in the years to come will offer standing room only. We aspire to nothing less than world leadership in an emerging area of twenty-first century science.

On March 26, 1986, Bill Stwalley sent me a report on the activities of the several search committees looking for candidates for the endowed chairs. He indicated that potential candidates had been identified from the chemistry and engineering pools and enclosed a letter from one who had commented, in a general way, about space, equipment, and support staff requirements, all suggesting that if Iowa could provide them he would be willing to consider the possibility of a move. Bill proposed that, as the candidates were identified, they should be invited to visit the campus and, if they were willing, to participate in the designing of the new spaces that we might be able to provide them. At that point the possibility of building a special facility for the purpose was only in the talking stage.

In July 1986 we got word that the Iowa Department of Economic Development had allotted us $3.25 million in lottery revenues to endow six professorships: three in laser science and engineering and one each in biocatalysis, hydraulics, and manufacturing productivity. Matching private funds brought the funds available to $6.5 million. Now we could proceed with some certainty in making plans for the laser center's space and the people to occupy it. In October 1986 the Board of Regents approved our request to build a $25.1 million laser science laboratory. That was only the first step, of course. The legislature would have to provide the funds, and we knew we would have to do some "selling" before the funds were at hand. In retrospect, we had already started to walk down the primrose path of our own undoing when it became known that "three top laser scientists have indicated that they would like to work in the new facility." While they were not named at this point, their present institutions were identified: the National Bureau of Standards, MIT, and Northwestern. (Later they were identified as William Phillips, physicist, Bureau of Standards [one of three scientists who would later share the 1997 Nobel Prize in physics]; Aram Mooradian, engineer, Lincoln Laboratories at MIT; and Richard Van Duyne, chemist, Northwestern.)

The estimate of 12,000 laser-related jobs coming to Iowa that we used in some of the talks and news releases was not just idle speculation on our part but an extrapolation of other predictions. It was a composite based on projections carried by such periodicals as *Newsweek*, *Time*, the *Wall Street Journal*, the *Economist*, *Photonics*, *Spectra*, and *Fiber/Laser News*. Based on these projections, Bill Stwalley suggested that at least 800,000 new jobs would be created in laser-based industries in the U.S. during the period from 1991 to 2000 and that Iowa would attract its fair share. Assuming that the percentage of the U.S. population living in Iowa would be 1.5 percent, Iowa could expect its share of the 800,000 jobs to be 12,000.

It was clear that we would have to build space designed and dedicated for use by the researchers who would occupy it, particularly if we stood a chance of recruiting the world-class scientists that we were seeking. President Freedman was of the view that a building specifically designed for laser science and engineering should not be one with humdrum architectural design but something that was both functional and symbolic of the science and the age.

On January 15, 1987, only the fourth day of the 1987 session of the legislature, the Iowa Senate passed legislation allowing the regents to sell $25.1 million in bonds to finance the laser center. It took the action only after defeating a move that would have prohibited classified research in the building (a gratuitous action since university policy already forbade it). Action would not be forthcoming so soon in the Iowa House, which raised questions about the nature of the research that would be done in the center. This was the era of the DOD Strategic Defense Initiative, or Star Wars, and questions arose about the possibility of the center's becoming an integral part of that initiative, and, if so, was that an appropriate activity for the university.

When the bonding measure reached the Iowa House, the Appropriations Committee handily approved authorization for the bonding but inserted a clause that would restrict the conduct of classified research in the Laser Center. Shortly after that, the Board of Regents passed a resolution that condemned such a restriction and endorsed a statement by President Freedman and Gordon Eaton, then president of Iowa State University, that said in part: "It is unwise and undesirable to include restrictions on research in bonding indentures that have a life of twenty-five years because, unlike a statute, indentures cannot be changed by legislation alone." It wasn't until May 11, 1987, that the bonding bill was finally passed and, after weeks of debate on including the classified research restriction, without any such restriction. Nevertheless, the extended discussion of the bonding bill (there were funds for other regents projects as well) kept the laser center on the news and editorial pages of the local newspapers through the intervening weeks. Not surprisingly, questions about the Nobel-class scientists' intention of joining the university and the projected economic impact of the center kept roiling up as well.

After lots of discussion and an initial unanimous vote against the site, the Campus Planning Committee voted unanimously on June 9, 1987, to recommend that the Laser Center be built in the parking lot north of the Union. It was the recommendation of the design team because "it allows a design which could interact well with the Iowa River and student needs, provides for adequate expansion without crowding the site and is in a location that has a public as well as campus image." At the same time the committee recommended that the parking lot be replaced with a parking ramp (now the North Campus Parking Ramp). The decision needed to be made early in planning for the building since a location was necessary before the architects could proceed with its detailed design.

Dick Gibson, then director of Facilities Services Group, had the assignment to find the architect and supervise the planning and construction of the building. Here is his account of that effort:

About that time you . . . had three potential faculty people identified. I . . . visited all three of them on site so I could get a little bit better understanding of what this thing was. We persuaded them to assist us in the planning project because we didn't have anybody else but Bill Stwalley who might tell us what a laser center was. They came out here. I can think of at least two sessions we had with them, sitting right here in our conference room, helping us design this building.

Jim Freedman told me that he wanted a world-class building. I thought, how in hell do I guarantee a world-class building? The first step was to get a world-class architect. One of the architecture magazines had a story about really hot architects. So we sent the invitations out to this whole group of people — twenty-five or thirty — world-class architects and ultimately interviewed at least four for this project. Frank Gehry got it. It was Frank's first big project.

When we bid it, we were over budget by four or five million. We rebid it and took some of the components out, got it bid again and got it built. It was really not a difficult time to get the building built except for the skin, which was a major issue.

Somewhere during that design process, we pulled in those three scientists, and they helped us design the basic form of the building. The notion of the open-office environment, the notion of the generic laboratory that was not even going to have walls in it at the time we did it. . . . A lot of people who have seen it think that it is one of Frank Gehry's best works. . . . That building, if it isn't already, will be an icon on this campus. There is no doubt in my mind about it. People love it or hate it.

On August 26, 1987, Interim President Dick Remington made a formal offer to Mooradian of an endowed chair in laser engineering, a lead role in recruiting six new faculty for the center, six specialized support persons, and $3.5 million for equipment during the initial three-year period, much of which would come from external sources. On October 1, 1987, Remington made an offer to Van Duyne of an endowed chair in laser chemistry, the lead role in recruiting four new faculty for the center, plus equipment and support persons similar to that offered to Mooradian. Since it was understood that Phillips's decision depended on Mooradian's decisions, an offer to Phillips was held in abeyance.

In late November 1987 we got word that Mooradian had received an attractive offer from private industry and probably would not be coming to Iowa after all. Since Phillips had indicated that his coming to Iowa was contingent upon Mooradian's acceptance, we had doubts about either of them coming. In January Van Duyne, citing "personal reasons," declined our offer to move to Iowa. Mooradian's decision was disappointing, to say the least, since he had emerged as the nominal leader of the three and, with the other two, had come to campus several times to participate in planning the details of the building to make sure that spaces were designed precisely to meet their needs. While they had not accepted formal offers at that planning stage, it seemed reasonable to assume that persons as busy and as in demand as they were would not invest such time on the Iowa campus idly if there weren't serious intent to follow through when formal offers were made and the new space was available to them.

Following the declination of our offers, the finger pointing began on all fronts, legislators and university administrators in particular. Distinctions were made between "promised" and "expected." The "you saids" and "no we didn'ts" overshadowed the fact that there were, after all, other world-class laser leaders yet to be recruited. Dick Remington, clearly not deterred by the declinations, said on January 22, 1988: "Before long we will be filling these open positions with top-level scientists. We have not lowered our sights one millimeter. We are aiming high and we will score."

Dick was true to his word. On May 21, 1988, Arthur Smirl, chairman of the Center for Applied Quantum Electronics and distinguished research professor of physics at North Texas State University, accepted his offer of the endowed chair in laser engineering. Today, Smirl occupies space in the laser center building, now called the Iowa Advanced Technology Laboratories.

On June 20, 1988, Bill Stwalley sent President-designate Rawlings a letter summarizing the planning, commitments, and negotiations for faculty and staff appointments, equipment, and support staff that had been made up to that time for the laser center. He discussed a possible candidate for the endowed chair in physics and plans for identifying a person for the chemistry chair. The tone of the letter was positive and upbeat, based on the assumption that our plans were on track to fulfill the design that had been fashioned for a world-class laser center at Iowa. His letter received no response.

November 9, 1988, was an important day in the life of the center — groundbreaking for the construction of the building. Governor Branstad, other state and local officials, and university folks gathered for the event. President Rawlings was the principal speaker:

This is truly a brilliant day for the University of Iowa and for the state of Iowa. For the past two years, some of the most far-sighted leaders in the university and around the state have been working together to make this moment possible. As we prepare to break ground for the Center for Laser Science and Engineering Building, I am happy to welcome all of you to this celebration of pure and brilliant light.

I mean not only the laser light that will be studied and put to new uses in this building, but also the light of the scientist's curiosity, the force that is driving our professors and investigators and students to reach ahead of what has been known, toward the science of the future. And I mean the light of the artist's imagination, the force that has urged Frank Gehry to break the molds of the past and create the architecture of the future. And, finally, I mean the light of faith and optimism that all of us share in the future of the university and the future of the state of Iowa.

. . . We're going to start laying the groundwork for a building of the twenty-first century that is going to house the scientific research that will take the university and the state of Iowa into the forefront of the next century.

The *Daily Iowan* for that date noted that "the Laser Center will have 24 faculty members and three endowed chairpersons. The program is searching for 14 faculty members. Arthur Smirl, the first of the three endowed chairpersons to be hired, will help the UI fill the remaining positions." Clearly, the thrust was positive; there was no hint that the plan would ultimately be sacked.

However, there were other voices that seemed, at least from my point of view, to cast a pall on the whole concept of a Midwest citadel for laser science. On February 7, 1989, Andy Brownstein, a *Daily Iowan* reporter, wrote a column in the *DI* with the headline: "Laser Center Fate Remains a Mystery," with the subtitle, "Where's the force behind the UI laser center?" In his column he reported on some comments from Iowa Representative Jack Hatch to the effect that Hatch was disappointed in the way in which the president and the governor had presented the proposal, and that President Freedman had given members of the legislature the impression that "three professors had promised to come, and a great window of opportunity would be passing us by if we didn't act immediately." He reported that Hatch felt that the "12,000 jobs was a shot in the dark" and that Rawlings would not have presented the project as Freedman had, saying that Rawlings "knows what the legislature wants."

What did Jack Hatch mean when he said Rawlings knew what the legislature wanted? Hatch was one of the loudest exhorters of the university to do something for economic development, and we had supplied him with reams of documentation about lasers and the laser center. Did the legislature want us to call the whole thing off? In effect, that was what President Rawlings was about to do.

On May 26, 1989, Bill Stwalley wrote to President Rawlings, frustrated by silence and inaction from the president's office. Here are some excerpts from that letter:

Is there any compelling reason for changing the scope of the Laser Center? If so, how should it be changed? Given that the scope is either reaffirmed or modified, how can the Laser Center be managed most effectively for achieving its research, educational and outreach goals?

... I feel that our Laser Center recruiting efforts, already significantly damaged by the current uncertainty, must be suspended until the scope is hopefully reaffirmed or, if necessary, modified. This scope implies not only University of Iowa commitments to Art [Smirl], Susan [Allen, a professor in the Department of Chemistry with complementary research interests], myself and others here who have worked tirelessly for years to develop the laser center, but it also implies commitments made to the Board of Regents, the legislature, the governor, and the people of Iowa. I find the current rumor-laden environment positively Kafkaesque and urge you to clear the air.

President Rawlings responded to Stwalley on July 14 to the effect that, given the fact that a new vice president for research had not yet been appointed, he was asking Leo Davis, acting associate vice president for academic affairs in the office of Acting Vice President for academic affairs David Vernon, to assume oversight of the center. Both President Freedman and Interim President Remington had chosen to centrally involved; clearly, Rawlings had not, indicating, to me, by his action that his heart was not in the center's success.

The negative drumbeats continued. In an effort to move the building along, contracts had been let for the building's foundation and footings. However, the completion of the design of the building had been delayed because the bids for the original design had been over budget. For some months the foundation stood naked — no workmen were in sight — another sign that perhaps all was not quite right. Then the university made clear to the Board of Regents at its September 1989 meeting that it would be necessary to make a request for a supplemental budget increase to cover the cost of equipping the center. Ordinarily, this would not have seemed unusual since it has been common practice for the legislature to appropriate funds for construction first, to be followed in a subsequent year by another appropriation for building equipment. In this instance, however, critics of the project, including some members of the Board of Regents, pointed at the upcoming need as another indication of misrepresentation. David Vernon did his best to answer the questions, but the president was noticeably silent.

In October 1989 the board approved the appointment of Arthur Smirl as director of the Laser Center, succeeding Bill Stwalley, who would continue to teach and do research in the center. In the ten months since the center had been established, there had been substantial accomplishments: Five of the seventeen primary appointments associated with the center had been filled; nine postdoctoral research associates and seventeen students were conducting research with laser faculty. Two million dollars in external funding had been received, and three university laboratories — the Iowa Laser Facility, directed by Bill Stwalley, the Laser Microfabrication Facility, directed by Susan Allen, and the Ultrafast Photonics and Electronics facility, directed by Arthur Smirl — were in place.

In December 1989 the Board of Regents approved the redesign of the building, with its completion scheduled for 1992, a year after it was originally scheduled to be completed. The bids on the redesigned building came in within budget. At the same meeting Arthur Smirl is quoted as saying:

> We fumbled the ball. While kicking it around, trying to pick it up, trying to decide whether we wanted to be in the game, other states have more efficiently put larger resources in place. If we do nothing else and this continues to trickle along at the rate at which we've been making appointments over the last five years, then we are going to have missed a real opportunity. The University of Central Florida, University of Michigan, Princeton University and the University of Alabama at Huntsville have surpassed us. Five years ago only the University of Rochester and the University of Arizona were ranked above us.

On April 26, 1991, James Morrison, then vice president for research, wrote a memo to Bill Stwalley, directing him to discontinue the operation of the laser facility forthwith. It was, he said, based on his conclusion "that there exists for the facility a continuing pattern of unsatisfactory financial management, an insufficiently broad client base and a cost/research benefit ratio that is inappropriately large, requiring a greater cost subsidy than I am willing to impose on this office." It was to be one of Morrison's last actions; the very next day he left the university!

On August 13, 1991, the *Des Moines Register* printed a little piece entitled "Laser Center: $25 Million 'Sting.'" "The facility is now behind schedule, its avant-garde design by noted architect Frank Gehry has been scaled back and it has become synonymous with 'boondoggle.'" It quoted Don Avenson, former speaker of the Iowa House of Representatives, as saying, "It was a wonderful, wonderful sting." I felt compelled to respond the next day with a letter, which was printed in the August 23, 1991, issue of the *Des Moines Register*.

> Shame! Shame!
>
> Don Avenson, former speaker of the Iowa House of Representatives, has characterized as a "sting" the efforts of former University of Iowa's President Jim Freedman to convince state government to provide funds for the building a laser center at the University of Iowa. My dictionary includes in its definition of "sting" the following: "overcharge, cheat, ... an elaborate confidence game; specifically: such a game worked by under-

cover police to trap criminals." To characterize Mr. Freedman's efforts to get funds for that building that way is scandalous! Mr. Freedman believed in that cause, and believed that it would prove to be a beneficial project for the economy of the state. Critics may believe that the proposition was misguided but it most certainly was not an elaborate effort to deceive. What unearthly good would come to the university and the individuals involved if such had been the case? An apology is in order, Mr. Avenson!

Congressman Neal Smith quotes Mr. Freedman as saying that only a tiny fraction of the research funding for the laser program would come from NASA and DOD. Mr. Smith took that response as evidence "that he [Mr. Freedman] didn't know what he was talking about." Quite the contrary! The University of Iowa has an outstanding record for competing for research dollars (well over $125 million annually over the last several years). The source of those funds are primarily from the National Institutes of Health, reflecting the world-class quality of the research conducted by the university's faculty in the area of health, broadly defined. Historically, the DOD and NASA, with the exception of space physics, have not been major sources of research support at the University of Iowa. I am certain that Mr. Freedman was reflecting that history in his reply to Congressman Smith's question. Mr. Freedman might have responded that it was the university's intention, with the assistance of Congressman Smith, to secure major, directed awards through specific congressional appropriations for that purpose, but such had not been the university's strategy since it was, and still is, doing very well, thank you, through the competitive channels available to it. An apology from Mr. Smith is also in order.

The Laser Center building is coming to completion. And believe it or not, the original dream could still be valid. Lasers are far from being an outmoded fad. Fill the building with $15 million in state-of-the-art equipment, and recruit two or three world-class laser researchers, in addition to Arthur Smirl and his faculty colleagues who are already here, and the consequences will be significantly felt both in the academic and economic realms. What is needed now are state leaders with vision and guts. Any volunteers?

Some Reflections

You have just read of some of the circumstances and events that were involved in the conceptualization and implementation of the Laser Center. Some ten years later, I asked several people who were directly involved in the effort to reflect on those times.

Dorsey (Dan) Ellis, then vice president for finance and university services, was responsible for the Campus Planning Committee. "I take the credit or the blame, as the case may be, for what ultimately happened here. We were pleasantly surprised that architects of the caliber that we were seeing were interested in this process. One was Frank Gehry from Los Angeles, a controversial architect. He came up with a conceptual design that many of us found to be quite exciting. The location on the banks of the Iowa River was a wonderful location, very visible, and made it a central part of the campus. I was the point person for persuading the regents to accept Frank Gehry as the architect and the design that he had come up with conceptually. Although very daring and forward looking, and perhaps a little jarring to some people, nonetheless . . . exciting.

"The building that was actually built was not the design I took to the Board of Regents! The concept that Gehry showed us was a building that took advantage of the river and had a plaza out overlooking the river, that kind of tied into the Union. I thought it was dramatic, it was contemporary, it was forward looking, but I thought it very appropriate and fit in on this campus in the location. The building that's actually been built — I don't see any relationship to that and the conceptual design that he had presented."

William Stwalley recalls: "I began to appreciate lasers before I went to the National Science Foundation [1975–1976] on a year's leave from Iowa, although we didn't have any lasers or do any work with lasers there until after my return. But it was clear in the late 1970s that the laser was probably the most powerful technique available for a variety of applications after the computer.

"I think the original idea to establish a laser center at Iowa was an outgrowth of the activities in the laser facility which I was directing, which involved interactions with people in many different departments — chemistry, physics, many engineering departments, some people in the medical school, and some other departments as well. It was clear that there was a big advantage in the shared use of equipment. Many people were reluctant to get lasers or get involved with lasers because that involved a fair amount of learning and a fair amount of expense.

"We had an international search, and we identified three really outstanding people in the area of laser science and engineering: Mooradian, Phillips, and Van Duyne. Each of them had a broad perspective on lasers and their applications and doing frontier research in their own areas.

"The clear projections in the trade magazines in the area of laser science and engineering were that this field was going to grow very dramatically — it was growing very dramatically at 50 percent per year — and that it was expected to rival electronics in 2010 in terms of total magnitude of the investment. Of course, there are lots of common examples: check-out counter readers, universal product code readers, the CD players, fiber optics telecommunications — all of those are laser-based and those things are going to continue to expand.

"I don't think our projection of 12,000 laser-related jobs in Iowa was a completely unreasonable number over a decade or possibly two decades. But universities don't create jobs. Universities can provide research support for the companies that want to create jobs, and they can provide talented students to work in those companies, but the climate of the university is not going to determine the climate for business in the state. That's a complicated issue. You have to get venture capital, and you have to have the right tax laws and all of that. In Connecticut there were 113 photonics companies when I arrived in 1993, and now [1997] there are 148 and that's going to continue to grow. It's one of the biggest growth areas in Connecticut, along with biotechnology.

"I really thought the three laser stars that we identified were excited about our proposal. They were very interested. They spent a lot of their time on this project, and they were all busy people who had lots of other things to do. Even so, they came out and reviewed plans for the building. I think they thought of themselves as being part of it. But they didn't just make personal suggestions. They made suggestions on how to build up the center as a whole, not just with their personal goals in mind. They really had a sense of participation in what was happening. They knew they would be getting offers from us, detailed offers, and we discussed the details of the offers, and those were discussed with other people in the administration here. There were offer letters for all of them. Those offers were the result of significant negotiations, but those negotiations were over by the time the final building plans were being reviewed.

"We not only talked to them, they talked to each other. I think Mooradian, for example, got cold feet — he had a good business opportunity in Massachusetts where he was. He did want to leave Lincoln Labs. So it was a competing offer, I would say, that surfaced after he was being interviewed here. He went to a small start-up business in Massachusetts, where there's very good infrastructure for the business, and I think the business has done very well.

"But we had very many other good candidates in the pool, well over a hundred, and a number of those were outstanding people as well. There were people who were recruited later. Art Smirl did come. Dick Powell, who was the director of a laser center at Oklahoma State, of smaller scope than what we had planned, became the head of the Optical Sciences Center at the University of Arizona, instead of being recruited here. Dan Griscowski, who was at IBM, who was a real leader and set up, for example, an international council on quantum electronics, and is very active in lots of things. He went to Oklahoma

State to replace Powell. Those were people we could have had here, but it didn't work out.

"It's hard to tell why the center proposal didn't proceed. Nothing came out from central administration. People would say very good words. We had a groundbreaking. President Rawlings presented all this nice stuff for the building. But when it came to identifying resources, for example, to hire Dan Griscowski, we couldn't get $500,000 to $600,000 in start-up commitments, which was very modest for somebody of Griscowski's caliber, and, in fact, I think he ended up with over $1 million in start-up going to Oklahoma State, and he brought a lot of equipment with him from IBM.

"The administration's response was to make other projections, consider another way of doing things, asking that new materials be prepared, but nothing seemed to jar anything loose in terms of support for proceeding with the center. So, it was a frustrating experience that was not there when President Freedman was working with the laser center before he left to go to Dartmouth. Acting President Remington was also very supportive.

"I still think the laser center for Iowa was a great idea. Now I think Iowa really has missed an opportunity. It's probably too late to do a lot about it. For example, one school that is developing a very nice program, not as ambitious as the program here, is Montana State. And there are a number of photonics companies in Montana, because in Bozeman they have some very good laser physicists and laser chemists.

"Our projection of 12,000 jobs was not off the wall. I don't know how you assess those things. Prediction is tremendously difficult. I think the photonics area is a great one, materials area is a great one for economic growth, biotechnology is very good. All of those are being invested in by the state of Connecticut in their Critical Technologies Program. Iowa just needed to follow through."

Hunter Rawlings III, then president of the University of Iowa, now president of Cornell University, from a 1997 interview: "[The establishment of the University of Iowa as a national center for laser science] was certainly a difficult issue to deal with because, when I came to the university, there had already been the public difficulty, and there was a lot of dissatisfaction with the university's selection of that research priority and with the failure to recruit the top faculty members who had been invited to come. There was a strong sense that the effort had gotten off to a weak start, and that the building was not going to be used in the ways that had been planned. We tried to make the best of that, and to scale down the program in such a way that the money we did receive could be well used. But it continued to be a very difficult public issue for us. And I would say we never built the kind of research momentum that we had hoped."

Jim Freedman, from a 1997 interview: "Any public university has to expect that, in most instances, it will be asked to choose architects from that state, and that's totally appropriate. But you also want new architectural gems, which means you have to take chances on internationally known architects, and this seemed to be one of the great opportunities to do it. As we looked at all those lists of names, Frank Gehry was one of those people. I think that building is gorgeous. I think it's stunning and elegant. Many people don't agree with that, but I think that that building is really one I'm most proud of here; that we got in world-class architects to do it.

"You don't launch these kinds of things unless you are prepared. And I think you launch these with a little bit of faith that if these people are as good as we believe, and if the facilities are as good as we believe, that it's going to attract support and attract grants, and it's going to be worth every effort. But obviously every time you put up a building with people, you're making a commitment for the future."

In my opinion this is a story of an unrequited dream. Some of the characters did not prove to be white knights but masquerading peasants. The reflection of the laser center building, now used to house a number of advanced technology laboratories, falls on the Iowa River, which keeps rolling quietly along. But the luster is missing. In my view it could have been striking indeed.

1995—1997

During my interviews with university observers for this history, people commented on a variety of university developments and issues that I have not addressed directly as I have recounted the day-to-day events of the twenty-five years. To add a helpful perspective, I am including reflections about those times from some with whom I talked.

Graduate College

Sam Becker, professor emeritus, communication studies, and former acting vice president for academic affairs: "There were clearly relationships with the Graduate College when I became chair of the department and, before that, to get some support on some projects. . . . The kind of support then available has died now. It encouraged more of us to do projects. . . . There was always a little seed money. . . . Some of our early research on teaching by television and working with interactive television — some of the seed money for those projects came out of the Graduate College. My impression was that somehow there were always a few loose dollars to encourage people do some things, and, even though it was never a lot of money, it was terribly important, especially for some of us relatively young faculty, before we really had the reputations that enabled us to bring in some grant money. I think that was the kind of support that helped to push this university ahead in development and grant getting. I don't think that it existed at all before Sprie was in that office. It did two things: First, the money itself was helpful, but, secondly, it showed that somebody had some faith in you; somebody had some confidence that you were important enough to be supported, and I think that makes a lot of difference."

The College of Medicine and the University

John Eckstein, professor emeritus of internal medicine and former dean of the College of Medicine: "I had come to realize how important the Vice President for Research Office was because I was active in getting grants at the time that position was established. I remember how hesitant we were in the College of Medicine to have someone other than our own department head or dean sign off on them. People would want the animal house, for example, to be all in the College of Medicine, people on our faculty. And it became obvious that we didn't have the general administrative focus that would permit us to do that well. But it was made a sensible, rational process, and by the time I became dean of the College of Medicine, it was very comfortable to work with [the vice president for research]. There were so many things that were done, major programs, big program-project grants, SCORE [Specialized Center of Research] grants, center grants, things of that sort that the College of Medicine participated in.

"I remember participating in a couple of AAU meetings with Sandy [Boyd] and talking about research, and I realized that in many places, perhaps most of the places that I knew anything about, the Office of the Vice President for Research and the Office of the Graduate College were together; that was not unusual in my mind at all.

"I thought the Sponsored Programs Office really grew in competence and understanding of the national scene during the years I was in the dean's office. I found more and more I didn't have to rely on my own connections in government, in Washington, at NIH to get information, that it was much easier to call Marge Hoppin. And it was always done so well that perhaps we weren't holding up our share all the time, at least in our office.

"When I became the dean, the general attitude of the faculty, particularly with people who had a lot of grant money, was that they should get some of that indirect cost recovery back some way. I approached the president a couple of times about it. The third time, Sandy got me in the office, alone I think, and we sat down and looked at some exhibits that I had about the College of Medicine. I remember one in which I talked about tuition, grant money, faculty practice plan money, and so on, and made estimates about how much indirect costs we were bringing in. Sandy said, 'All right, if you're going to push me on this, here's what we'll do. Your indirect costs are coming back to you under the heading of "A Funds" or "State Money."' He said that state money is made up of tuition, indirect costs, and appropriation. He said, 'I'll be responsible for the appropriated money and the tuition component of it. We'll make you responsible for generating the indirect costs in the college. Possibly we could work something out.'

"I thought a lot about what a terrible chore it was, the other deans around the country fighting with the administration, with their faculty, trying to walk some kind of middle line. I think I told you and Sandy that I was going to stop this, and that I'd try to explain to the faculty that I would trust the administration that it was taken into account when decisions were made that we were bringing in a lot of money into the university. There wasn't much choice, but as time went on, I think periodically I'd be able to make a case for a special need or something of that sort that headquarters would take into consideration. I became a pretty strong advocate for not fooling around with indirect costs. I think, in general, our faculty within this college was very quiet compared with faculties I know in other medical schools.

"I don't remember any major conflicts with your office. Usually the posture of everyone in both offices was to try to work things out. If there was something we didn't understand, we'd get it straightened out.

"The establishment of the Central Research Support Facilities played well. I didn't have as much to do with that as I would like to take credit for. The ideas came from your office, and Rex Montgomery [associate dean] jumped on those in a hurry over here. With the construction of the [Eckstein Medical Research Building], he insisted that we should set space aside for a variety of those special facilities. It was just wonderful, and so many of those, which were accessible to everybody in the university, were right here in the college. It helped our recruiting in ways you just can't believe. Take an assistant professor who was coming in, say, internal medicine, and they were trying to recruit him. We'd walk through that building and show him these things. Once, I think it was in the electron microscopy facility, this young fellow asked the director of the facility how long it would take before he could do some work. He was told, 'If you came here tomorrow, we would be able to have you doing something the following day.' I think it was true, and the kind of response you would get, 'My God! At Michigan it would take me months, perhaps years, to get access to somebody who had an electron microscope who would let me use it!' That was a very fine thing, and I certainly hope it continues.

"The evolution of the Human Subject Committee began a good many years ago. In its early days researchers felt that they didn't need to have some committee telling them that they couldn't stick needles in people or catheters or something; they understood what was right and wrong, and the institution didn't have to take charge. Well, gradually, as events happened, it was a wonderful thing to have that Institutional Review Board in place. Gradually, it came to be accepted; it took time. The people who were appointed in some cases were overly conscientious, overly scrupulous about some things, and faculty members would come around and ask if I could do anything about it. I'd tell them that was Spriestersbach's job. I thought that was a valuable thing.

"You had very good people, and they had liaison roles with government agencies and the congressional delegations, and they were on top of things. It became clear that your office was way ahead of things, and you knew when we had to have a policy, and you were pretty much getting it in there; it seemed to me you always had a policy, or had something in the works, that would kind of protect us or cover us or help us do a better job if we got into some kind of difficulty.

"Sandy talked a lot about the university being a unified place. I think he had a very clear vision of what he thought the university should be. It wasn't just whimsy; he had a picture of the university and he proclaimed it. He didn't want a great huge bunch of centers and things that were outside the real academic framework. I bought into that. I think the future could be awkward because now the Health Science Center administratively appears to be, at least from a distance, becoming like other places, where the Health Science Center is somewhat remote from the university. I think it will be hard to make it like a lot of other places because we're physically so close. But that kind of stuff can hinder progress."

External Funding

James Van Allen, professor emeritus, physics and astronomy: "During the period when I first came here, research in the department was on a small-scale basis. I should say that an annual grant of 50K was considered to be big money in physics in the early 1950s and the preceding years. . . . [Then came the] massive movement from the federal government to appreciate the role of science, specifically in the area of national defense. That became overwhelmingly clear in WWII and was under the guidance of Vannevar Bush, who was the most important proponent and practitioner of that fact, and it permeated the whole system of government.

"The University of Iowa lagged behind in exploiting that. I think that stemmed in part from [President Hancher's] reluctance to accept government support for any work at the university. He had more or less what I call a pre-WWII attitude that universities were primarily teaching institutions, primarily engaged in scholarly research which had no particular relationship to federal policy or federal investigations of any sort. He exercised a certain reluctance, and I experienced that reluctance myself in dealing with him during that period when I was first here, although there was a small externally supported research effort by the then Atomic Energy Commission. In my field the first major development in my life was a small grant from the Research Corporation, a private corporation, and followed fairly soon after by my first grant, in 1952, and I have had continuous support from ONR to the present day; I just got news three days ago [October 1995] that my proposal for the coming year had been approved. That level of integrity on the part of a federal agency is really extraordinary in my experience and I have been very grateful for that.

"Meanwhile we started branching out beyond that. During what was called the International Geophysical Year in 1957–1958 we had fairly strong and mas-sive support from the National Science Foundation. It was charged with ad-ministering the U.S. component during the National Geophysical Year, and we were one of the principal participants in a proposed earth satellite days during the mid to late 1950s, so we were immediately helped by success of some of the early missions. We were sort of catapulted into a position of con-siderable prominence in this new field of research and space by using artificial satellites and spacecraft. In our field the level of activity grew very sharply in the early 1960s, and it went up to levels of a million dollars a year of external support within our department alone.

"The post-WWII sort of spin off, if you want to call it that, went into a 'peaceful' period of the wartime role of science in the development of weap-onry which was quite revolutionary in the military system. Previously, univer-sities and university-type people had virtually no role in the development of weaponry and techniques or tactics of warfare, strategy, policy of warfare, or military policy; they were totally excluded. It was a totally different world, and that was clearly evident in the terribly primitive and low level of operation of many weapons. The most famous, in my naval experience, were the torpedoes which had been developed under high secrecy entirely within the military sys-tem, most of which did not work in combat, and the other was in the general area of fire control and antiaircraft defense, which I had a special role in dur-ing the war. The whole thing was so primitive that it was really ridiculous by any standard of technical savvy. That was recognized by the government and military people during the war by virtue of the contributions that various people made in radar, proximity fuses, torpedo development, and, most no-tably, the atomic bomb.

"The second main element in my impressions is what I would call the gen-erally optimistic expansionistic period in the United States when everything was going great, everything was expanding, life was getting better, people were delighted to recover from the stringency of the wartime period, the great loss of life, individual sacrifices, the deprivation of many things in ordinary life. In fact, we were sort of finally released from that at the end of the war, and things were booming: housing, transportation, building of highways, development of new cities, anything you could mention was in a great overwhelming period of postwar optimism, building a great future. Money was no object. That phi-losophy had been quite evident during the war, and I worked in a laboratory in which the director declared, 'I don't want anybody wasting time trying to save money.'

"I think that feeling, although in a different context, carried into the post-WWII period and, of course, to the new agencies that were being created. This persisted up to and including the success of the Soviets in first orbiting Sputnik I in October 1957, which sort of electrified the world and almost paralyzed, shocked the whole United States and most of the civilized world because the whole vein of thinking was that the Soviets were a terribly backwards nation, and here they were, beating us to the highest technological achievement of the day. The other thing is the Cold War apprehension that the Soviets were flying over our heads and looking down our necks so to speak, and there was a great apprehension about their recognizance capability. It didn't, of course, exist at that point, but that was the general level of apprehension which was part of the Cold War neurosis, and the general popular impression of science was extremely favorable. The atomic bomb was a very impressive demonstration, and, for every knowledgeable human being in the world, it was a matter of physics and engineering.

"Those were the two main elements — the impetus from the war and the common impression that science was great stuff. The Sputnik experience sort of resulted in what, in my opinion, was a totally mistaken but nonetheless important general national feeling that science education — the education in science I would rather call it — in the United States was rather backward and had dwindled away over the years and was really pretty second rate as witness the Soviet success and also the German success with rocket development. Those were taken to show that the U.S. was really the backward nation when it came to science. Of course, the fact of the matter is that all of those achievements were done by people who had been educated long before WWII for the most part, and had nothing to do with the post-WWII decay in the sciences in academic institutions, though the general influence was affirmative and aggressive in terms of improving sciences and the teaching of science in both.

"During WWII almost every scientist that I can think of joined in the 'war effort.' They went to national laboratories to perform contract work. They migrated to places like Los Alamos, the Radiation Lab at MIT, the Applied Physics Lab at Oakridge, and some of the other major federal institutions. They migrated on the expectation that it was only temporary, and they intended to go back to their own universities and resume more or less a normal academic form of life after the war. Nonetheless, they established a very large network of contacts within the federal institutions, and, as the prospect for support became imminent, they, like I, made the almost monthly trips to Washington to serve on consulting committees, advisory committees, and planning committees for developing programs in science, so a very strong contact relationship developed between the academic people and the federal establishment. It was by and large a mutually both agreeable and profitable relationship because the bureaus themselves had usually limited scope and confidence which was greatly enlarged by having advisory committees of significant people working with them. This developed into a huge network of grants and contracts with universities and a contract is a contract; it is an agreement for mutual benefit of both the contractor and the contractee, so that the obligation of the university faculty member to the sponsoring federal agency became a very important part of his life. In fact, the support by those agencies was by and large the principal element by which he [sic] advanced his own research interest, even though those were not particularly military. Nonetheless, ONR and others supported work in that field in the general advancement of human knowledge.

"More and more, these relationships tended to diminish the institutional authority of a faculty member. But, as the university made my work in research possible, it did not support it by and large. That was kind of a torture that we underwent, and it greatly diminished the institutional loyalties; they became shifted towards the federal supporting agencies and toward national organizations of one kind or another; that persists to the present time.

"There is no doubt in my mind that if you want a way to do research supported by an external agency, you have to do research that is broadly related to its mission; there is no doubt that the definition of mission on the part of various agencies of the federal government [does] have influence and continue[s] to influence the direction of research within universities. I don't think that has been necessarily ominous, because, for one thing, there has been a great diversity in agencies in the federal government, and that is one of the strengths of federal support. If the Atomic Energy Commission is not interested, then maybe NSF is or ONR is or maybe the Office of Air Force Research; they have a great diversity of interests. . . . By and large, support by the agencies that I have dealt with have been extremely beneficial to our program and to the university in general and have been basically unrestricted.

"The construction of [Van Allen Hall] was strictly within that scope, but it was on the beginning edge. That was, of course, a very important development in the life of the department and the future of the department. The approval [for its building] and the legislative appropriation was accomplished during President Hancher's tenure. I was principally responsible in getting about one third of the support from the National Aeronautics and Space Administration [NASA], in a very helpful but short-lived program that they had for construction of facilities, and by the National Science Foundation, and so the state got a terribly good bargain on this building. I think it was something like 1.5 million dollars from the state and roughly a similar amount from the federal agencies. Nowadays, a building like this would cost about 15 million dollars.

And then soon thereafter, I worked with HEW, and we got another roughly 50 percent support for the second portion of the building."

David Vernon, professor of law and former vice president for academic affairs: "In many of the institution's units we expect people to support themselves. And there's a different attitude about someone who, in effect, is generating his or her own money, than someone who is being paid by the institution, in terms of what he or she sees as their role. It does make a difference, I think, in attitude. Good people have a great institutional sense. Some who support themselves completely are some of our greatest institutional loyalists, and some of them who don't do anything and live on what we pay them are far from loyalists.

"I think, during the time that I have been here, that the face of the university has changed. We've gotten a lot better than we were, and, to a large extent, funded by the research activity that we generated through the efforts of the faculty. The fact is that we would not be where we are today at all if it hadn't been for that kind of development. That is, I think, the major funding difference. The state's portion probably has fallen back over those years. It was, I suppose, the single most dramatic development.

"When I came in 1966 we were just starting to develop. The times were good. In the early days when NSF was getting in the business we had a lot of support from the central administration generally. I think Howard Bowen was a person who understood all this from his background in economics, and Sandy [Boyd] carried that on. So I think about the single most significant thing that happened since I have been here was actually that. I think it was the one development that made the most difference to us. Even with that, I have never figured out why we don't have more people in the National Academy of Science.

"The university is a national asset. It never occurred to me that what we were doing was limited to state effort. It seemed to me that we were a state institution, but with national and international dimensions. I was taken aback when people started fussing about the state. I thought our research should be on a worldwide basis."

Federal Government Relations

Derek Willard, associate vice president for research: "There were mixed feelings about the practice of pork barrel activity both within this institution and also outside of it in our state legislature and in the Congress. We never attempted to pork barrel a project on a very large scale. There were two reasons for that. One was there was a high degree of distance and skepticism among our own faculty and professoriat who believed that, though you might make some short term gains with earmarked activity, in the long run it could hurt the scientific enterprise. The peer review system was the strongest system we had to guarantee that the science was going to be the best possible science that we could get, and we could hold this out to the public and, with that guarantee or safeguard in place, the public gave to us the responsibility of making decisions on what was important to do and what was not. When you entered into a pork barrel situation the safeguard was gone and suddenly your institution was deemed very similar to other institutions that were simply competing for scarce funds; you were all in the same field.

"Our position here has always been that you don't build a building unless you have a program that is going to go into that building that you have decided as an institution you would like to support and would be important to you over the long run. The problem with institutions that seek funds for a building, hoping that will jump-start activity on the campus, is that it rarely does. It in fact can have the opposite effect by draining funds from the institution and from the state, in the case of a state-run institution, in order to try to attract people to work in that building. The problem is that good people who are on the cutting edge of research are already existing in some fairly strong research environments at other institutions. This kind of work group is built up over a period of years, typically a decade, to amass a concentration, a critical mass of people, who move forward with that research. Typically state legislatures do not have the patience to wait a decade after they have made a major investment in a building to see it be productive."

State Relations

Hunter Rawlings III, president of the University of Iowa, 1988–1995: "There were several efforts during those seven years [of my presidency] to have the state intrude more into the life of the university by setting policies, or by establishing reviews and audits of the university, that I felt went too far. We were able, often at great length and effort, to fend off, I thought, most of those attempts to politicize university policymaking. And that's very important. . . . Those efforts will always come, in any state, and I know they're coming again in terms of teaching loads and that kind of thing. But they need to be resisted if at all possible, partly by the university taking responsibility to put in wise policies of its own."

State of the University

Willard (Sandy) Boyd, president of the University of Iowa, 1969–1981: "I used to say not only are we all physically present in one place but we're all intellectually present. And I felt that truly this institution was arts and sciences surrounded by professional colleges, and that this was a great opportunity for this kind of interaction. I think it helped that we were physically together, but I think it's unusual that the health colleges have been as integrated into the university as they have been here, and in an intellectual sense and with high standards — not trying to pull away from the institution and wanting to go their own way. This has given us a great opportunity. I wish more people took advantage of the opportunity of getting out of their own disciplines and seeing what was going on elsewhere."

George Chambers, professor of education, formerly executive vice president, University of Iowa: "We have now bypassed the Vietnam era and we're on a roll with regard to revenue. During that era the university moved away substantially from a decentralized organization to centralization, which, I believe, has had a devastating negative impact and that is still continuing. I think one of the great strengths of this place was the fact that it was decentralized and central administrators recognized that was a strength. But it no longer exists today, and that's the way of life. I think it's always easier to centralize than it is to decentralize, so what took two hundred years or one hundred years to come about was destroyed perhaps in five to ten, and it might take another twenty to fifty to get it back there, if ever."

Deirdre McCloskey, professor, Departments of Economics and History: "For several years I have been saying to people that there should be 'intellectual cross dressing,' and economists should be talking, for example, to psychologists — when they talk about the mind they actually know what they are talking about. Where did it come from? I think about 10 percent of a faculty have this willingness to talk outside their 'invisible' college. The other 90 percent want only to stay within the economic history or microbiology of specialists in their own narrow field. [But others] run their intellectual lives in the 10 percent way and do the work of the disciplines with an interdisciplinary perspective. Some of my colleagues and I have stressed that it does not damage the specialized work; it does the work of the disciplines with an interdisciplinary perspective.

"The 90 percent won't try because they're afraid of not knowing. They want to be experts. I know a lot of people who can't learn new things because it frightens them. It reduces their self-esteem. I wish they were more confident. I didn't know anything about literary criticism, and so I went to the Dartmouth School of Criticism and Theory. My colleagues were assistant professors and graduate students: I was a forty-eight-year-old full professor in economics and history. It was wonderful! I had a poetry class and I worked on term papers. You know Harry Truman said that an expert is someone who doesn't want to learn anything new because then he wouldn't be an expert! And I asked an important American philosopher, a friend, 'John, have you ever read Hegel?' and he said, 'No, and I propose never to do so,' as though he was proud that he was ignorant.

"What makes a university interesting is chance-taking, and that's all Iowa can ever be if it's to be first rate. Unlike Harvard or Michigan, we can't just follow and depend on our weight of prestige. Spriestersbach understood it, Seashore understood it, I understand it. That makes three of us! Following the conventional 'plumbing diagram' of the usual disciplines will only guarantee mediocrity, followership."

Arthur Bonfield, professor, College of Law: "Bowen, Boyd, and Freedman had enormous strengths. My view of the three of them is that they were three very good presidents with very different strengths and that each made a very different contribution, a very substantial contribution, to this place. I think the one who clearly had the most difficult job was Sandy Boyd, because he was president during the most tumultuous and difficult time and had different problems. Nevertheless, the other two made enormous contributions as well. Howard [Bowen] was the dreamer. Howard dreamed the great dream of taking the university forward, which was a very modest place when I came thirty-six years ago. . . . I'm not denigrating what had been before. . . . There was a great leap forward in the three administrations we're talking about [Bowen, Boyd, and Freedman] in this university's position in the educational hierarchy of this country. A great leap forward.

"At the beginning of this period, and I'm generalizing, this was a very ingrown university. You had departments where 80 percent of the people in the departments were graduates of this university. Faculty, I'm talking about. Howard Bowen, president, and Sandy Boyd, vice president for academic affairs, decided to change all that. Starting in 1964–1965, we began increasing the faculty on a geometric scale. And by looking outward, hiring people from all over the United States, other universities, to diversify in intellectual orientation, in educational background, in educational experience, to diversify this institution. There was an enormous qualitative as well as quantitative change in what went on in this university. Again, I'm not in the slightest bit denigrating what existed before. It was a good place. But the enormous qualitative progress was made as a result of this recruiting effort.

"Next was the addition of programs. One might say too many programs, but we were in a period of time when the student body was growing. There was, even though there were financial hard times, more money available for growth, hiring faculty left and right, the whole focus of the university changed. Places like the College of Medicine, during that period, went from good but sleepy places into national powerhouse research places. Places like the College of Law, which was a very good law school when I came here, went from a good law school to a nationally recognized law school of competitive national proportions in the top group.

"Jim Freedman's great strength, even though he was a lawyer, was that his heart was in liberal arts. He did a lot for the liberal arts at this university. As a matter of fact, one of his most conspicuous contributions, I think, was in the importance of relating to and strengthening of liberal arts. Sandy dealt with some of the most difficult times imaginable in terms of upheaval. Howard was at the beginning of the period of charted growth and tried to figure out how he could start diversifying and nationalizing, even then, in making the university nationwide and international more than it had been before. Jim Freedman made a very positive contribution educationally. Jim was a great educational theoretician with great intellectual messages, great intellectual leadership of a kind that was just right for the times. Sandy provided stability, leadership, courage. While his predecessors needed courage, too, of course, the particular kind and degree of courage during Sandy's period that was required was extraordinary. He was faced with the potential of thousands of people rioting, people taking over buildings, violence.

"The university, as a result of student unrest, really adopted numerous policies, and, frankly, I think they are the right policies. I worry sometimes now that students want to be protected from the outside and not be subject to the police and want to go back to the old system, which, by the way, is not unusual; everyone wants their cake and they want to eat it, too, but the emancipation of students ending *in local parentis* meant that if the student committed a crime, the police would come in and punish them.

"I just named a number of areas where I think the university made positive advances. When I say none of this is an unvarnished good, it was clearly, from where we started, sound to have more responsiveness to students' desires about teaching, more responsiveness to the students about shared participation in governance, more responsiveness to students' complaints about us acting as their parents and limiting them.

"I think we made progress in all those areas; in some of those areas I think we went too far. I think it's one thing to listen to students and another thing to cede any share of actual governance authority. I think it's a positive thing. However, we've sometimes now gotten to the point at the university that, it seems to me, we have to consult and share seeming authority almost with students, and I think that is a bad consequence. But we made progress about opening this place and trying to end or reduce hopefully the racism and issues like that. That's also a positive thing. And also to be more concerned about student teaching. I worry now that we're so concerned about student teaching, for example, that the student teaching questionnaires may dampen good teaching because faculty members at the other extreme may feel they have to cater to these numbers and therefore don't do what they think is best because they're worried about the numbers.

"I've become a little bit worried today about whether that openness is an openness only to one point of view. And I am a little bit concerned as to whether or not we are trying to foster within this university diverse viewpoints even when they are so-called politically incorrect viewpoints. But again, I think one of the things we brought forward from that era and that was firmly reaffirmed was that this would be an open forum. I hope that we continue to maintain it, and I believe most of the time we have."

EPILOGUE

I want to close this book on a personal note because this has been a personal account of the course steered by the University of Iowa during the quarter century 1964–1989. Others came and went during the period, including presidents, vice presidents, and deans with all of their associates. Some stayed. I did.

Over the years I have identified a number of principles by which I have endeavored to deal with academic administration. Some have been culled from previous experience. Some have been borrowed from colleagues from this or other institutions related to the academy. Others have been forced upon me by my supervisors or by circumstances. Still others have come, I think, from whatever strengths I have that I either brought to the job at hand or developed along the way.

It may be presumptuous to offer them here, because, in doing so, I may be giving them undeserved credence. Still, it may be that some other person, present or future, may find these principles useful. So, in humility, I present them in no particular order of priority:

Don't accept a position unless you believe in its mission and that of the institution of which it is a part.

Remember that there are major limitations on what you know. Strive always to be open to new ideas, new ways of doing things.

Cultivate your sense of curiosity about the whys and wherefores of traditions, policies, and procedures as they are. Remember that they were established by persons like you and they may not represent the ultimate.

Dream the dream; no one else will dream for you.

Leaders must lead with more than waving flags. Those who are following you are there because they have confidence in you and your ideas. Just remember that, being out in front, you are vulnerable to criticism.

Respect your colleagues as you expect them to respect you. Remember that they come in all shapes and sizes, some of which you may not care for. Nevertheless, their worlds are real and you must seek to understand them.

Remember that professors are persons who need encouragement and praise; a figurative pat on the back is always welcome.

Select your staff with care; having made your choices, define their responsibilities, and give them the authority and support to follow through with their assignments.

Go the extra mile; doing so, you may discover unexpected rewards.

Do more than identify issues and problems; propose solutions as well.

Remember, even though there may be times when you may prefer not to, that the faculty is the professional core of a decentralized institution; if academic strategies and priorities are to be put in practice effectively, faculty consensus is required.

Be an attentive and patient listener, showing respect to the speaker by doing so.

You will be involved in group meetings ad nauseam; attend them with patience, participate in the discussions when appropriate. Be prepared to offer solutions to problems identified; the groups will welcome them.

You won't be able to be affirmative to all requests placed before you. Support your decisions with your rationale for doing whatever you decide to do. Don't be cryptic in your turn-downs; always be respectful of the proposer.

Academic executives must seek advice from a wide representation within the institution; in the end, however, only persons with line responsibilities are held accountable, and you will be, too.

Be decisive and timely in making decisions; wishy-washy leaders do not, and should not, survive.

Remember that the academy works with ideas, creating them, teaching them, and archiving them; don't allow the bureaucracy to shackle their full exploitation.

Never pull your punches when you are sure of your facts; even if your boss chooses to kill the messenger, he or she can't kill the message that must be reckoned with, one way or the other.

By your practices, establish the reputation of a person whose word is your bond.

All in all the history of the University of Iowa, including these twenty-five years, is a very positive one. It derives from persons of many different hues, with many different interests, values, and points of view. But it has an intellectual core that is very real, if seldom articulated, or even appreciated by many. It has kept the university on course for one hundred and fifty years and shows every sign of continuing to do so far into the future. I feel very privileged to have been allowed to travel along with it during part of its journey.

APPENDIXES

APPENDIX 1.

Graduate Deans, 1900–1999

Dean	Department	Years
L. C. Weld	Mathematics	1900–1907
Thomas H. Macbride	Botany	1907–1908
Carl E. Seashore	Psychology	1908–1936
George Stoddard	Psychology	1936–1942
Carl E. Seashore	Psychology	1942–1946
Carlyle Jacobsen	Psychology	1946–1948
Harvey H. Davis	Education	1948–1950
Walter F. Loehwing	Botany	1950–1960
Stow Persons	History	1960–1961
John C. Weaver	Geography	1961–1964
Orville Hitchcock	Speech	1964–1965
D. C. Spriestersbach	Speech Pathology	1965–1989
Leodis Davis	Chemistry	1989–1990
Rudolph W. Schulz	Psychology	1990–1991
Leslie B. Sims	Chemistry	1991–

Number of Faculty, 1965–1990

Year	Number	Year	Number
1965–66	733	1978–79	1,487
1966–67	781	1979–80	1,503
1967–68	849	1980–81	1,532
1968–69	916	1981–82	1,536
1969–70	941	1982–83	1,574
1970–71	987	1983–84	1,622
1971–72	992	1984–85	1,617
1972–73	1,378	1985–86	1,632
1973–74	1,334	1986–87	1,601
1974–75	1,368	1987–88	1,598
1975–76	1,395	1988–89	1,630
1976–77	1,426	1989–90	1,642
1977–78	1,450		

Note: Includes tenured and tenure-track professors, associate professors, and assistant professors.

Number of Students by College, 1965–1989

Year	Business Administration		Dentistry		Engineering		Graduate	
	Men	Women	Men	Women	Men	Women	Men	Women
1965	426	41	208	1	588	3	2,925	950
1966	645	61	214	1	577	2	3,325	1,166
1967	759	75	215	1	477	0	3,493	1,277
1968	734	88	227	1	472	2	3,492	1,397
1969	713	67	235	0	443	3	3,500	1,519
1970	759	72	246	2	423	7	3,463	1,621
1971	833	90	252	3	400	11	3,426	1,501
1972	758	101	273	3	356	14	3,286	1,571
1973	738	115	302	8	380	19	3,150	1,660
1974	762	155	314	25	446	26	3,194	1,987
1975	858	236	319	38	523	62	3,299	2,210
1976	841	294	324	43	531	87	3,241	2,333
1977	837	309	328	47	553	103	3,087	2,414
1978	773	359	332	50	614	143	3,102	2,455
1979	795	429	320	54	616	147	3,077	2,599
1980	817	487	314	63	711	164	3,039	2,641
1981	749	491	287	81	827	190	2,960	2,601
1982	736	510	272	84	926	222	2,993	2,643
1983	810	485	248	78	958	219	3,145	2,854
1984	854	532	224	80	1,023	246	3,013	2,898
1985	999	627	226	67	1,014	250	3,025	2,857
1986	1,003	649	212	69	1,027	253	3,059	2,898
1987	1,103	688	208	76	1,033	250	3,136	2,951
1988	875	564	204	84	1,034	232	3,296	2,988
1989	750	478	194	92	1,020	219	3,329	3,039

Note: Numbers are fall enrollments. Figures from 1971 forward include the Saturday and Evening Class Program enrollments.

Law		Liberal Arts		Medicine		Nursing		Pharmacy		Total	
Men	*Women*	*Men*	*Women*	*Men*	*Women*	*Men*	*Women*	*Men*	*Women*	*Men*	*Women*
432	16	5,045	4,358	696	46	6	398	178	38	10,504	5,851
448	15	5,102	4,757	725	48	4	412	209	44	11,249	6,506
428	12	5,346	5,078	757	46	2	416	218	59	11,695	6,964
381	13	5,712	5,463	778	34	4	430	216	62	12,016	7,490
378	26	5,979	5,786	785	48	5	449	225	75	12,263	7,973
432	39	6,152	5,679	854	51	4	492	211	97	12,544	8,060
500	54	5,949	5,594	884	68	7	494	218	103	12,469	7,918
514	69	5,823	5,382	900	101	24	539	239	99	12,173	7,879
519	90	5,953	5,564	962	123	31	534	268	112	12,303	8,225
486	98	5,873	5,834	948	138	42	542	270	131	12,335	8,936
476	127	6,247	6,052	982	159	38	472	270	144	13,012	9,500
460	140	5,961	6,097	992	180	47	409	270	143	12,667	9,726
459	166	5,961	6,400	989	213	45	452	251	152	12,510	10,256
455	175	5,805	6,606	963	231	35	480	254	158	12,333	10,657
419	191	5,833	6,761	968	272	35	453	230	150	12,293	11,056
404	206	6,651	7,445	970	296	37	482	202	171	13,145	11,955
395	231	7,459	8,059	955	336	31	486	171	155	13,834	12,630
404	239	8,185	8,800	934	339	25	489	160	179	14,635	13,505
413	233	8,643	9,407	932	346	23	454	164	187	15,336	14,263
414	216	8,640	9,221	935	400	38	608	169	201	15,310	14,402
423	216	8,366	9,322	921	391	31	513	176	227	15,181	14,470
406	243	8,198	9,255	946	396	27	478	163	222	15,041	14,463
424	248	7,850	9,073	925	404	18	382	135	229	14,832	14,301
407	230	8,045	9,178	978	439	21	299	124	232	14,984	14,246
416	297	7,878	9,066	966	465	23	313	111	228	14,687	14,197

APPENDIX 4.

Graduate College Enrollment by Degree Objectives, 1968–1989

Year	Masters	Doctorates	Other	Total
1968	2,566	1,913	410	4,889
1969	2,558	2,038	423	5,019
1970	2,348	1,956	780	5,084
1971	2,469	2,048	410	4,927
1972	2,388	1,862	607	4,857
1973	2,404	1,816	590	4,810
1974	2,540	1,854	787	5,181
1975	2,804	1,809	896	5,509
1976	2,818	1,885	871	5,574
1977	2,775	1,884	842	5,501
1978	2,822	1,853	882	5,557
1979	2,902	1,947	827	5,676
1980	2,900	1,864	916	5,680
1981	2,924	1,835	802	5,561
1982	2,980	1,877	779	5,636
1983	3,183	2,017	799	5,999
1984	3,041	2,055	815	5,911
1985	2,943	2,148	791	5,882
1986	3,013	2,186	758	5,957
1987	3,150	2,246	691	6,087
1988	3,132	2,375	777	6,284
1989	3,113	2,467	788	6,368

Note: Enrollment figures taken from fall semester reports. Prior to 1968 the registrar recorded totals only for those seeking graduate degrees.

Advanced Programs Offered in the Graduate College, 1966–1989

Department or Interdepartmental Program	Catalog Degrees Offered	Program Changes	Date of Approval
Accounting	M.A.	Nonthesis degree added	7/12/68
Afro-American Studies[†]	M.A.[1]	Program addition	9/15/77
American Civilization	M.A., Ph.D.	American Studies[‡]	1/13/77
		Nonthesis degree added	3/19/69
Anatomy	M.S., Ph.D.	—	—
Anthropology	M.A.	Ph.D. added	9/10/70
Applied Mathematical Science[†]	Ph.D.	Program addition	6/25/71
Art	M.A., M.F.A., Ph.D.	Ph.D. changed to Art History	4/30/73
Art History[†]	Ph.D.	Program change	4/30/73
Asian Civilization[†]	M.A.	Program addition	3/14–15/74
		Nonthesis option added	11/24/87
		Asian Civilizations[‡]	6/24/88
Astronomy	M.S.*	—	—
Biology (Botany Department)	M.S.*	—	—
Biology (Zoology Department)	M.S.	—	—
Biomedical Engineering[†]	M.S., Ph.D.	Program addition	2/87
Botany	M.S., Ph.D.	—	—
Biochemistry	M.S., Ph.D.	—	—
Business Administration (Departmental)	M.A., Ph.D.	Nonthesis track added	2/19/76
Business Administration (Interdepartmental)	M.B.A.[1]	Changed to professional degree program in School of Management	10/93
Business Education	M.A.[1]	Ph.D. added	1968
		Suspended student entry	5/2/79
		M.A. degree terminated	1/30/81
Chemical Engineering	M.S., Ph.D.	Chemical & Materials Engineering[‡]	3/16/78
		Chemical & Biochemical Engineering[‡]	9/28/89
Chemical Physics	M.S., Ph.D.	—	—
Chemistry	M.S.,* Ph.D.	—	—
Child Behavior and Development	M.A., Ph.D.	Suspended entry	4/3/73
		M.A./Ph.D. degree terminated	9/15/77
Chinese Language and Civilization	M.A.	Suspended entry	11/6/72
		M.A. degree terminated	4/17/80
Civil Engineering	M.S.,* Ph.D.	Civil & Environmental Engineering[‡]	3/16/78

(*Continued*)

(Continued)

Department or Interdepartmental Program	Catalog Degrees Offered	Program Changes	Date of Approval
Classics	M.A., Ph.D.	—	—
Communication and Theatre Arts	M.A., Ph.D.	Name change from Speech & Dramatic Arts	1980
		Program terminated	1984
Community Dentistry[†]	M.S.	Program addition	7/13/72
		Community Dentistry & Dental Public Health[‡]	3/24/82
		Dental Public Health[‡]	9/89
Comparative Law	M.C.L.	Suspended entry	9/26/73
		Suspension lifted	10/28/82
Comparative Literature	M.A., Ph.D.	Nonthesis M.A. degree option added	3/6/69
Computer Science	M.S., Ph.D.	Nonthesis option added	11/9/66
Criminal Justice & Corrections[†]	M.A.	Program addition	6/27–28/74
Crown and Bridge Prosthesis	M.S.	Fixed Prosthodontics[‡]	6/72
Cultural Anthropology & Linguistics[†]	Ph.D.	Program addition	3/15/68
		Ph.D. degree terminated	3/16/78
Dance	M.F.A.	Program addition	11/86
Dental Hygiene	M.S.	—	—
Denture Prosthesis	M.S.	Removable Prosthodontics[‡]	6/72
Dramatic Art	M.A., M.F.A., Ph.D.	Theatre Arts[‡]	12/16/80
		M.A./Ph.D. terminated	2/17–18/88
Economics	M.A., Ph.D.	Nonthesis M.A. option added	11/12/69
Education	M.A.,* M.A.T.,[1] Ed.S.,[1] Ph.D.	—	—
Electrical Engineering	M.S.,* Ph.D.	Electrical & Computer Engineering[‡]	3/16/78
Endodontics[†]	M.S.	Program addition	9/13/79
English	M.A.,* M.F.A., Ph.D.	—	—
French	M.A.,* Ph.D.	—	—
Geography	M.A.,* Ph.D.	—	—
Geology	M.S.,* Ph.D.	—	—
Genetics[†]	Ph.D.	Interdisciplinary program added	6/23/75
German	M.A.,* Ph.D.	—	—
Greek	M.A.	Nonthesis M.A. degree approved	2/19/69
History	M.A.,* Ph.D.	—	—
Home Economics	M.A.,* M.S.*	Suspension of grad. student admission	12/4/89

APPENDIX 5.

(Continued)

Department or Interdepartmental Program	Catalog Degrees Offered	Program Changes	Date of Approval
Hospital and Health Administration	M.A., Ph.D.	Student entry suspended—Ph.D. program	6/25/75
		Student entry into M.A. program suspended	4/8/76
		Nonthesis option added to M.A.	2/7/77
		Suspension of student entry into M.A./Ph.D. programs lifted	2/7/77
Industrial and Management Engineering	M.S.,* Ph.D.	—	—
Instructional Design & Technology†	M.A.,* Ed.S., Ph.D.	Program addition	2/19/76
Journalism	M.A.*	—	—
Latin	M.A.*	—	—
Law Enforcement & Corrections†	M.A.	Program addition	4/14/67
Library Science†	M.A.	Program addition	4/14/67
		Library and Information Science‡	11/83
Linguistics	M.A.	Nonthesis subtrack added	2/12/76
		Ph.D. added	3/16/78
Mass Communications	Ph.D.	—	—
Mathematics	M.S.,* Ph.D.	—	—
Mechanical Engineering	M.S.,* Ph.D.	—	—
Mechanics and Hydraulics	M.S.,* Ph.D.	Suspended student entry; termination approved when remaining students finish	3/16/78
Microbiology	M.S.,[2] Ph.D.	Hours reduced from 45 to 30 for M.S.	11/20/72
Molecular Biology†	Ph.D.	Program addition	10/19/88
Museum Methods	M.A.	Suspension of M.A. degree	3/10/71
Music	M.A.,* M.F.A., D.M.A., Ph.D.	—	—
Neuroscience†	Ph.D.	Interdepartmental program approved	9/84
Nuclear Science and Technology	M.S.	Student entry suspended	10/19/77
		Program termination approved	9/13/79
Nursing	M.A.[5]	Revised M.A. to min. 45 s.h. plus thesis	4/5/78
	Ph.D.	Approved program	9/17/87
		Reduced from 45 to 39 s.h. for some M.A. students	11/24/87

(Continued)

APPENDIX 5.

(*Continued*)

Department or Interdepartmental Program	Catalog Degrees Offered	Program Changes	Date of Approval
Nutrition	M.S.,* Ph.D.	Suspended student entry	2/13/73
		Reactivation of Ph.D. program	11/12/79
		Human Nutrition (Ph.D. program)‡	9/16/86
Obstetrics and Gynecology	M.S.	M.S. degree termination	2/9/73
Office Management	M.A.	M.A. degree termination	9/10/70
Operative Dentistry†	M.S.	Program addition	9/13/79
Operative Dentistry and Endodontics	M.S.	Separated into M.S. in Operative Dentistry, M.S. in Endodontics	9/13/79
Ophthalmology	M.S.	Program discontinued	7/21/83
Oral Diagnosis	M.S.	M.S. degree suspended	9/11/74
		Degree termination	4/9/76
Oral Pathology	M.S.	Degree suspension	1/23/75
		Approval for 1 student entry to program	2/12/76
		Major designation changed to Stomatology	9/89
Oral Surgery	M.S.	Oral and Maxillofacial Surgery‡	9/14–15/83
Orthodontics	M.S.	—	—
Orthopedic Surgery	M.S.	Degree termination	2/9/73
Otolaryngology	M.S.	Otolaryngology—Head and Neck Surgery‡	5/17/84
		Degree termination	2/89
Pathology†	M.S.	Degree addition	6/25/71
Pedodontics	M.S.	Pediatric Dentistry‡	12/12/84
Periodontology	M.A.	36 month variant of M.A. in Periodontology	1/3/72
Pharmaceutical Sciences†	M.S.[1]	Program addition	12/16/70
Pharmacology	M.S., Ph.D.	—	—
Pharmacy	M.S.,* Ph.D.	—	—
Philosophy	M.A.,* Ph.D.	—	—
Physical Education (Men's)	M.A.,* Ph.D.	—	—
Physical Education (Women's)	M.A.,* Ph.D.	—	—
Physical Therapy	M.A.[3]	—	—
	M.P.T.[1]	M.A. degree approved	9/17–18/86
Physician Assistant†	M.P.A.[1]	Program addition	10/13/87
Physics	M.S.,* Ph.D.	—	—
Physiology and Biophysics	M.S., Ph.D.	—	—
Political Science	M.A.,* Ph.D.	—	—
Preventive Medicine and Environmental Health	M.S.,* Ph.D.	—	—

(Continued)

Department or Interdepartmental Program	Catalog Degrees Offered	Program Changes	Date of Approval
Prosthodontics†	M.S.	New degree combining Fixed and Removable Prosthodontics	12/10/87
Psychiatry	M.S.4	Degree termination	9/13/73
Psychology	M.A.,* Ph.D.	—	—
Public Affairs†	M.A.	Program addition	3/14–15/74
Quality Management and Productivity†	M.S.*	Interdisciplinary program addition	10/86
Radiation Biology	M.S., Ph.D.	—	—
Recreation Leadership	M.A.*	Leisure Studies‡	6/86
Religion	M.A., Ph.D.	Nonthesis option added to M.A.	12/15/83
Russian	M.A.	—	—
Science Education	M.A.,* Ph.D.	—	—
Social Studies	M.A.*	—	—
Social Work	M.S.W.1	Thesis option added	10/22/79
Sociology	M.A.,* Ph.D.	—	—
Spanish	M.A.,* Ph.D.	—	—
Speech	M.A., Ph.D.	Communication‡	12/16/80
		Communication Studies‡	9/84
Speech Pathology and Audiology	M.A.,* Ph.D.	—	—
Statistics	M.S.,* Ph.D.	—	—
Stomatology	M.S.	—	—
Surgery	M.S.	Student entry suspension	2/13/73
		Degree termination	3/14/74
Urban and Regional Planning	M.A., M.S.	Nonthesis master's approved	3/4/70
Zoology	M.S.,* Ph.D.	M.S. and Ph.D. degrees changed to Biology	10/84

Note: All degrees listed were in place by May 24, 1966; subsequent additions and deletions of degrees are noted.

*Department offers both program with thesis and a prescribed program without thesis.

†Program addition approved after May 24, 1966

‡Program name change.

1. Nonthesis degree.

2. Forty-five semester hours required for M.S.

3. Certificate awarded at end of twelve months; 15 additional semester hours required for M.A.

4. Three-year master's program.

5. Thirty-seven semester hours with thesis; 45 semester hours without thesis.

APPENDIX 6.

Enrollment of International Students, 1965–1989

Year	Total Number University Students	Total International Students	International Graduate Students	Total Graduate Students	Percent Graduate International Students	Total Percent International Students
1965	16,355	377	309	3,875	8.0	2.3
1966	17,755	399	328	4,491	7.3	2.2
1967	18,659	400	327	4,770	6.9	2.1
1968	19,506	404	329	4,889	6.7	2.1
1969	20,236	480	376	5,019	7.5	2.4
1970	20,604	507	393	5,084	7.7	2.5
1971	20,387	521	407	4,927	8.3	2.6
1972	20,052	511	368	4,857	7.6	2.5
1973	20,528	535	359	4,810	7.4	2.6
1974	21,271	601	401	5,181	7.7	2.8
1975	22,512	641	428	5,509	7.8	2.8
1976	22,393	749	485	5,574	8.7	3.3
1977	22,766	826	500	5,501	9.1	3.6
1978	22,990	935	597	5,557	10.7	4.1
1979	23,349	1,030	671	5,676	11.8	4.4
1980	25,100	1,235	786	5,680	13.8	4.9
1981	26,464	1,286	728	5,561	13.1	4.9
1982	28,140	1,408	804	5,636	14.3	5.0
1983	29,599	1,513	929	5,999	15.5	5.1
1984	29,712	1,521	939	5,911	15.9	5.1
1985	29,651	1,662	1,074	5,882	18.3	5.6
1986	29,504	1,874	1,183	5,957	19.9	6.4
1987	29,133	1,957	1,303	6,087	21.4	6.7
1988	29,230	1,937	1,350	6,284	21.5	6.6
1989	28,884	1,866	1,354	6,368	21.3	6.5

APPENDIX 7.

Gifts, Grants, and Contracts Accepted by the Board of Regents, 1962–1989

Year	Applications Forwarded	Percentage Change	Funds Accepted	Percentage Change
1962–63	$14,678,000		$11,338,121	
1963–64	18,779,000	28	11,707,727	3
1964–65	24,588,000	31	16,553,899	41
1965–66	44,732,000	82	15,501,809	−6
1966–67	50,968,205	14	19,902,533	28
1967–68	62,519,905	23	35,404,346	78
1968–69	49,769,852	−20	32,763,920	−7
1969–70	79,259,236[1]	59	25,687,358	−22
1970–71	50,886,546	−36	30,858,355	20
1971–72	72,405,535[2]	42	31,731,805	2
1972–73	69,841,938	−4	33,264,481	5
1973–74	91,097,664	30	41,301,291	24
1974–75	86,744,844	−5	44,732,618	8
1975–76	89,943,900	4	42,208,622	−6
1976–77	97,069,723	8	44,295,403	5
1977–78	112,783,175	16	49,331,472	11
1978–79	125,160,017	11	59,038,639	20
1979–80	115,346,036	−8[3]	67,078,431	14
1980–81	115,221,757	n/a	67,211,915	n/a
1981–82	107,892,489	−6	70,235,254	4
1982–83	128,621,967	16	66,711,793	−5
1983–84	144,236,444	12	82,953,267	24
1984–85	156,005,932	8	88,121,488	6
1985–86	184,873,876	21	89,440,177	1
1986–87	166,113,408	−5	100,777,980	13
1987–88	213,630,970	29	115,145,963	14
1988–89	232,673,757	9	140,532,796	22

1. Includes $25,104,450 proposal for hospital addition.
2. Includes $9,750,125 for hospital addition.
3. Unusually large multiyear proposals from physics to NASA accounted for this wide discrepancy.

APPENDIX 8.

Gifts, Grants, and Contracts from Selected Major Sources

Year	Public Health Service	Office of Education	National Science Foundation	NASA
1962–63	$ 4,542,408	$ 276,468	$2,298,145	$ 1,565,894
1963–64	6,070,925	175,130	1,904,296	972,826
1964–65	7,158,588	746,691	876,563	1,752,750
1965–66	6,902,972	1,692,068	1,120,870	2,236,561
1966–67	9,740,150	3,053,916	1,950,922	885,050
1967–68	18,362,346	4,395,597	6,834,414	2,736,536
1968–69	18,723,690	4,149,172	1,926,286	1,443,478
1969–70	11,891,771	2,931,534	2,303,854	2,473,576
1970–71	14,728,314	2,812,609	3,521,230	2,015,543
1971–72	14,589,162	3,113,133	1,297,959	5,326,291
1972–73	19,943,886	3,053,939	1,533,201	1,166,170
1973–74	24,304,083	2,148,070	1,156,780	5,961,607
1974–75	29,457,775	3,376,164	1,576,704	884,433
1975–76	22,952,573	4,622,494	2,036,664	1,055,881
1976–77	23,098,351	4,321,245	2,348,831	1,208,451
1977–78	24,674,582	4,947,682	2,346,025	3,072,299
1978–79	31,099,604	3,534,090	1,827,830	6,096,511
1979–80	34,578,382	7,023,937	3,046,041	3,181,715
1980–81	36,144,901	6,553,493	2,601,801	2,804,861
1981–82	36,568,934	7,084,677	2,875,568	3,802,235
1982–83	34,788,315	7,087,303	2,464,536	4,061,742
1983–84	44,611,572	7,295,299	3,373,785	4,129,685
1984–85	47,861,979	7,622,621	3,104,035	3,519,294
1985–86	49,044,769	10,053,297 [1]	3,422,168	3,998,902
1986–87	53,900,453	8,462,397	4,260,288	4,965,601
1987–88	58,455,604	9,107,707	3,932,077	5,802,379
1988–89	62,518,036	14,374,982	4,974,968	15,350,511

1. Increase due in part to timing of the earlier arrival of the award documents from the government for student support.

2. Represents money given directly to the University by the University of Iowa Foundation, Individuals, and Alumni (1971 and years following: gifts under $500 not included here).

3. System changes have been implemented resulting in June 1977 figures for the U of I Foundation being excluded from this report. In the future, figures for the U of I Foundation will be from June through May.

4. Gifts from individuals given directly to the University. Funds transferred into the University from the University of Iowa Foundation are no longer included in this report.

Department of Defense	Corporations	Foundations	Individual, Alumni, & U. of I. Foundation[2]
$ 917,566	$ 219,770	$ 507,378	$ 149,231
617,604	188,868	233,315	208,140
1,484,539	284,311	1,503,122	1,390,758
844,414	338,402	565,103	222,845
632,092	299,764	259,330	1,409,419
475,135	234,219	276,240	270,863
1,794,315	381,252	429,971	1,983,784
1,377,538	432,410	1,443,175	683,170
1,120,578	475,160	812,895	481,332
976,483	355,602	1,022,670	1,010,274
614,624	400,578	789,133	1,289,644
954,326	638,859	1,309,017	861,978
664,222	1,204,238	713,441	695,153
808,236	845,405	1,391,529	3,012,545
906,139	1,220,477	1,088,119	2,722,079
864,003	1,265,811	1,409,208	1,298,872[3]
1,628,810	1,335,869	1,544,951	1,217,143
1,370,993	2,138,368	2,444,881	2,322,311
1,284,496	2,332,149	4,092,738	1,794,453
2,629,617	2,804,042	2,711,165	3,446,012
2,530,472	2,653,511	2,704,895	2,091,568
3,064,004	3,257,943	3,779,917	2,257,860
2,830,171	4,622,252	2,754,880	2,993,757
3,633,267	3,902,419	4,420,565	953,071[4]
3,504,251	5,366,500	3,934,460	70,785
2,893,175	6,077,226	4,461,703	265,567
3,484,164	12,927,054	5,646,638	19,650

Gifts, Grants, and Contracts Received by Purpose (in Thousands)

Purpose	1962–63	1963–64	1964–65	1965–66	1966–67	1967–68	1968–69	1969–70	1970–71
Research	$5,315	$7,721	$10,451	$10,127	$10,231	$11,527	$12,437	$12,374	$13,608
Training	1,483	1,945	2,320	2,532	3,127	3,502	3,194	3,872	5,003
Fellow./Scholar.	387	805	473	565	763	1,560	2,832	2,365	2,147
Cap. Impr.	3,109	803	1,470	831	1,730	9,524	7,670	1,218	3,093
Loan Funds	324	6	55	30	1,366	1,912	1,319	1,088	1,522
Misc.	718	427	1,785	1,418	2,686[1]	7,379[2]	4,806	4,770	5,487

Purpose	1971–72	1972–73	1973–74	1974–75	1975–76	1976–77	1977–78	1978–79
Research	$19,102	$17,313	$24,602	$20,025	$20,736	$24,181	$29,066	$37,618
Training	4,640	5,969	5,619	7,488[3]	4,192	4,166	7,331	7,705
Fellow./Scholar.	2,846	3,073	2,726	2,456	3,961	2,094	3,377	3,949
Cap. Impr.	510	973	1,008	4,503	3,415	887	115	428
Loan Funds	1,642	1,636	1,303	1,268	1,760	4,414	995[4]	1[4]
Misc.[1]	2,991	1,282	376	401	863	958	856	538
Ed. Dev.[5]	—	2,783	3,813	5,000	4,499	4,061	3,586	2,772
Commun. Serv.[6]	—	1,862	—	2,612	2,552	3,534	2,541	3,612
Continuing Ed.[7]	—	—	—	—	—	—	1,465	2,415

	1979–80	1980–81	1981–82	1982–83	1983–84	1984–85	1985–86	1986–87	1987–88	1988–89
Research	$43,228	$43,325	$49,335	$47,043	$58,415	$61,633	$65,541	$74,444	$88,808	$108,798
Training	6,786	7,893	6,278	4,725	4,573	4,514	4,501	6,632	7,241	6,760
Wk. Study										
Fellow./Scholar.	5,855	6,586	7,500	6,906	8,218	8,358	10,327[8]	8,670	6,972	13,689[8]
Cap. Imp. & Equip.	515	178	549	694	90	1,875	886	1,369	968	1,332
Loan Funds	897	1,198	20	42	46	—	—	—	—	—
Misc.	1,888	480	347	398	1,166	267	300	506	673	798
Ed. Dev.[9]	3,666	2,391	1,947	1,538	1,918	2,019	346	744	567	455
Commun. Serv.	3,802	4,415	3,403	5,183	7,884	9,119	7,302	8,036	8,049	8,163
Continuing Ed.	442	640	255	182	374	320	233	376	85	512
Endowed Chair	—	—	—	—	—	—	—	—	1,775	—

Note: For years July 1, 1979–June 30, 1989: Reports are based on notification date of award, not effective date; the figures do not reflect expenditures.

1. Includes regional medical planning grant, library resources, Upward Bound from 1966–1974.

2. Includes NSF Center of Excellence grant.

3. A system was introduced to report grants at time of receipt rather than beginning date. Thus, receipts will appear higher than usual because of overlapping reporting. This is particularly true of training grants that begin on July 1 and Financial Aid grants in FY 1976 from Office of Education.

4. Some 1977–78 funds were reported in 1976–77 since report is based on notification date. Similarly, 1978–79 funds were not received until July. Drop is, therefore, artificial.

5. Capitation and curriculum development.

6. Regional Medical, Family Planning, etc.

7. Included under Miscellaneous prior to 1977–78.

8. Increase due in part to timing of the earlier arrival of the award documents from the government for student support.

9. Curriculum development and instruction improvement, formerly included U.S. capitation grants, which no longer are funded.

APPENDIX 10.

Committees, 1988–1989

University committees advisory to the vice president for educational
development and research
  Academic Computer Services
  Research Council
Committees advisory to the vice president for educational development
and research
  Aging
  Animal Care and Use
  Child Behavior and Development
  Editorial Review
  Electron Microscopy Facility
  Environmental Health and Safety
  Fermentation Facility
  Foreign Students
  Health Services Research
  High Speed Computing Facility
  Human Subjects
  Image Analysis Facility
  International Education
  The *Iowa Review*
  Iowa State Water Resources Research Institute
  Laser Facility
  Mass Spectrometry Facility
  Nuclear Magnetic Resonance Facility
  Occupational Health Service
  Patents
  Protein Structure Facility
  Public Policy Center
  Radiation Protection
  Recombinant DNA
  State Archaeologist's Office
  Study Abroad
  Technology Innovation Center
  University House

Video

Windhover Press

Committees advisory to the dean of the Graduate College

Affirmative Action

Evolutionary Ecology and Biology

Graduate Council

Iowa Quaternary Studies Group

INDEX